FÁTIMA REVISITED

Other books in this series

Heavenly Lights: The Apparitions of Fátima and the UFO Phenomenon

Celestial Secrets: The Hidden History of the Fátima Incident

FÁTIMA REVISITED
The Apparition Phenomenon in Ufology, Psychology, and Science

Compiled by
**DR. FERNANDO FERNANDES,
DR. JOAQUIM FERNANDES,
& RAUL BERENGUEL**

Translated from Portuguese and Edited by
ANDREW D. BASIAGO & EVA M. THOMPSON

Foreword by
WILLIAM J. BIRNES

Introduction by
RALPH STEINER

Aɴᴏᴍᴀʟɪꜱᴛ Bᴏᴏᴋꜱ
San Antonio • New York

An Original Publication of Anomalist Books

Fátima Revisited:
The Apparition Phenomenon in Ufology, Psychology, and Science
Copyright © 2008 by Andrew D. Basiago & Eva M. Thompson

ISBN: 1933665238

Cover art by Roy Young
Book design by Seale Studios

"Evidence For Enhanced Congruence Between Dreams And Distant Target Material During Periods Of Decreased Geomagnetic Activity" by Stanley Krippner, Ph.D. and Michael Persinger, Ph.D., was originally published in the *Journal of Scientific Exploration*, 10(4), 487-493, 1996, 0892-3310/96, Copyright © 1996 by the Society for Scientific Exploration.

For information, go to anomalistbooks.com, or write to:
Anomalist Books, 5150 Broadway #108, San Antonio, TX 78209

ACKNOWLEDGEMENTS

The editors wish to thank Meredith Daniel and Chaz V. Adams for helping to prepare this anthology for publication.

Dr. Frank McGillion wishes to thank Dr. Joaquim Fernandes for inviting him to contribute his paper, Eve McGillion for providing assistance translating relevant text from German, and George Docherty for providing similar assistance with text originally published in Spanish.

Dr. Mario Simões wishes to thank Mrs. Rita Baumeister Simões for revising his manuscript in English.

EDITOR'S NOTE

This anthology is the result of an ongoing and ever-growing exchange of ideas between leading researchers and scholars throughout the world who have, in an informal manner, joined Project MARIAN (the Multicultural Apparitions Research International Academic Network), in the last several years. The papers gathered here have appeared in both peer-reviewed journals and original works inspired by the intense and productive process of "brainstorming" about the "visionary" phenomena of Fátima in 1917 that has taken place under the aegis of MARIAN, which is coordinated by the Center for Transdisciplinary Studies in Consciousness (CTEC) at the University Fernando Pessoa, in Porto, Portugal. This international project seeks to create a forum in which the great mysteries of human existence might be solved.

AUTHORS & CONTRIBUTORS

AUTHORS

SCOTT ATRAN is director of research in anthropology at the Centre National de la Recherche Scientifique in Paris, visiting professor of psychology and public policy at the University of Michigan, and presidential scholar in sociology at the John Jay School of Criminal Justice in New York. His books include *Cognitive Foundations of Natural History*, *In Gods We Trust*, *Plants of the Petén Itzá Maya* (with Ximena Lois and Edilberto Ucan), and *The Native Mind* (with Douglas Medin). In addition to his work on the ideology and social evolution of global network terrorism, he conducts research in Guatemala, Mexico, and the U.S. on universal and culture-specific aspects of biological categorization and environmental reasoning and decision making among the Maya and other Native Americans.

RAUL BERENGUEL, M.S. is a research associate of the Center for Transdisciplinary Studies on Consciousness (CTEC) at the University Fernando Pessoa, where he began his investigations in 1971. He has been affiliated with the Center of Astronomical Studies and Unusual Phenomena (CEAFI) and the National Commission of Investigation of UFO Phenomena (CNIFO). He was the founder of the Portuguese Society of Scientific Exploration and is the author of several publications covering diverse borderland science issues.

IRENE BLINSTON earned her Ph.D. in Transpersonal Psychology from the Institute of Transpersonal Psychology in Palo Alto, California in 2005. Her doctoral research focused on adults who experienced religious apparitions in childhood. Her dissertation, *When Children Witness the Sacred*, provided a new body of knowledge showing the impacts, lifelong after-effects, and consequences of the disclosure of religious apparitions. A rising figure in the field of transpersonal psychology, Blinston appeared in the documentary *Science of the Soul* (2005). A researcher, writer, and speaker, she studies apparitional encounters around the world.

JANET ELIZABETH COLLI is a psychotherapist specializing in Post-Traumatic Stress Disorder (PTSD) and matters of transpersonal spirituality. She holds a Ph.D. in Clinical Psychology and has authored numerous articles about near-death experiences (NDEs). She has investigated inter-species communication and animal-assisted therapies, especially as developed for children with cancer. During her career, she has served on diverse commissions of academic evaluation within the field of psychology in the United States.

RYAN J. COOK is visiting assistant professor in the Department of Anthropology at Loyola University Chicago. He holds a doctorate in Anthropology from the University of Chicago. An expert on marginalized religious and scientific groups, he has published works based on his ethnographic investigations in North America and Latin America. His interests include the convergence of technoscience and spirituality in the new religions, the dynamics of stigmatization and boundary-work, and the uses of UFOs in popular culture and the media.

ERIC DAVIS, who holds a Ph.D. in Physics, is an investigator for Warp Drive Metrics of Las Vegas, Nevada. As research director for the National Institute for Discovery Science, he developed theoretical works in advanced physics and a new propulsion strategy for possible eventual use in interstellar travel. At the University of Tucson, he has participated in programs of astronomical observation and space exploration related to Jupiter, Uranus, and Neptune. He has served as a consultant to NASA, the U.S. Air Force, and other aerospace agencies.

FERNANDO FERNANDES is a professor at the Superior Institute of Engineering in Porto. He has a Ph.D. in Electronic Engineering and Computing from the University of Porto. He was a co-founder of the Portuguese Society of Scientific Exploration (SPEC), is an associate investigator at CTEC at the University Fernando Pessoa, and is a member of the collective CDU of the Anomaly Foundation in Spain. Prominent among his areas of interest are parapsychology, paranormal experiences and beliefs, and altered states of human consciousness.

JOAQUIM FERNANDES is a professor of History at the University Fernando Pessoa in Porto, Portugal, where he is a member of the Center for Transdisciplinary Studies on Consciousness (CTEC). He holds a Ph.D. in Contemporary History. His doctoral thesis explored "The Imagined Extraterrestrial in Portugal from the Middle of the 19th Century to the Modern Era." He is the co-editor of CTEC's journal *Cons-sciences*. His interests are the history of science and the comparative anthropology of secular and religious visionary experiences, emphasizing the Fátima apparitions of 1917, about which he has co-authored three works with Fina d'Armada.

DAVID M. JACOBS is Associate Professor of History at Temple University, where he specializes in 20th century American history and culture. He received his Ph.D. in U.S. Intellectual History in 1973. Since 1977, he has taught the only regular curriculum course on UFOs in America. He began researching UFOs in the mid-1960s, and has amassed over 40 years of primary research data and analytical hypotheses on the subject. Since 1986, Dr. Jacobs has devoted most of his professional energies to researching the UFO abduction phenomenon. Having investigated over 1,100 abductions with over 145 subjects, he is one of the foremost UFO abduction researchers in the world. His books include *The UFO Controversy in America, Secret Life: Firsthand, Documented Accounts of UFO Abductions, The Threat: Revealing the Secret Alien Agenda*, and *UFOs and Abductions: Challenging the Borders of Knowledge*, for which he served as editor.

STANLEY KRIPPNER is an internationally renowned psychologist involved in the study of human consciousness and altered states. He holds a Ph.D. in Educational Psychology from Northwestern University. He was the director of the Maimonides Medical Center in New York City and now guides research at the Saybrook Graduate School in San Francisco. He is a member of international associations in psychology, parapsychology, sleep studies, dissociation, and clinical hypnosis. Widely recognized as the person principally responsible for promoting the academic investigation of human consciousness, he has published approximately 500 articles in the field.

FRANK McGILLION, an investigator of the works of Freud and Jung, participates in numerous scientific and literary societies in the United Kingdom. He obtained his Doctorate in Medicine with a specialty in Neurophysiology and Psychophysiology from the University of Glasgow and then pursued postgraduate studies at Oxford. He has investigated the history of medicine and traditional belief systems. His recent papers include a review of Jung on synchronicity and an account of the esoteric interests of Sigmund Freud. His autobiographical novel *On the Edge of a Lifetime*, published in 2002, was widely praised.

AUGUSTE MEESSEN is professor emeritus at the Catholic University of Louvain in Belgium. A Ph.D. in Science, he lectures on theoretical physics, quantum mechanics, and mathematical physics. He has conducted fundamental and theoretical investigations in nuclear and solid state physics. A research associate at the Massachusetts Institute of Technology, he is the author of the important scientific papers "Optical Properties of Thin Metal Films" in

Progress in Optics and "Space-time Quantization, Elementary Particles, and Cosmology" in *Foundations of Physics*.

GILDA MOURA is a psychotherapist who specializes in hypnosis and past life regression. Her work focuses on the treatment of traumatic situations and extraordinary experiences. A graduate in Psychology from the University of Gama Filho, she founded the Center for the Study of Altered States of Consciousness in Rio de Janeiro, Brazil. In the United States, she has worked as a consultant for the Chicago-based Kairos Foundation, where she co-directed a project on altered states of consciousness and "mapping" of the affected areas of the brains of four different groups of subjects – alien contactees, "psychic surgery" patients, mediums, and members of Saint Daime's Church.

MICHAEL A. PERSINGER is the research director of the program in Behavioral Neuroscience at Laurentian University in Ontario, Canada. He holds a Ph.D. in Physiological Psychology, with a specialization in Clinical Neuropsychology. He is considered a leading world authority on the effects of electromagnetic fields upon human behavior and perception, including those in the extra-low frequency (ELF) and very low frequency (VLF) ranges, a field of research that he pioneered. He is the author of six books and more than 200 articles in this discipline.

VITOR RODRIGUES earned a license in Clinical Psychology from the University of Lisbon in 1984 and a Ph.D. in Educational Psychology from the University of Lisbon in 2002. He is an adjunct professor at the Superior School of Nursing in Évora. Between 1988 and 2001, he was an assistant professor in the Psychology and Sciences of Education at the University of Lisbon. He is a delegate of the European Association of Psychotherapy, president of the Luso-Brazilian Transpersonal Association, and a board member of the European Transpersonal Association.

MARIO SIMÕES is a psychiatrist and professor on the Faculty of Medicine at the University of Lisbon. The director of ALUBRAT, the Associação Luso-Brasileira de Transpessoal [the Portuguese-Brazilian Transpersonal Association], he investigates modified states of consciousness and transpersonal psychology. A graduate in anthropology and ethnology from the Technical University of Lisbon, he holds a Master's degree in Psychiatry and a Ph.D. in Psychiatric Medicine. He was trained in clinics in Zurich, Vienna, and Madrid and at the Freiburg Institute. He was an organizer of the Bial Foundation symposium, "Beneath and Beyond the Brain."

JACQUES F. VALLÉE is an astrophysicist and information systems specialist who holds a Ph.D. in Computer Science. He developed the ARPANET, a precursor to the Internet, for the U.S. Department of Defense. He has served as a consultant to companies, universities – including Stanford University – and government agencies in France and the United States – including the National Science Foundation and NASA, where he developed the first map of Mars. A writer about the frontiers of science, he is also a recipient of the Jules Verne Prize.

CONTRIBUTORS

ANDREW D. BASIAGO is a lawyer, journalist, and environmental scholar educated at UCLA and Cambridge. He is the American writer and book editor who was responsible for bringing *The Fátima Trilogy* to the English-speaking world. He is now writing a book about secret time-space exploration activities undertaken by the Defense Advanced Research Projects Agency.

WILLIAM J. BIRNES is a New York Times best-selling author who has written and edited over 25 books in human behavior, true crime, current affairs, history, psychology, business, computing, and the paranormal. The publisher of *UFO Magazine*, editor of *The UFO Encyclopedia*, and consulting producer and host of *UFO Hunters* on The History Channel, he co-authored *The Day After Roswell* with Lt. Col. Philip Corso, *A Worker In The Light* with George Noory of Coast-to-Coast AM, and *Space Wars* with William B. Scott and Michael J. Coumatos.

RALPH STEINER is an investigative journalist and documentary producer specializing in science, technology, and public policy issues. His in-depth reporting for the Pacifica radio network won several awards from the Corporation for Public Broadcasting. In recent years, his work has explored anomalies within the context of modern science, ethics, and philosophy.

EVANGELINE M. THOMPSON is an accomplished poet, singer/songwriter, translator, and interpreter fluent in the Romance languages. She has translated essays, poems, lyrics, musicals, operas, television scripts, and feature films, including motion pictures made by such leading international filmmakers as Bertolucci, Diegues, Herzog, Kurosawa, Malle, Wajda, and Zhang.

ROY YOUNG is the artist who designed the cover images for the Anomalist Books edition of *The Fátima Trilogy*. He is considered a leading illustrator in science fiction. His work has appeared in albums, books, comic books, and movies. He created the award-winning graphic novel series *The Villikon Chronicles* and was production designer for the film *Genesis of Evil*.

CONTENTS

FOREWORD

The secret of UFOs is hard to penetrate. Where do they hide? Why can't the world's leading scientists get a handle on this phenomenon? Why is academia so afraid of talking about UFOs? And, why can't reasonable people study the UFO mystery from the perspective of their disciplines without getting into fights with one another over such things as what constitutes evidence and testimony? One would think that, given all the ways that researchers in the social sciences, in the field of law, and in the physical sciences have been able to contribute to forensic science over the past 200 years, they might be able to approach a subject like UFOs with a measure of academic collegiality.

But this has not been the case.

Rather than finding ways to share information and develop common approaches, researchers have too often fought pitched battles over the smallest of issues. Ideally, in UFO research, we would draw a logical line from physical evidence to eyewitness testimony and from there, to some sort of common ground, even if the common ground means that we have to be satisfied with a lack of conclusion. But when one looks at the UFO field, what one finds is that researchers not only fail to do that, but they sometimes heap scorn upon researchers in different fields.

There are many examples of this pattern.

Let's start with the Roswell Incident of 1947. What constitutes evidence that the UFO crash at Roswell took place? Can we rely on eyewitness testimony, even when some of the eyewitnesses are dead? Tom Carey and Don Schmidt show, in *Witness to Roswell*, how many different stories all point to the same event happening at the same time. We can even use the testimonies of different Roswell witnesses to triangulate who saw what, when, and where. But for the physical scientists, this is by no means sufficient. They ask: Where is the smoking gun? Where is the evidence? If one is to believe that the Roswell crash actually occurred, what happened to all the evidence?

In fact, historians can theorize about what happened to the Roswell crash evidence. We can point to Lt. Walter Haut's affidavit that he went to the crash site and recovered a piece of the wreckage and put it on his desk. We can refer to Dr. Jesse Marcel, Jr.'s testimony that he saw and handled pieces of the UFO wreckage. We can cite Major Jesse Marcel, Sr.'s statement that he accompanied the wreckage to Carswell Air Force Base in Fort Worth, Texas. We can add to these accounts Major Marion Magruder's claim that he saw the wreckage at Wright Field. And we can even rely on Lt. Col. Philip Corso's story that he saw some of the Roswell debris at Fort Riley in 1947 and then again at the Pentagon in 1961.

Why is such evidence not good enough?

Ask the skeptics and they will say that without the evidence itself, descriptions of the evidence are insufficient. Ask trial lawyers and they will say that corroborative descriptions of evidence – even if the evidence has been removed by another party, say, the government – are enough to establish that such evidence existed, even if the descriptions vary in small details. Ask historians and they will say without a doubt that people saw something even if we don't have that something in front of us. Then ask psychologists, and they will say that there was an event, which was traumatic enough to cause a major impact, no pun intended, upon the lives of the different witnesses. In other words, just by getting people from different disciplines to stop arguing with one another over details only relevant to separate disciplines and to look at where the different fields of study overlap, we can get some agreement as to what researchers accept as truth.

In the social sciences, when different people approach a solution only from within their own perspectives and cannot see the correspondences between perspectives, we call this "linkage blindness." In management-speak and in military-speak, when people only approach solutions up and down the chain-of-command, without looking outside their cubicles for any other perspective, that's called "stovepipe thinking." In other words, if a solution to a problem doesn't exist within the acceptable bounds of a settled discourse or the confines of an organizational chart, then there is no solution.

Over the years, this kind of thinking has bedeviled both Ufology and the paranormal field in general. Physicists have only talked to physicists; photo experts have only communicated their expertise to other photo experts in the language of "histograms," "spectrum analysis," and other terms, but have not tried to explain what they do to either historians or psychologists. As a result, people from the various disciplines have not communicated with each other about the evidence that underlies the most significant cases.

I would cite as another relevant example the legendary Barney and Betty Hill abduction case of 1961, which is still debated after 46 years. I am certain that if the psychologists could talk to the chemists that analyzed the dress that Betty Hill wore on the night of her abduction, and if the historians could get access to the records at Pease Air Force Base, then maybe a greater truth would emerge than what we have seen, namely, endless speculation over whether the Hill case falls within a statistical norm or whether the Hills were suffering from a shared delusion.

The solution to this problem, of course, is the interdisciplinary approach that has been evolving in the social sciences for the past 20 years and that is, in fact, also beginning to emerge in Ufology. Interdisciplinary investigations of the UFO phenomenon work. They have proven successful in such colloquia as the Rockefeller-sponsored Pocantico Hills conference and the French COMETA report.

Ufologists should consider making the interdisciplinary approach the standard one for investigating important cases in the field. We should re-open such critical cases in Ufology as the UFO sightings over Washington, D.C. in 1952, the Kecksburg crash of 1965, and the Cash-Landrum Incident of 1980. These are examples of the kinds of UFO incidents that lend themselves to the interdisciplinary approach.

Fátima Revisited is a fine example of the promise that this approach holds. In its pages, a profound and complex understanding of the Fatima Incident of 1917 is articulated. And this is achieved only through the alchemy of synthesizing insights from diverse disciplines – for example, what Ufology has to say about alien contact experiences, what psychology has to say about altered states of consciousness, and what science has to say about the effects of geomagnetic fields on human consciousness.

This book also reveals the degree to which Ufologists around the world are eager to create an international discourse in Ufology. *The Fátima Trilogy*, of which this anthology is the third and final volume, grew from one exchange of emails between a Portuguese researcher and an American journalist into a multidisciplinary collaboration involving 35 individuals from 10 countries.

What resulted is the kind of work that can rescue Ufology from parascience on behalf of science. If who the alien beings are, where they are from, and what they want remain among the abiding mysteries of our time, then humanity's place in the Cosmos might depend on international, interdisciplinary collaborations of this kind.

William J. Birnes

INTRODUCTION

Y ou are about to enter the wonderland that lies between observation and belief.

As of this writing, almost a century has passed since three Portuguese children encountered a luminous mystery in the sky above Fátima, Portugal, a small town north of Lisbon. By October 13, 1917, tens of thousands more had observed the "Miracle of the Sun." The solar disk was said to have turned gray and spun wildly, casting off colorful rays and discharges, swaying and rushing forward and backward in the firmament. This day capped six months of similar events, all taking place on the 13th of each month. The children believed they were being visited by angels, the Virgin Mary, Jesus, and Joseph, and that prophecies were spoken to them. Perhaps the best known of all Marian apparitions, the enigmatic events at Fátima in the waning days of World War I have continued to prompt thoughtful questioning.

The riddle persists to this day as to exactly what was seen, and whether or not something verifiably paranormal occurred. This volume, the last in the famed trilogy that examines Fátima from a position of serious scholarship, endeavors to reopen multiple windows of inquiry. The authors' objectives are to bring those long-ago events into the light of modern speculation, and thereby broaden our comprehension of the relationship between the mind and "objective" reality.

The Fátima Incident of 1917 was not a singular event. Even today, episodes of this nature occur, haunting the sky of human knowledge.

Barely a century ago, visions and revelations were often accorded the ring of absolute truth and were used to affirm religious belief. In the Western world, the Church of Rome spent two millennia sanctifying such claims, anointing saints, and proclaiming the validity of officially recognized "miracles." For most of our history, the numinous and the supernatural have occupied central positions in the pantheon of influences shaping both our sense of identity and our sense of connection to a larger world.

The empirical methods of science are relative newcomers to the arsenal of human understanding. As the 19th and 20th centuries unfolded, humanity earnestly began to apprehend natural phenomena through the focused lens of disciplined observation. A new secular myth based upon allegedly objective facts became the basis for a new orthodoxy. The prodigiously mechanistic powers of science were unleashed to explain the world to us in new ways that were at odds with the age-old subjective traditions of faith.

Natural science and its offspring, technology, have radically altered how we perceive and think, and how we live on the Earth. They have not, however, changed the essential makeup of the human psyche. What we collectively believe largely determines how we act. Understanding mass psychological phenomena, like those that took place at Fátima, can yield significant insights into human motivations and social movements. This, in turn, can help us prepare to deal with a world whose social and technical complexities are increasing at an alarming pace.

Fátima was a mass phenomenon. At the height of its ongoing manifestations in 1917, an estimated 70,000 people witnessed the "Miracle of the Sun." Some claimed to have seen, and even heard, the Blessed Virgin, the Christ Child, and other deities. World War I was reaching its abysmal depths. The prophecies and warnings that were supposedly uttered by supernatural beings reflected the anxious zeitgeist of the times. In today's world, teeming with political instability, corporate plunder, environmental destruction, and resurgent religious fundamentalism, observations gleaned from the Fátima experience strike a powerfully resonant chord.

Several of the scholars contributing to this book assert that modern physics and neuroscience offer tidy explanations for what was initially perceived. The events associated with Fátima were, they say, the product of electrical discharges from within the Earth that stimulated the brains of witnesses, inducing common hallucinations.

Others state that prolonged sun-gazing can, in fact, replicate the main sighting experience, that of a wildly spinning and gyrating, multi-colored solar disk. The interplay of mass psychology and widely shared religious beliefs are then credited for the emergence of the prophecies and warnings attributed by the percipients to Our Lady of Fátima.

From a psychological point-of-view, the emergence of compelling Jungian archetypes, such as the Great Mother, at a time of terrifying global conflict, is explored. The interplay between unknown sensory stimulation and the formation of a powerful myth upholding traditional religious beliefs helps to ground the discussion from a social and cultural perspective.

There are, however, other aspects of the Fátima phenomena that are now becoming recognizable within the context of a far more controversial mystery, one that is at once very ancient and quite contemporary. That mystery demands that we approach the matter with unswerving eyes and unbiased minds. *Fátima Revisited* ventures into this unconventional territory while maintaining the highest standards of scholarship and inquiry. I am referring to the UFO mystery.

At mid-century, the skies opened up yet again, forcing upon the sure-footed disciples of science a number of manifestations that they could not easily reconcile. As humanity moved quickly from being earthbound into the age of powered flight, we were inspired, once more, to gaze upon the primal

"Chariots of the Gods" and ask the deepest question of all: Are we alone?

This volume, like the two definitive histories of Fátima that preceded it, makes a powerful argument that Fátima may represent the first mass UFO sighting event of the modern era. If one omits the traditional religious interpretations of the witnesses, what was seen appears to conform to many aspects of the classic UFO phenomenon as it was later observed during and following World War II.

Points of commonality abound between "Marian apparitions" of the Fátima typology and the more subjective aspects of modern UFO encounters. Both are provoked by sensory stimuli that can be perceived in mass while being documented by photographic equipment. Indeed, black and white photos of the "Miracle of the Sun" in 1917 exist, and they depict what could be interpreted as a luminous, silver disk in the sky similar in many ways to the "flying saucers" captured on film from the late 1940s onward.

Descriptions of communication between the Virgin Mary and the Fátima witnesses are remarkably reminiscent of telepathic interactions with alien beings reported by modern UFO abductees and contactees. Witnesses reported hearing a buzzing in their heads prior to perceiving a voice that spoke to them internally. The Blessed Virgin Mary's lips did not move.

Neuroscientists included in this tome suggest this may indicate that microwave radiation was beamed at witnesses to induce voices in their heads. They cite as a further indicator of an electro-magnetic presence the rapid drying of the witnesses' clothes; October 13th had been a rainy day. They show convincingly that the use of sophisticated technology might explain most, if not all, of what was observed, heard, and felt at Fátima by literally tens of thousands of people.

We are reminded that throughout the past century, apparitional events have continued to occur around the world in concert with waves of such things as mass UFO sightings, crop circle formations, and alien contact experiences. Is there evidence of a connection between these various manifestations? *Fátima Revisited* makes a strong case that the answer to this question is, undoubtedly, "Yes."

This is a work that is both bold in its choice of subject and comprehensive in its approach. Its Portuguese compilers, Fernando Fernandes, Joaquim Fernandes and Raul Berenguel, have created an anthology that leaves no stone unturned. The judicious editing and fluid translating of American journalists Andrew D. Basiago and Eva M. Thompson have produced a compelling work of scholarship that stands by itself in the field of paranormal research. It is up to the reader to accept the challenge.

Ralph Steiner

THE FÁTIMA PHENOMENA

— Michael A. Persinger, Ph.D. —

One of the best documented cases of the 20th century involving luminous phenomena framed within the UFO typology occurred in Fátima, Portugal in October 1917. Approximately 70,000 people observed a sphere of unusual light. Many of these witnesses also saw several images that included variants of Joseph, Mary, and Jesus, sacred symbols of the Christian religion. This paper attempts to establish a causal relationship between these visions and the physiological and neuro-physiological alterations experienced by witnesses, as well as tectonic conditions within the Fátima region. The author theorizes that stimulation of the cerebral-temporal lobe may be the actual cause of the apparition phenomenon.

THE REPORT

Several books have been written about the Fátima phenomena. One of the most systematic texts, although steeped in religious interpretation, is *The True Story of Fátima* by João de Marchi (1952). The following descriptions highlight the details reported in his book.

The major luminous event occurred in the early afternoon on October 13, 1917. Stimulated by the previous observations of other people and the notoriety of three young children (Lúcia, Jacinta and Francisco) who had some religious experiences when they closely approached some luminous displays, thousands of people gathered along the side of a mountain near an oak tree. On top of this tree, low-level luminous events had appeared previously.

Before the appearance of the luminosity, the day had been characterized by incessant rain and cool weather. At about one o'clock in the afternoon, one of the children (who had reported the most vivid religious experiences) told everyone to kneel down since she had seen the sign that "the woman in light" was coming. A lightning flash preceded the luminosity.

Shafts of brilliant red light were emitted from the rim of the revolving luminosity and reflected off the trees and people on the ground. Other colors included green, violet, and blue, in various mixed arrays. Not surprisingly, considering the odd event and the religious context, many people were frightened and prayed for forgiveness or yelled, "I believe!"

1

To appreciate the detailed similarity of the Fátima phenomenon to more contemporary UFO displays, the descriptions from people who were actually there are useful. According to de Marchi, Almeida Garrett, a professor at Coimbra University, recorded the following observations:

> I do not agree with the comparison that I have heard made in Fátima – that of a dull silver disc. It was a clearer, richer, brighter color, having something of the luster of a pearl. It did not in the least resemble the Moon on a clear night because one saw it and felt it to be a living body. It was not spherical like the moon, nor did it have the same color, tone or shading. It looked like a glazed wheel made of mother-of-pearl...

> The clouds passed from west to east and did not obscure the light of the Sun (the word used for the luminosity) . . .giving the impression of passing behind it, although sometimes these flecks of white took on tones of pink or diaphanous blue as they passed before the Sun.

> It was a remarkable fact that one could fix one's eyes on this brazier of heat and light without any pain in the eyes or blinding of the retina. The phenomenon, except for two interruptions when the Sun seemed to send out rays of refulgent heat, which obliged us to look away, must have lasted for 10 minutes.

> The Sun's disc did not remain immobile. This was not the sparkling of a heavenly body, for it spun round on itself in a mad whirl. Then, suddenly, one heard a clamor, a cry of anguish breaking from all the people. The Sun, whirling wildly, seemed to loosen itself from the firmament and advance threateningly upon the Earth as if to crush us with its huge and fiery weight. The sensation during those moments was terrible.

At the beginning of the phenomenon, Lúcia apparently instructed the people to look at the Sun (the luminosity), an event that she could not recall later. Lúcia reported she could see and hear the "woman in light" talking. Apparently, the apparition had told her that the war (World War I) would end that day. The war did not end — a factor that unnerved both the children and religious leaders, who had seen this event as a miracle and a prophecy fulfilled.

The children and other people, especially those people nearest the children and the luminosity, reported a variety of figures:

2

The lady of Rosary is no longer ascending. She stands in glory to the right of the Sun and her light is such that the great fixed stars are by comparison pallid and weak. For a moment, she is gowned in white precisely as the children have known her each time she has appeared above the stubby oak. Yet as quickly, and as strangely, then she is wearing a mantle of blue and with her, in fidelity to the promise she has made is St. Joseph, with the Christ Child in his arms...

These visions are brief and they succeed one another rapidly. Three times St. Joseph has traced the sign of the cross above the people. St. Joseph fades away and Christ appears at the base of the Sun. He is cloaked in red. With Him stands His Mother. She is gowned now in neither white nor blue, but as Our Lady of Sorrows, gazing on the Earth. She has not the traditional sword in her heart.

The major phenomenon, however, did not occur as an isolated event. It had been preceded several times by low-level luminosities (balls of light) and close encounter experiences. Most of the luminous events occurred near the top of the same oak tree and were paired with a buzzing sound, "like a mosquito in a bottle." Just before each event, the Sun became hazier, the air smelled fresher (sometimes with a breeze), and a flash of lightning occurred.

During the months preceding the October display, severe claps of thunder and odd noises were reported in the neighborhood. Villages reported local "pops and bangs." One month before the main luminosity, a luminous ball (quite unlike the cloud-like displays that had been reported before) was seen by many people to move away from the top of the same tree and to travel down into the valley.

The psychological and neurobiological aspect of the phenomena center primarily around the three children: Lúcia, Jacinta, and Francisco. They were the first to report the luminous displays and had approached the events on several occasions between May and October of 1917.

The first and consequent occasions were paired with experiences of seeing a young woman within the luminosity. The woman, who was identified as the "Mother of God," was experienced in great detail by all three children. Only the two girls, Lúcia and Jacinta, heard the woman speak. The boy did not. Lúcia reported most of the auditory experiences or "messages." The apparition-like experiences followed the first sighting of a wispy, cloud-like phenomenon at the top of the tree. Before this occurrence, the children had been taking care of sheep and engaging in various religious behaviors, such as counting rosary or saying prayers. They had played games, but most of the time (according to reports at least), they concentrated on religious themes.

The experiences associated with the "woman in the luminosity" varied from personal application to world instruction. For example, the children were told to say their prayers daily and that if the world did not change, it would be destroyed. In short, humanity was told to mend its ways or else. World War I was at its peak.

The experiences occurred on several different occasions, allegedly on the 13th of every month between May and October of 1917. They were near the same tree and involved great detail. The dress and outlines of the young woman were clearly evident to Lúcia, in particular, and followed the contemporary images of the Virgin Mary.

Various experiences, however, were noted. The boy thought the first image was that of a headless angel. During the major event in October 1917, the children were alleged to report seeing several images in quick progression: Joseph, Mary, and Jesus. People, especially those closest to the children, also reported a variety of religious figures.

The psychological profiles of the young children are difficult to assess from secondary reports. No direct methods of testing were available at that time. Lúcia was perceived as the leader of the group and was known for her interest in games and dancing. She had an excellent memory although she was illiterate.

According to his peers, the young boy, Francisco, was obsessed with religion. His main desire in life was to "die and go to Heaven." Francisco was also prone to epileptic-like attacks. For example, he would be found prostrate in a dazed condition on the rocks. He would only "awaken" when someone shook him or screamed loudly at him. He was clearly masochistic and had bizarre obsessions. Francisco spent a great deal of time considering what type of punishment or sacrifice he should follow. On one occasion, as punishment, he decided to feed his lunch to the sheep and to eat acorns.

The youngest girl, Jacinta, was apparently happy and normal. She was a follower and quite religious. She was seen as gentle and sweet. Jacinta was Francisco's sister and both were the first cousins of Lúcia.

Within three years following the major phenomenon, Jacinta and Francisco died. Francisco died during the influenza epidemic of 1918 while Jacinta died of what appears to be lung cancer. According to the description of the time, after a siege of bronchial pneumonia, a punishing form of pleurisy set in. An abscess formed in the delicate membranes of her chest cavity and there was "an agony of unrelenting pain." She died after several months of slow attrition. Only Lúcia survived this period. She became a nun.

Repeated experiences were reported by the two girls and implied by the boy. Before her death, while bedridden in her village, Jacinta reported that the woman in light had appeared again and told her she would be taken to Lisbon. Lúcia had several more experiences. One most notable occurred when, as a novice, she was forced to clean a filthy toilet. She returned, covered with feces. Her face, however, "was radiant and showed great countenance"; apparently, she had just had another experience.

THE INTERPRETATION

The large Fátima phenomenon on October 13, 1917, and the smaller, less spectacular events earlier that year, were luminosities associated with the tectonic strain within the region. This area is well known for its intense strain and deep foci quakes. In fact, the most intense quake ever recorded was the Lisbon earthquake of November 1, 1755. The area is still active, as indicated by the deep focus quake of 1954.

As predicted by the theory that links seismic activity to luminous displays, the luminosity occurred along a fault region. In many respects, the Fátima luminosity was more of a "ghost light" variety than a single event UFO. Consequently, like the New Jersey light (although it is much dimmer), the Fátima phenomena would begin near the same charge collector: the top of an oak tree.

Several factors suggest that the tectonic strain was of the "slow accumulation" variety. First, the event occurred at least six times with an interepisodic interval of about one month. (Except for the last two events in September and October, independent witnesses did not verify the actual dates.) The most likely trigger for this synchrony was lunar phase. Secondly, the phenomena increased in intensity over time. Initially, the luminosities were barely detectable, except as a light haze or cloud. As the number of presentations continued and the strain increased, the luminous component of the EM field became more and more intense. By September 1917, luminous displays were clearly seen by many observers independent of the young children.

The electromagnetic component of the surface manifestation was intense. Even during the earlier displays, when the strain levels were far below those of October 1917, the electric fields achieved discharge intensities. As the field increased in strength, ozone was generated, thus producing the experience of "fresh air." Finally, an actual discharge occurred, which the children perceived as a "lighting flash."

Each time, the sequence of events was the same. Since they occurred within the children's work-play area, the contiguity of the pattern was soon learned. The sequence reflected the increasing intensity of the electric and magnetic fields as the strain levels increased within the Earth.

The October manifestation was a classic and very large luminosity that lasted for about 10 minutes. It was similar to the type observed by "abductee" Travis Walton in 1975 and his friends, except the context involved religious themes. Quite unlike the Walton luminosity, however, the Fátima manifestation remained at significant altitudes since it could be seen from at least 20 miles away.

No doubt, the Fátima event was bright. People observing it mistook it for the Sun. Since there was cloud cover that day, the actual Sun was not seen. The fact that the luminosity was well below the clouds is indicated by the observation that the clouds "moved behind it."

If the people had had the label "UFO" or "flying saucer" at the time, they would have called the Fátima luminosity, the Fátima spaceship. The only label available to them, however, was "the Sun." This daily object was the only experience that matched this odd phenomenon. Under the assumption that the luminosity was the Sun, a miracle was the only contemporary explanation. The Sun could not display these odd effects without terrestrial devastation.

The spinning and color alterations of the Fátima ball indicate that it was passing through energy changes. It emitted different dominant wavelengths and discharged multicolored streamers into the air. Occasionally, it emitted infrared in sufficient intensities to induce warmth in the observers. On several occasions, the brightness was painful.

As the luminosity hovered and moved above the witnesses, it also underwent changes in boundary condition. The opacity, which gave it a metallic sheen, altered with the pearl-like luster. Since its boundary oscillated and moved, it appeared "alive."

The core of the luminosity was quite bright and hot. Lúcia found this part of the luminosity too bright and in fact did not look in this direction. The images of saints were seen along the edges of the luminosity, in the halo region produced by the ionization of the air.

The altitude of the luminosity was maintained by the source field, which was vast, and the presence of tens of thousands of people in the vicinity. Towards the end of the display, during the maximum instability, the ball of light dropped to a lower altitude. Since the onlookers assumed the ball was the Sun, this movement induced panic: "the Sun was falling."

If the numbers of viewers had been less or the source field had been diminished more quickly, then the luminous display would have approached the ground. People in the vicinity would have been knocked unconscious or electrocuted. The history of Fátima would have been much different.

Close proximity to the manifestation, even before it developed the luminous component, was sufficient to stimulate the body and brain. The three children, whose brains were already sensitive, experienced a series of temporal lobe stimulations.

The religious content of the experiences was determined by their obsession with religious themes, their lack of education, and their behavior at the time of the experience. The only label they had for any unusual event was loaded with religious associations. When they said to each other, "Look! An angel!" at the time of first stimulation, the psychological set for the intense imagery was determined. (If they had grown up in a world of *Star Wars*, they would have seen and heard some variant of Luke Skywalker.)

Predictably, the "experiences" of the children, particularly Lúcia, during each stimulation by the surface manifestation, reflected their reinforcement history. First the "lady in light" told them to say their prayers and be good. As more and more people ridiculed them, however, the hallucinatory experiences became increasingly persecutory. The "lady in light" began to show scenes of death to people who did not believe her (and implicitly Lúcia).

The themes and details of the Fátima images were a hodgepodge of Lúcia's own childhood revelations and religious clichés. She had heard a wealth of religious statements (far more than children from the 1980s) and had been taught multiple rituals. They became the source materials for the experiences. The other children, who had a similar learning history, reported comparable (but not the same) perceptions.

Like contemporary *close encounter* experiences, Lúcia heard both truth and falsehood while stimulated by the surface manifestation. Whereas her prediction of the October event was true, the prediction that World War I would soon end was totally false.

The prediction of the Fátima event was no more fantastic than anticipation of lunar phase since the luminosities had already demonstrated a clear periodicity. The prediction of the end of the war had been derived from a different source altogether, namely, Lúcia's fantasy.

Indeed, information obtained during dissociated states and brain dysfunction can be enlightening. It is, however, not always correct. It has the same limits as any other form of interpolation. Unfortunately, it is also influenced by the wishes and personality of the perceiver.

There was, initially, individual variance. The young boy did not hear "the woman" speak. In fact, he remembers a haze that looked like a headless angel. The similarities in their stories occurred after the experiences, as they talked and compared events. Still unstable from the stimulation of their brains, each remembered each other's experiences as if they were his or her own. By the time they reached home after each experience, the memories were "the same."

That the experiences followed a direct stimulation of the brain, primarily the temporal lobe, is indicated by the objective amnesia shown by the children. Lúcia remembered many details that were actually the images stimulated in her brain by the intense EM manifestation. Yet she could not remember what she said during that period. The bright, detailed order of religious images is similar to the serial scenes and details noted by patients whose temporal lobes are stimulated. As the intense EM fields from the luminosity stimulated Lúcia's brain on that day in 1917, she experienced EM illusions that changed from Joseph to Christ to Mary.

Lúcia was certainly the expected core source for the detailed experiences. She had an excellent memory and enjoyed imagery-inducing activities such as games. She, like the other children, had vivid imaginations that were stimulated and embellished by direct contact with the surface manifestation. This stimulation was reinforcing as indicated by the consequences. The children felt sensations of ecstasy and great meaningfulness as the brain discharges continued. They were convinced of their own truthfulness. With such profound and real experiences (the children were not really lying), social derision was trivial.

The Fátima episodes, however, produced long-term damage. The repeated stimulations and discharges within their brains produced a marked instability within the temporal region. On several consequent occasions, they had repeater experiences in places other than the oak tree.

By far a more serious development, especially in Jacinta, was the development of cancer. The lung cancer was due to the radiation emitted around the tree (their major playground) before and after the luminosities. No doubt, the other forms of radiation emitted from the brighter displays added their component.

Lúcia survived the damage from radiation but still suffered from temporal lobe discharges. During these discharges, she again experienced words from the "Blessed Virgin." These experiences occurred even without the stimulation from the EM field near Fátima. The "experiences" occurred following conditions that stimulated her temporal lobe. Periods of anxiety or fear were associated with "hearing voices." Not surprisingly, smells such as the stench of cleaning the toilets unleashed one of her attacks. Her peers misinterpreted a twilight state as a "face of godly transcendence."

PHYSICAL ASPECTS OF THE "MARIAN APPARITION" EXPERIENCES IN FÁTIMA, 1917 — PRELIMINARY SYSTEMATIZATION AND MODELING

— Joaquim Fernandes, Ph.D. —

This paper intends to systemize a collection of physical sensations and reactions reported, by different witnesses, at the time of the religious events that took place at Cova da Iria in 1917. It proposes the possibility that what occurred at Fátima during the "apparition" experiences was a series of phenomena, linked by causal nexuses and an economy of hypotheses, which are plausible and identifiable today as the result of accumulated scientific knowledge and the intelligent reflections of various researchers. We can assume that these witnesses could not have anticipated that, in cases of exceptional phenomenological situations, similar events would later be explained in different cultural contexts. Recent laboratory experiments and their resulting models can be enumerated, which result from convergent multidisciplinary areas, that have the potential to lead to new insights into the psychophysical processes, of which apparitional manifestations, in general, are a part. Eventual new developments also appear to take shape in the domains of anthropology and the noetic sciences. Some theoretical models are taken from literature or developed from information that was directly given to the author.

INTRODUCTION

The genesis of the well known Fátima apparitions of 1917 in Portugal's mythical and cultural fabric must be perceived in the context of the Marian tradition of popular Catholicism, which was itself informed by sediments of Neolithic matriarchal cults. During its 80 years of history, the mental complex of Fátima's phenomena established itself and flourished in Portuguese society within the narrow bounds of a dichotomy of acceptance and denial, with no discussion of alternatives. This system of belief generated its own protective mechanisms, finding strength in the clarity of the immediate and the comfortable versus the indeterminate and ineffable. Consequently, it determined the way in which we perceive and reconstruct the "reality" of Fátima, within the boundaries of sensory and cultural "grids" that are recognized and identified.[1]

Recently, there has been growing curiosity on the part of researchers and scientists, spanning the physical, human, and social sciences, about the public, indeed famous, episodes of 1917. This convergence of a concrete and dispassionate approach to phenomena reputed to be extraordinary, even miraculous, by many, should not and does not intend to impact the status of religious and devotional meanings given by the dominant belief system to the events at Cova da Iria in 1917. Nevertheless, this surge of interest by the scientific community contradicts the alleged impossibility of analyzing objectively the phenomena deduced from the Fátima reports.

Scientific research must reaffirm its autonomy, and exercise its right to question, in all its plenitude, with no coercive boundaries or supposed unapproachable "territories" imposed to satisfy the circumstantial convenience of religious and temporal powers. Of paramount importance, it must overcome the classic dichotomy between belief and disbelief, between faith and reason, in a time when those "mental self-sufficiencies" are poised for redefinition.

None of this has anything to do with elitist and positivist presumptions, which are a recurring excuse for those who are not interested in confronting the new data and perspectives that the march of time has made possible. The integration of new facets of the Real on the outskirts of Knowledge comes from the capacity of human curiosity to erase successive impossibilities.

The first sign of a new, pluralistic, and non-conformist reading of "Marian" phenomena was seen in the publication, for the first time, in the 1980s, of works about Fátima that were historically based, notably, research performed by the author in cooperation with historian Fina d'Armada.[2]

Our review of the "Marian apparitions" at Fátima from the perspective of universal knowledge gave Fatimist discourse a new legitimacy. Gradually, we realized that our correlations and suppositions were gaining momentum and worthy allegiance as far as scientific collaboration was concerned. Among these collaborations, with researchers from various backgrounds, we must point out the continuing and fruitful dialogue that we have kept, since the early 1980s, with Auguste Meessen, a theoretical physicist at the Catholic University of Louvain. He combines a faithful adherence to the Catholic religion with an exemplary feeling of "not feeling imprisoned by dogma and believing that our duty will always be that of searching for the truth."[3]

MATERIALS AND METHODS

Our sources have included the original interrogations of the three child seers, as well as first-hand reports, selected according to their informative wealth. With these documents – approximately 100 testimonies – we have elaborated a factual database that in its variety and subjectivity presents both a possible and a historically verifiable portrait of what took place on that wasteland of the Portuguese countryside in 1917.

This material, because of its intrinsic wealth, was thoroughly and systematically compared to a variety of effects and characteristics found in close encounter experiences involving Unidentified Aerial Phenomena (UAP) and the literature of "communication" and "contact" recorded in eyewitness accounts during the course of the last 50 years.

One of the most curious and intriguing pieces of evidence comes from Lucia's original description in the "Parish Inquiry" of 1917, where she speaks of a "very luminous lady… who held a *glowing ball* in her hands, and turned her back on the seers when she went away."[4] A careful evaluation of the witnesses' descriptions allows us to consider the means of "locomotion" of the "luminous lady," how she appeared at the top of the tree and how she was removed from it. She ascended via the gradual manifestation of a cone-shaped luminous beam that was retractable and came from "up high" – from within a supposed cloud that moved in a peculiar pattern since it traveled *against* the wind, and that enveloped the feminine figure in its core. There are examples in the available literature consistent with this kind of luminous beam, which some authors describe as "solid light."[5]

Another determining factor was the search for an eventual mapping of the sightings of the so-called "Miracle of the Sun" on October 13, 1917, which we selected as a possible source of new information. We were able to show, by direct localization or by probable and indirect extrapolation, that most of the witnesses were distributed on the grounds of Cova da Iria along a 70-meter wide strip oriented roughly on a north-south axis. All of the known testimonies in which witnesses alleged physical effects and physiological reactions during the ten-minute time frame in which the "solar object" appeared to come close to the crowd were placed within that strip of land. The sensations described during that phenomenon were:

- A sudden and intense wave of heat;
- Immediate drying of rain-soaked clothing and soil; and
- Instant physiological effects, such as "miraculous cures."

All of these reactions followed the apparent descent of the "solar object" over the crowd gathered there. The triple effect described seems to support the hypothesis of a manifestation of great thermal amplitude coming from a source outside the witnesses. The anomalous movements of the "object," which supposedly "imitated the Sun," together with the simultaneity of its physical consequences, present some obstacles for the different explanatory models regarding the hallucinatory nature of such events. Within this context, we remind the discussion, which is still open, about proposals of "image projections" typical of several hypnotic states.[6]

RESULTS

We are, therefore, in a position to promote a necessary evaluation of the results, one as objective as possible, which will allow us to go beyond the emotional adhesion to the events at Cova da Iria in their sociological and anthropological contexts as manifestations of popular religiosity.

Among the documented material elements mentioned above, we must underline a set of references produced by the little seers and/or simple circumstantial witnesses of the apparitions, in which they claim to have heard a noise defined in the original documents of the time as "a buzzing, like a bee inside a jug, which was heard every time the Lady spoke to the seers *without moving her lips*" (emphasis added).[7]

Until not long ago, such analogies would have no other expression or meaning besides that of picturesque details, common to the language and folklore that characterize the region of Serra de Aire, to be found in the more or less naïve testimonies of believers who experienced the cyclical episodes around the small tree.

But it so happens that this "buzzing" phenomenon, which has been repeated here and there around the world, at different times, and in different cultural settings, could represent a coherent factual nexus if inserted within a global physical model. Hearing a sound such as this could relate to a "source" that is responsible for the remaining physical evidence reported at Fátima. The first association or correlation that emerges is a manifestation of electromagnetic radiation within the microwave spectrum, the physical and biological effects of which have been verified by scientific teams in French, Canadian, and American laboratories since the 1950s.[8]

This single clue, ignored both by the devotional dogmatism of pious believers and by the innocuous positivism of scientific skeptics, could be a viable starting point for the elaboration of a coherent hypothesis that explains the three phenomenological processes, and their simultaneous effects, that took place during the "solar" episode on October 13, 1917, including intense heat, the drying of clothing and soil, and other physiological effects.

This fundamental cause-and-effect relationship was initially advanced by the American nuclear physicist James McCampbell who, aware of our conclusions, strengthened the pertinence of this hypothesis in his deductions about the effects produced by an electromagnetic source of that magnitude upon living beings and the environment.[9]

Although subject to future verification, the electromagnetic radiation hypothesis would offer the possibility of having served as a communication "channel" between the luminous "Being" and the seer Lúcia, as the already mentioned experiences tend to corroborate.[10]

In fact, since McCampbell framed this hypothesis, laboratory initiatives have produced noteworthy results in support of this model, if we take it as a given that the witnesses of the Fátima apparitions heard a noise like the "buzzing of a bee." Among these corroborations are experiments, run by elements of the Canadian Institute of Electrical and Electronic Engineers, as well as privately by James C. Lin, Sergio Sales-Cunha, Joseph Battocletti, and Anthony Sances, which produced what is known as "Microwave Auditory Phenomenon" or "MAP."[11]

MAP could help us identify the kind of communication involved in the apparitional experiences of 1917 and other exceptional lay experiences, both of which have included altered states of consciousness. Whether in its religious context – like the example of Fátima – or lay context, both "contact" experiences are characterized by the reception of a "message" by the "chosen ones," who are then made receivers and keepers of it.[12]

Cultural variations of an identical process imply a "contactee syndrome" that by itself takes an ontogenetic path that varies, generally culminating in a vector of transformation (in the lay context) or is metanoic in nature (in the religious or mystical one).

In regard to the Canadian experiments, it is worth noting that short discharges of microwave radiation produced noises reverberating in the skulls of the test subjects. The subjects' heads were placed in line with a cone-shaped antenna, inside an appropriate and isolated compartment. The perceptions obtained consisted of a combination of audible sounds.

These studies showed that *the individuals subjected to these tests perceived "buzzing" noises* inside their heads when exposed to microwave radiation between 200 and 3,000 MHz, with an average strength of between 0.4 to 2mW/cm². The modulated frequencies varied between 200 and 400 Hz. In general, *the sounds were perceived inside the head, mostly in the occipital area.*

On the matter of this sound effect, we must recall the statement of a fourth and ignored seer of the 1917 phenomena, Carolina Carreira – whose testimony constitutes one of the most suggestive discoveries that we found in the original archives that had been kept at the sanctuary of Fátima. This almost ignored witness described to us the reception of some sort of "commands" *inside the head*, heard when she observed an "angel" of small stature and blond hair in the vicinity of the holm oak tree that cradled the descent of the "luminous lady." Those commands were repetitions of "Come here and pray three Hail Mary's; come here and pray three Hail Mary's…"[13]

To this suggestive framework of experiences are added new scientific approaches, which were personally transmitted to us by Jean Pierre Petit, a CNRS astrophysicist. This scientist informed us of experiments conducted at the CNES of Toulouse in 1979, which, as confirmed by the personal testimony of Professor Thourel, director of the DERMO, involved the reception of a kind of sensation *through a non-hearing path*, produced after he accidentally exposed himself to a modulated emission of the previously mentioned EM frequency.[14]

It seems obvious that the situations described open the way for inevitable comparisons. Something similar may have occurred at Cova da Iria and in the Canadian lab. Whatever, in fact, may have been the eliciting "agent," it is easy to see that these auditory sensations were reported by the seers and by others in close proximity, which supports the hypothesis of a radiant, "energetic," external, and non-subjective source in some way serving as a channel for a kind of non-verbal communication between the luminous Being and the child witness Lúcia dos Santos.

DISCUSSION

The experimental stages achieved by scientific and laboratory research in the areas of so-called "mind control" are very well illustrated in the available literature, although not all information on this important subject has been totally disclosed to the public by governmental authorities. [15]

Meanwhile, the discussion of verifiable hypothetical and explanatory models that can confirm the physical cause-effect nexus considered here is being advanced by prominent figures in several areas of borderland science.

As an example, the Swiss biologist Claude Rifat, having considered the narratives and representations of the contents of the "apparitional" experiences, suggests that we should pay attention to the *Locus Coeruleus*, an important region of the mammalian brain that could play a part in these "unreal" situations. Rifat suggests that the source of radiation X from the luminous Being, etc. would interfere with the normal functions of that region of the brain. There is the possibility, therefore, of the creation of induced "images," adapted in consonance with the cultural contents of the "messages" transmitted by the protagonists of those singular events that shatter our subjective "normalcy."[16]

Similarly, we draw your attention to the emergence and development of a new scope of analysis, inspired by advances in the neurosciences, that intends to approach in a particularly original way the global interdependencies and relations between the brain and the effects of religious and transcendent experiences. It is the field of Neurotheology, exemplified in the work of psychiatrist Eugen d'Aquili and neurologist Andrew Newberg at the University of Pennsylvania, in particular, their long-term study of brain function and blood flow during the practice of meditation by Tibetan Buddhist monks.[17]

Another important clue may exist in the interference of the EM spectrum that was recently found in "crop circles" by a team led by U.S. biophysicist C. Levengood of the BLT Research Team at the University of Michigan. By investigating the interiors of "crop circles," it was possible to observe in the laboratory that the physiological alteration of these plants – including such effects as drying, dehydration, and withering – were identical to the ones produced by an emission of microwave EM radiation and corresponded to different levels of absorption of this type of radiation by the plants.[18] Undoubtedly, this verification will prove helpful in explaining the three effects observed during the "Miracle of the Sun" on October 13, 1917.

When we set out to establish models and hypotheses based on subjective testimonies, deficiently informative and imprecise, affected by a universe of constraints both in space and time, not all is linear or within reach. The minimum selection that we have brought to this anthology, however, puts together some of the vital signs with which we can draw some semblance of coherence and objectivity. This is so precisely because the writers whose work is represented here anticipated parallel situations as "impossible" as the ones presently taking place before our very eyes.

The great methodological problem facing evanescent, uncontrollable, and hardly replicable phenomena is determining, as consistently as possible, their internal coherence, backed by a comfortable number of independent observations. In complex frameworks such as these, it is very important, as stated by Auguste Meessen, to consider first, the reliability of particular information, second, the number of similar cases, and third, the scientific analysis of the physical effects at stake.[19]

The sequence of physical aspects, which will eventually become a model because of further investigations, cannot be put aside or minimized only by caprice, coincidence, or collective hysteria. Laboratories do not sympathize with subjectivity. In the same sense, the exploration of these connections, at the neurological level, has the potential to become an open road for the analysis of the formation of the "messages" elaborated by the "contacted," ancient and modern, religious and lay, in different cultural times and places. Of special interest are the implications for the formulation of a model of non-verbal communication, extensive to "contact" experiences, both lay and religious, transcultural and timeless, and the emergence of a new transdisciplinary area – the neurotheology or neurobiology of religion itself.

As will certainly be verified, the future of science – as told by its past history – promises new and stimulating "readings" of what is temporarily "unexplainable" and exists on the margins of current knowledge and belief systems.

Notes

[1] Cf. MORIN, E., *O Método III: O Conhecimento do Conhecimento/1* [*Method III: The Knowledge of Knowledge*], Mem Martins, Publicações Europa-América, 1987.

[2] Cf. d'ARMADA, F., *O que se passou em Fátima em 1917* [*Fátima – What Happened in 1917*], Amadora, Livraria Bertrand, 1980; d'ARMADA, F. and FERNANDES, J., *Intervenção Extraterrestre em Fátima – as aparições e o fenómeno OVNI* [*Extraterrestrial Intervention at Fátima: The Apparitions and the UFO Phenomenon*], Amadora, Livraria Bertrand, 1982; d'ARMADA, F. and FERNANDES, J., *As aparições de Fátima e o fenómeno OVNI* [*The Apparitions of Fátima and the UFO Phenomenon*], Lisbon, Estampa, 1995; d'ARMADA, F. and FERNANDES, J., *Fátima – nos bastidores do segredo* [*Fátima – Behind the Secret*], Lisbon, Âncora Editora, 2002.

[3] Personal communication, July 12, 1980.

[4] d'ARMADA, F. and FERNANDES, J., *Intervenção Extraterrestre em Fátima – as aparições e o fenómeno OVNI*, Amadora, Livraria Bertrand, 1982, p. 33.

[5] HEERING, J., "A comparative analysis of 62 'solid light beam' cases," in *UFO Phenomena*, Bologna, 2, 1977; Cf. also MEESSEN, A., in *Inforespace*, Brussels, May/September, 1978; Cf. for an exposition of physical and physiological results, NIEMTZOV, R.C., "Physiological and radiation effects from intense luminous unidentified objects," in *UPIAR Research in Progress*, Bologna, II(2 and 3), 1984.

[6] OLMOS, V.J.B. and GUASP, M., *Los Ovnis y la ciencia* [*UFOs and Science*], Madrid, Plaza & Janes, 1981, cap. XI, p. 314 *et seq.*; Cf. also PERSINGER, M.A. *et al.*, "Issues forum: Tectonic stress theory," in *Journal of UFO Studies*, Chicago, 1990, 2, pp. 99-176; LAWSON, A.H., "Hypnosis of imaginary UFO 'abductees,'" in *UFO Phenomena*, Bologna, 1978-79, III(1), pp. 219-258.

[7] d'ARMADA, F. and FERNANDES, J., op. cit., *supra*, pp. 64-70.

[8] See the paper in this volume written by Raul Berenguel.

[9] McCAMPBELL, J., *Ufology*, Belmont, Jaymac Company, 1973.

[10] See footnote 8, *supra*.

[11] See *Proceedings of the IEEE*, 68(1), January 1980.

[12] For the lay cases studied from the viewpoint of psychotherapy, see MACK, J.E., *Sequestro* [*Abduction*], Lisbon, Planeta, 1994, and more recently, by the same author, *Passport to the Cosmos: Human transformation and alien encounters*, New York, Crown Publishers, 1999.

[13] d'ARMADA, F. and FERNANDES, J., op. cit., note 4, pp. 361-372.

[14] Personal communication, December 3, 1983.

[15] See the paper in this volume written by Raul Berenguel and the vast body of historical research into the defense establishments of the United States and the former Soviet Union.

[16] RIFAT, C., "A theoretical framework for the problem of non-contact between an advanced extraterrestrial civilization and mankind: Symbolic sequential communication versus symbolic non-sequential communication," in *UFO Phenomena*, Bologna, 3, 273-288, 1978-79; see also by the same author, "Is the *Locus Coeruleus* an important anatomical center of the brain, involved in the most bizarre aspects of UFO reports? – The induced dream hypothesis," in *UFO Phenomena*, Bologna, II(1), 1977.

[17] NEWBERG, A.B. and d'AQUILI, E.G., "The Neuropsychology of Religious and Spiritual Experience," in ANDRESEN, J. and FORMAN, R.K.C. (eds.), *Cognitive Models and Spiritual Maps*, Thorverton, Imprint Academic, 2000, pp. 251-266.

[18] LEVENGOOD, C. and TALBOT, N., "Dispersion of energies in worldwide crop formations," in *Physiologia Plantarum*, Stockholm, 105, 615-624, June 1999.

[19] "Note about Marian apparitions," personal communication, January 8, 2001.

POSSIBLE PSYCHOLOGICAL AND PHYSICAL FACTORS RELATED TO MARIAN VISIONS

— Dr. Frank McGillion —

The text attempts a composite revision that is differentiated from the factors that could unleash the Marian apparition phenomena. Causal heterogeneity is present in this proposition, which also includes geo-magnetic and environmental stimuli, individual and cultural expectations, as well as pineal gland and central nervous system intervention, as framed by the psychodynamic theories of Carl G. Jung. The explanation reduces itself at various levels wherein several visionary typologies in different epochs are analyzed historically and symbolically. The Jungian legacy is once again invoked to analyze the phenomenology from a point-of-view of matriarchal archetypes, among others.

INTRODUCTION

The phenomenon of purported visionary experiences of the Virgin Mary, generally termed Marian visions, is a complex one and undoubtedly requires ongoing, multidisciplinary investigation to assess its origins and significance. Certain phenomena and hypotheses associated with such visions, however, can be usefully addressed with a view to helping us understand at least some aspects of their possible genesis and form.

In this article, I shall address specific phenomena and hypotheses that might assist our comprehension of such visions and that may be linked, through some connection of greater or lesser importance, to the actions of the temporal lobe of the brain and the pineal gland and its hormones.

It is hoped that by so doing, a general schema will emerge that could account for certain aspects of the genesis of such visions, who is most likely to experience them, and in what form they might be expected to appear. To this end, the following will be considered:

- How such visions may be induced by exposure to ambient

geomagnetic and similar physical phenomena, and whether, or not, these are necessary or sufficient for their occurrence;

• How our interaction with ambient physical forces might be associated with certain physiological processes in the central nervous system that correlate with these visions, which in turn might relate, directly or indirectly, to relevant actions of the pineal gland and its hormones, which include melatonin;

• How certain aspects of Carl G. Jung's psychodynamic theories might provide a common context for such visions, suggest who might be expected to experience them, and presage in what form they might be expected to manifest in different cultures.

In considering all of these, due significance will be given to the fact that such visions are frequently reported as being perceived by more than one person simultaneously, at one or more locations, and on an ongoing basis.

POSSIBLE PHYSICAL FACTORS OF RELEVANCE

A great deal of modern scientific thought suggests that many religious phenomena, including visionary experiences, have specific biological correlates. (1) In particular, such experiences are often associated with alterations in the activity of the temporal lobes and other areas of the central nervous system. (2-4)

Biological Origins
From this perspective, religious experiences are thought to occur as a result of physical, pharmacological, or psychopathological actions on the central nervous system. Indeed, the religious experiences of specific individuals ranging from the time of the Old Testament to modern times, and considered by many to be genuinely visionary, have been attributed to such phenomena (5-8). So, too, have apparent revelations formally attributed, by their percipients, to the Virgin Mary and Christ. (9)

Presences
The general sense of an alien presence being close to an individual, or the experiencing of visions of various types, has been produced virtually on demand by artificial electrical stimulation of the temporal lobe area of the

brain by electrodes placed on the crania of volunteers. Similar phenomena have been reported as a result of such stimulation by naturally occurring geomagnetic and other geophysical forces. (10-18)

Personality
Related studies suggest that temporal lobe lability correlates with certain personality indicators defined by the Swiss psychiatrist Carl G. Jung, in a manner consistent with the view that individual cognition is derived from a temporal lobe lability factor: something that could predispose individuals to visionary and related experiences to a greater or lesser degree. (19)

Religious Experiences
Subjective phenomena of the sort commonly referred to as "mystical experiences," and phenomena commonly associated with religious visions, such as distortions of perception of space and time, also show a significant correlation with geomagnetic activity. (20-25) In addition, individuals with "psychic interests" show specific alterations in temporal lobe activity. (26)

Egyptian Visions
More specifically, visions of the Blessed Virgin Mary have been reported in Zeitoun, Egypt, where, in 1968, visions of a figure, considered by many to be the Virgin, appeared on a number of occasions on the roof of a Coptic Church. Again, these apparitions have been shown to correlate with geophysical variables, in this instance, tectonic strain-related emissions. (27)

Biological Considerations
Whatever the phenomenological status of Marian visions, a possible candidate in terms of the biological correlates of their occurrence, in addition to the temporal lobes, is the pineal gland. The general sense of alien presences of one sort or another, and associated experiences produced by transcranial stimulation, is more evident in people who demonstrate a significant alteration in circulating levels of the pineal hormone, melatonin. (28)

The Pineal Gland
In addition, in response to electromagnetic stimulation, the pineal secretes a number of hormones, which show widespread biological activity including significant psychoactive actions. (29, 30) Such effects on the pineal gland and its hormones can also be produced by electromagnetic fields of various types and strengths including those of the geomagnetic field type. (31-34)

Electromagnetic Fields

Accordingly, electromagnetic fields of appropriate types at specific geographical locations could, by way of a mechanism involving the pineal gland, correlate with various types of visionary experience, including those referred to as Marian visions.

Visions by Groups of Individuals

A major feature of many religious visions is that they are often reported by groups of individuals. Obviously, therefore, any hypothesis, or set of hypotheses, that addresses the issue of such visions has to account for the fact that it is often reported that more than one percipient perceives these visions simultaneously. So how could such collective experiences occur?

Geomagnetic Effects

While still relatively speculative, there is a significant body of evidence that suggests that geomagnetic, ambient and other electromagnetic radiations, and the like, are capable of causing qualitatively similar subjective effects in individuals as objectively assessed by changes in EEG patterns. Such actions could produce a greater or lesser degree of commonality of experience in a group of individuals, and it has been postulated that such psycho-physiological effects of these fields could literally "brainwash" groups of people. (35-39)

Visions in the Sky

Jung described an example of what he considered to be a collective exteriorization phenomenon related to his concept of the collective unconscious, which we discuss in greater detail below. This concerned what we now call unidentified flying objects, which he collectively termed: "a modern myth of things seen in the sky." (40)

Pharmacological Assistance

In addition, when, after appropriate pharmacological preparation, individuals are exposed to certain stimuli, each person experiences what we can reasonably say are identical visionary experiences, which those of us not so primed cannot perceive. Again, the associated biological mechanism involved may well involve the pineal gland. (41)

Mesmer's Magnetism

Hence, in a manner not dissimilar to the effects reported by Anton Mesmer during his magnetically induced healing of what he termed his "sickly ladies," it appears that perception beyond the ordinary human range can occur, in a predictable and regular manner, in a group of people of similar physical and/or psychological predisposition and constitution. (42)

General Effects of Geomagnetism

There appears to be no doubt either that, in a number of ways, geomagnetic and other physical phenomena can influence groups of people more or less simultaneously, producing a variety of subjective and objective effects that range from the relatively innocuous to the overtly fatal. (43- 48)

Dietary Factors

The role of possible dietary contaminants in individual and collective instances of visionary experience – including that causing the condition known as "ergotism" – are also worthy of mention in this general context. It seems highly unlikely, however, that contamination of any sort could provide consistent, sequential visionary experiences in a discrete group of individuals over a protracted period of time. (49)

More Speculative Examples

At a more speculative level, there are reports in the parapsychological literature of group experiences of specific types of beings, including those of groups that in some manner believe they can "create" such entities. One of the most dramatic was the apparent creation of an active entity by a group who practiced techniques similar to those employed by Spiritualists of the Victorian era in the United Kingdom. (50)

Eastern Entities

Whatever the merits, or otherwise, of such reports, from a phenomenological perspective, they certainly suggest that a group of appropriately motivated individuals can collectively experience, and possibly in some sense, "manufacture" a presence of a type that appears to physically manifest; much as, in the Eastern tradition, the entities referred to as *tulpas* are allegedly produced by intent.

WHAT A MARIAN VISION MIGHT LOOK LIKE

Once apparent by whatever means, can we predict what a vision of the Marian variety might be expected to look like? Obviously, this is a question difficult to address without being tautological. After all, religious visions are defined as such because of their content. A deeper insight into this question, and a possible basis for attaining a cross-cultural view of such visions might possibly be obtained, however, from considering visionary phenomena in a general psychological context.

Jung's Collective Unconscious

Carl G. Jung's theory of the Collective Unconscious in general, and his concept of the archetypes in particular, appears to provide a viable theoretical context within which to predict the possible form a Marian-type vision would take, with the specific archetype he referred to as the Mother Archetype, being of special interest in this respect.

According to Jung, in addition to our *personal unconscious* – the contents of which are defined solely by what we have experienced – we also have an inborn *collective unconscious*, the contents of which are hereditary and composed of a "...common psychic substrate of a super personal nature." (51)

Archetypes

While the personal unconscious is deemed to be composed of "feeling-toned" complexes, the collective unconscious is composed of what he termed "archetypes," empirical contents of the collective unconscious that have not been submitted to conscious awareness. These are the dynamic psychological entities that Jung suggested provide us with a basis for universally common aspects of cultures, such as myths, legends, and so on. According to Jung, in dreams and visions, archetypes present in a form that is in great part defined by what tone and context the individual attributes to the overall experience.

Synchronicity

Jung states that when someone is under emotional stress and/or using active imagination, archetypes can become constellated: i.e., manifest in some apposite form in either a subjective or objective experience. He used the term *synchronicity* to describe external physical phenomena in the form of coincidence that occur within a specific context, and considered such coincidences to occur in great part as a consequence of archetypal constellation. (52) One of Jung's formal definitions of synchronicity is of particular interest here:

> "The coincidence of a certain psychic content with a corresponding
> objective process... perceived to take place simultaneously." (53)

In his autobiography, Jung gives several examples of such exteriorization phenomena, including one where physical phenomena were associated with his own charged emotional state, and another where the physical manifestation in question occurred in the presence of Sigmund Freud. (54)

Role of Emotion

Obviously, as with archetype constellation, Jung considered synchronistic events most likely to occur in individuals under severe emotional stress, or "active interest." Indeed, he attributed the apparently positive results of a celebrated experiment he carried out to test his ideas on synchronicity almost exclusively to his emotional involvement in the study. (55)

The Mother Archetype

Whatever one's view of Jung's ideas, one of his posited archetypes, the Mother Archetype, is of significant interest in terms of seeking a *general context* for Marian visions and, cross-culturally, those of a related nature. As he specifically stated, "The concept of the Great Mother belongs to the field of comparative religion." (56) According to this view, the constellated Mother Archetype would be expected to display specific attributes whether it appeared in dream, visionary, or other form.

General Form

Thus, it would assume the form of the literal mother, motherhood in any form, or the form of any individual such as, e.g., a teacher who was in a role commensurate with motherhood. More figuratively, it would be associated with more abstract mother figures such as goddesses in general and the Mother of God in particular.

Associations

In addition, it would be expected to be associated with anything representing fertility, arousing devotion or awe, giving succor or comfort, and with wisdom, intuition, or instruction.

Specific Form and Context

In more specific terms, the constellated archetype would be expected to manifest as a lady or maiden with otherworldly attributes, and be associated contextually with symbols of fertility and fecundity such as springs, trees, caves, rivers, rocks, stones, containers, vessels, protective items (such as relics or mandalas), and flowers – especially the rose or lotus, and other such symbols of containment. The constellation of this archetype would also be associated with secrets, prophecy, the underworld, the Moon, and by association, the Sun, and anything associated with redemption. (57, 58)

Converse Aspects

The opposite, or negative, aspects of this archetype could also be evident, in whatever form, to a percipient. In the Christian tradition, Jung specifically cites the Virgin as being "the Lord's mother and cross..." in this respect, and, in the Indian tradition, the goddess Kali as being the "...loving and terrible mother." (59)

The Virgin

In Jungian terms, therefore, the Mother Archetype, especially in the Christian tradition, could be expected to present itself in a visionary experience in the form of the Virgin Mary, the Mother of God, displaying some or all of the above attributes and characteristics.

Cultural Content

In addition, more specific features might be expected to occur, such as certain religious artifacts determined by projection of aspects of the percipient's or percipients' education, religion, expectations, and culture. Culturally specific attributes of an individual's predisposition towards a preferred choice of color and specific number, e.g., has been shown to reflect a region's religious and cultural milieu. (60)

Festum Asinorum

It is of interest to note that Jung passed specific comment on the fact that the feast called the *festum asinorum* was formerly held in Europe to commemorate the traditional flight of the Virgin Mary into Egypt. Hence, the ostensible appearance of an apparition of the Virgin Mary in Egypt, as referred to above, has an historical and cultural context, as Jung would suggest it must have. (61)

At first sight anyway, this general schema seems consistent with reports received from those who have claimed to experience visions of the Virgin Mary, Kali, Sophia, or other female religious figures.

As indicated, according to Jung, constellation of archetypes occurs most frequently in states of high emotion. Accordingly, they might be expected to occur more frequently, and/or vividly, in individuals or groups under duress.

It is possibly worthy of note, in this respect, that women can demonstrate certain behavioral problems during periods of increased geomagnetic activity, especially when they present with premenstrual syndrome, while women with spiritualistic interests demonstrate certain differences in temporal lobe function from those with no such interests. (62, 63)

Hence, in general terms, Marian and related visions might be expected to manifest in a specific cultural form to those who are most receptive due to factors such as gender, increased expectation, higher suggestibility, lack of formal education, or related factors. These might include those with constitutional and other pathologies, the young and poorly educated, and be expected to occur more frequently in females.

CONCLUSION

Given this, it seems perfectly possible that groups of people can and do collectively experience visions of whatever type for credible, if not common, psychological and physical reasons, that include interactions of geomagnetic and other fields with the temporal lobe, the pineal gland, and other possible biological structures and mechanisms.

In addition, it appears that Jung's system of analytical psychology in general and his views on archetypal forms in particular might be worthy of deeper consideration in this respect, especially given the fact individual lability of the temporal lobes appears to equate with Jung's personality types.

Accordingly, it is feasible that Marian visions are associated with quantitatively similar physical and/or psychological phenomena, which, if nothing else, might provide necessary, though possibly not sufficient, conditions for such experiences to occur.

Perhaps most importantly, such a general schema for visionary experience provides a basis for further empirical tests that may lead us to a deeper understanding of this phenomenon.

Notes

[1] PERSINGER, M.A., "The neuropsychiatry of paranormal experiences," *Journal of Neuropsychiatry and Clinical Neuroscience,* 13(4), 515-24, Fall 2001.

[2] TUCKER, D.M. and NOVELLY, A., "The remarkable symptoms of the temporal lobe dysfunction," *Annals of the Royal Academy of National Medicine (Madrid),* 118(3), 583-90, 2001.

[3] PERSINGER, M.A., "Paranormal and religious beliefs may be mediated differentially by subcortical and cortical phenomenological processes of the temporal (limbic) lobes," *Perceptual and Motor Skills,* 76(1), 247-51, February 1993.

[4] "Neurobiology of the numinous," *Annals of the Royal Academy of National*

Medicine (Madrid), 113(2), 513-27; discussion 528-31, 1996.

[5] ALTSCHULER, E.L., "Did Ezekiel have temporal lobe epilepsy?," *Archives of General Psychiatry*, 59(6), 561-2, June 2002.

[6] BRORSON, J.R. and BREWER, K., "St. Paul and temporal lobe epilepsy," *Journal of Neurology and Neurosurgical Psychiatry*, 51(6), 886-7, June 1988.

[7] LANDSBOROUGH, D., "St. Paul and temporal lobe epilepsy," *Journal of Neurology and Neurosurgical Psychiatry*, 50(6), 659-64, June 1987.

[8] "Neuropsychology of Swedenborg's Visions," *Perceptual and Motor Skills*, 88(2), 377-83, April 1999.

[9] SUESS, L.A. and PERSINGER, M.A., "Geophysical variables and behavior: XCV1. Experiences attributed to Christ and Mary at Marora Canada may have been consequences of environmental electromagnetic stimulation: implications for religious movements," *Perceptual and Motor Skills*, 93(2), 435-50, October 2001.

[10] COOK, C.M. and PERSINGER, M.A., "Experimental induction of the 'sensed presence' in normal subjects and an exceptional subject," *Perceptual and Motor Skills*, 85(2), 683-93, October 1997.

[11] PERSINGER, M.A., BUREAU, Y.R., PEREDERY, O.P., and RICHARDS, P.M., "The sensed presence as right hemispheric intrusions into the left hemispheric awareness of self: an illustrative case study," *Perceptual and Motor Skills*, 78(3), Part 1, 999-1009, June 1994.

[12] PERSINGER, M.A., TILLER, S.G. and KOREN, S.A., "Experimental simulation of a haunt experience and elicitation of paroxysmal electroencephalographic activity by transcerebral complex magnetic fields: induction of a synthetic 'ghost'?," *Perceptual and Motor Skills*, 90(2), 65974, April 2000.

[13] PERSINGER M.A., "Sense of a presence and suicidal ideation following traumatic brain injury: indications of right-hemispheric intrusions from neuropsychological profiles," *Psychology Reports*, 75(3), Part 1, 1059-70, December 1994.

[14] PERSINGER, M.A., "Personality changes following brain injury as a grief response to the loss of sense of self: phenomenological themes as indices of local lability and neurocognitive structuring as psychotherapy," *Psychology Reports*, 72(3), Part 2, 1059-68, June 1993.

[15] LAVALLEE, M.R. and PERSINGER, M.A., "Left ear (right temporal lobe) suppressions during dichotic listening, ego-alien intrusion experiences and spiritualistic beliefs in normal women," *Perceptual and Motor Skills*, 75(2), 547-51, October 1992.

[16] PERSINGER, M.A., "Personality changes following brain injury as a grief response to the loss of sense of self: phenomenological themes as indices of local lability and neurocognitive structuring as psychotherapy," *Psychology Reports*, 72(3), Part 2, 1059-68, June 1993.

[17] PERSINGER, M.A., TILLER, S.G. and KOREN, S.A., "Experimental simulation of a haunt experience and elicitation of paroxysmal electroencephalographic activity by transcerebral complex magnetic fields: induction of a synthetic 'ghost'?," *Perceptual and Motor Skills*, 90(2), 659-74, April 2000.

[18] PERSINGER, M.A., "Sense of a presence and suicidal ideation following traumatic

brain injury: indications of right-hemispheric intrusions from neuropsychological profiles," *Psychology Reports*, 75(3), Part 1, 1059-70, December 1994.

[19] HUOT, B., MAKAREC, K. and PERSINGER, M.A., "Temporal lobes, signs, and Jungian dimensions of personality," *Perceptual and Motor Skills*, 69(3), Part 1, 841-2, December 1989.

[20] PERSINGER, M.A., "Religious and mystical experiences as artifacts of temporal lobe function: a general hypothesis," *Perceptual and Motor Skills*, 57(3), Part 2, 1255-62, December 1983.

[21] COOK, C.M., KOREN, S.A. and PERSINGER, M.A., "Subjective time estimation by humans is increased by counterclockwise but not clockwise circumcerebral rotations of phase-shifting magnetic pulses in the horizontal plane," *Neuroscience Letters*, 268(2), 61-4, June 18th, 1999.

[22] PERSINGER, M.A., "On the nature of space-time in the observation of physical events in science," *Perceptual and Motor Skills*, 88(3), Part 2, 1210-6, June 1999.

[23] PERSINGER, M.A., "Feelings of past lives as expected perturbations within the neurocognitive processes that generate the sense of self: contributions from limbic lability and vectorial hemisphericity," *Perceptual and Motor Skills*, 83(3), Part 2, 1107-21, December 1996.

[24] PERSINGER, M.A., "Vectorial cerebral hemisphericity as differential sources for the sensed presence, mystical experiences, and religious conversions," *Perceptual and Motor Skills*, 76(3), Part 1, 915-30, June 1993.

[25] PERSINGER, M.A., "Neuropsychological profiles of adults who report sudden rememberings of early childhood memories: implications for claims of sex abuse, visitation/abduction experiences," *Perceptual and Motor Skills*, 75(1), 259-66, August 1992.

[26] PERSINGER, M.A. and FISHER, S.D., "Elevated, specific temporal lobe signs in a population engaged in psychic studies," *Perceptual and Motor Skills*, 71(3), Part 1, 817-8, December 1990.

[27] DERR, J.S. and PERSINGER, M.A., "Geophysical variables and behavior: LIV. Zeitoun (Egypt) apparitions of the Virgin Mary as tectonic strain-induced luminosities," *Perceptual and Motor Skills*, 68(1), 123-8, February 1989.

[28] PERSINGER, M.A., "Average diurnal changes in melatonin levels are associated with hourly incidence of bereavement apparitions: support for the hypothesis of temporal (limbic) lobe microseizuring," *Perceptual and Motor Skills*, 76(2), 444-6, April 1993.

[29] McGILLION, F.B., "The Pineal Gland and the Ancient Art of Iatromathematica," *Journal of Scientific Exploration*, 16/1, 19-44, 2002.

[30] RONEY-DOUGAL, S.M., "Recent Findings Relating to the Possible Role of the Pineal Gland in Affecting Psychic Ability," *Journal of the Society for Psychical Research*, 313-376, 1989.

[31] YAGA, K., REITHER, R.J., MANCHESTER, L.C., NIEVES, H., SUN, J.H., and CHEN, L.D., "Pineal Sensitivity to Pulsed Static Magnetic Field Changes during the Photoperiod," *Brain Research Bulletin*, 30(1-2), 153-6, 1993.

[32] SCHNEIDER, T., THALAU, H.P. and SEMM, P., "Effects of light or different

Earth-strength magnetic fields on the nocturnal melatonin concentration in a migratory bird," *NeuroScience Letters*, 168(1-2), 73-5, February 28, 1994.

[33] WEYDAHL, A., SOTHERN, R.B., CORNELISSEN, G. and WETTERBERG, L., "Geomagnetic activity influences the melatonin secretion at latitude 70 degrees north," *Biomedical Pharmacotherapy*, 55 Supplement 1:57s-62s, 2001.

[34] SOUETRE, E., SALVATI, E., BELUGOU, J.L., DOUILLET, P., BRACCINI T. and DARCOURT, G., "Seasonality of suicides: environmental, sociological, and biological covariations," *Journal of Affective Disorders*, 13(3), 215-25, November-December 1987.

[35] PERSINGER, M., RICHARDS, P.M. and KOREN, S.A., "Differential entrainment of electroencephalographic activity by weak complex electromagnetic fields," *Perceptual and Motor Skills*, 84(2), 527-36, April 1997.

[36] PERSINGER, M.A. and MAKAREC, K., "Possible learned detection of exogenous brain frequency electromagnetic fields: a case study," *Perceptual and Motor Skills*, 65(2), 444-6, October 1987.

[37] PERSINGER, M.A., "On the possibility of directly accessing every human brain by electromagnetic induction of fundamental algorithms," *Perceptual and Motor Skills*, 80(3), Part 1, 791-9, June 1995.

[38] HEALEY, F., PERSINGER, M.A. and KOREN, S.A., "Control of 'choice' by application of the electromagnetic field equivalents of spoken words: mediation by emotional meaning rather than linguistic dimensions?," *Perceptual and Motor Skills*, 85(3), Part 2, 1411-8, December 1997.

[39] PERSINGER, M.A. and MAKAREC, K., "Possible learned detection of exogenous brain frequency electromagnetic fields: a case study," *Perceptual and Motor Skills*, 65(2), 444-6, October 1987.

[40] JUNG, C.G., "Civilization in transition," in *Flying Saucers: A Modern Myth of Things Seen in the Sky*, pp. 309-433, in *Collected Works*, London, 10 RKP, 1959, second edition, 1968, pp. 307-418.

[41] PERSINGER, M.A., "Putative perception of rotating permanent magnetic fields following ingestion of LSD," *Perceptual and Motor Skills*, 87(2), 601-2, October 1998.

[42] ELLENBERGER, H., *The Discovery of the Unconscious – The History and Evolution of Dynamic Psychiatry*, New York, Basic Books, 1970, Fontana Press edition, 1994, pp. 58-83.

[43] PERSINGER, M.A., "Sudden unexpected death in epileptics following sudden, intense increases in geomagnetic activity: prevalence of effect and potential mechanisms," *International Journal of Biometeorology*, 38(4), 180-7, May 1995.

[44] O'CONNOR, R.P. and PERSINGER, M.A., "Geophysical variables and behavior: LXXXV. Sudden infant death, bands of geomagnetic activity, and pc1 (0.2 to 5 HZ) geomagnetic micropulsations," *Perceptual and Motor Skills*, 88(2), 391-7, April 1999.

[45] PERSINGER, M.A., "Out-of-body-like experiences are more probable in people with elevated complex partial epileptic-like signs during periods of enhanced geomagnetic activity: a nonlinear effect," *Perceptual and Motor Skills*, 80(2), 563-9,

April 1995.

[46] PERSINGER, M.A., "Geophysical variables and behavior: LXXI. Differential contribution of geomagnetic activity to paranormal experiences concerning death and crisis: an alternative to the ESP hypothesis, *Perceptual and Motor Skills*, 76(2), 555-62, April 1993.

[47] DE SANO, C.F. and PERSINGER, M.A., "Geophysical variables and behavior: XXXIX. Alterations in imaginings and suggestibility during brief magnetic field exposures," *Perceptual and Motor Skills*, 64(3), Part 1, 968-70, June 1987.

[48] PERSINGER, M.A., RICHARDS, P.M. and KOREN S.A., "Differential ratings of pleasantness following right and left hemispheric application of low energy magnetic fields that stimulate long-term potentiation," *International Journal of Neuroscience*, 79(3-4), 191-7, December 1994.

[49] MATOSSIAN, M.K., "Bewitched or intoxicated? The etiology of witch persecution in early modern England," *Medizinhist Journal*, 18(1-2), 33-42, 1983.

[50] OWEN, I.M. and SPARROW, S., "Generation of paranormal physical phenomena with an imaginary communicator," *New Horizons*, 1/3, 6-13, 1974.

[51] JUNG, C.G., *The Archetypes and the Collective Unconscious*, in *Collected Works*, London, 9/1 RKP, 1959, second edition, 1968, p. 3.

[52] JUNG, C.G., *The Structure and Dynamics of the Psyche*, in *Collected Works*, London, 8 RKP, 1960, second edition, 1969, pp. 417-532.

[53] De VRIES-EK, P. and McGILLION, F.B., "A Further Look at Jung's Astrological Experiment in the Context of His Concept of Synchronicity," in *Jaarbook van de Interdisciplinaire Verenniging Voor Analytische Psychologie* [*Yearbook of the Interdisciplinary Study of Analytical Psychology*], 13, 76-93, 1997; See also McGILLION, F.B., "The Influence of Wilhelm Fliess' Cosmobiology on Sigmund Freud," *Culture and Cosmos*, vol. 2/1, 33-48, 1998.

[54] JUNG, C.G., *Memories, Dreams, and Reflections*, London, Collins, Fount Paperbacks, 1961, pp. 178-179, 215.

[55] JUNG, C.G., *The Structure and Dyamics of the Psyche*, in *Collected Works*, London, 8 RKP, 1960, second edition, 1969, p. 477.

[56] JUNG, C.G., *The Archetypes and the Collective Unconscious*, in *Collected Works*, London, 9/1 RKP, 1959, second edition, 1968, p. 75.

[57] JUNG, C.G., *The Archetypes and the Collective Unconscious*, in *Collected Works*, London, 9/1 RKP, 1959, second edition, 1968, pp. 81-83.

[58] JUNG, C.G., *The Archetypes and the Collective Unconscious*, in *Collected Works*, London, 9/1 RKP, 1959, second edition, 1968, p. 81.

[59] JUNG, C.G., *The Archetypes and the Collective Unconscious*, in *Collected Works*, London, 9/1 RKP, 1959, second edition, 1968, p. 82.

[60] KULOGLU, M., ATMACA, M., TEZCAN, A.E., UNAL, A., and GEICI, O. "Color and number preferences of patients with psychiatric disorders in eastern Turkey," *Perceptual and Motor Skills*, 94(1), 207-213, 2002.

[61] JUNG, C.G., *The Archetypes and the Collective Unconscious*, in *Collected Works*, London, RKP, 1959, second edition, 1968, p. 258.

[62] RENTON, C.M. and PERSINGER, M.A., "Elevations of complex partial

epileptic-like experiences during increased geomagnetic activity for women reporting "premenstrual syndrome," *Perceptual and Motor Skills*, 86(1), 240-2, February 1998.

[63] LAVALEE, M.R. and PERSINGER, M.A., Left ear (right temporal lobe) suppressions during dichotic listening, ego-alien intrusion experiences and spiritualistic beliefs in normal women, *Perceptual and Motor Skills*, 75(2), 547-51, October 1992.

APPARITIONS AND MIRACLES OF THE SUN

— Auguste Meessen, Ph.D. —

One of the most peculiar aspects of Marian apparitions is their frequent association with environmental phenomena, in the near-atmosphere, known popularly as "miracles of the Sun," such as occurred on October 13, 1917, at Fátima. The author, a physicist and professor at a Catholic institution, makes an effort here to approximate the event's factors and natural causes that furnish an explicative model of the "solar" manifestations. After enunciating in detail the better-known hypotheses, he states his favor for the neuro-physiological interpretation, while interactions produced at the level of the visual cortex insinuate the involvement of solar kinetics on the Being observed.

THE PROBLEM AND POSSIBLE HYPOTHESES

The frequency of apparitions and their repetition rate at particular places has strongly increased during the last two centuries, but the number of "recognized apparitions" has remained rather small. The Catholic Church has thus become increasingly prudent in regard to them. An official recognition by the local bishop, pronounced in agreement with Rome, means only that a supernatural origin is *humanly* credible and that a cult of adoration is permitted. Catholics are not obliged to believe that apparitions are true, since they don't have the same dogmatic status as *divine* revelation, related to the life of Jesus. Nevertheless, there exists a problem, since we have *no satisfactory explanation* for apparitions, whether they are true or not.

The fundamental difficulty stems from the fact that "visions" are *subjective* experiences. Their authenticity can thus not be checked from the outside or by independent repetitions, as in scientific experiments. Apparitions are accompanied quite often, however, by "miracles of the Sun" that have been observed by hundreds and sometimes even by thousands of trustworthy persons. Since these perceptions have a more *objective* status, it should be possible to use them as a "lever" to start a rational study of all these phenomena. As is usual in science, we begin with the formulation of *conceivable hypotheses*. Our aim is then to test their validity by means of arguments that are based on *observations and logical reasoning.*

There are three possible explanations, and each one of them raises certain questions:

- The hypothesis of a supernatural origin;
- The hypothesis of a natural explanation;
- The hypothesis of an extraterrestrial intervention.

The hypothesis of *a supernatural origin* is the traditional one. It results directly from the statements of those who claim that they could "see" heavenly beings, usually the Virgin Mary, and that they could even "communicate" with them. Sometimes, there are also demonic elements. When apparitions are accompanied by "miracles of the Sun," the "seers" declare that they are *signs*, given to strengthen the belief of those who doubt. Is it possible to prove that these experiences and statements result from the intervention of a supernatural reality or could they be mental constructions? Whatever the case, it is possible to collect data on "miracles of the Sun." It appears then that they have always the same characteristics, wherever they occur. But this points towards the existence of *an underlying mechanism.* How does this come about?

The hypothesis of *a natural explanation* has to be considered, of course, at least for "miracles of the Sun." An astronomic or purely meteorological explanation is excluded, for physical reasons, but there would be no "miracles of the Sun," if the witnesses had not been able to look straight into the Sun during a relatively long time. How was that possible? What happened in their eyes and their brains?

The hypothesis of *an extraterrestrial intervention* may seem to be unrealistic to those who are not aware of the real dimensions of the UFO phenomenon. There is ample evidence, however, that it deserves serious attention. Extraterrestrial intelligences and civilizations could have much more advanced technical capabilities than our own, and they could perhaps perform large-scale *psychosocial experiments,* without letting us become aware of them. It is therefore conceivable that apparitions and "miracles of the Sun" could be produced by "alien visitors" to test our reactions and beliefs about religious matters. Can this be proved or disproved?

Having read numerous books and documents, visited places where recognized or unrecognized apparitions occurred, talked to seers, observed one of them very closely during apparitions and interrogated this unusual person, I am very conscious of the complexity of this problem. I am particularly sensitive to the feelings of those who pray with great fervor, since they are deeply suffering and hope to get help from a loving God. But I am also a scientist, who has to *search for the truth*. As a professor at a Catholic university, I feel particularly responsible with respect to the Church and all humans. If necessary, it would be much better to change some ideas, instead of dwelling in illusions or deception. I hope that everyone will understand this point-of-view.

MIRACLES OF THE SUN: FACTS AND EXPLANATIONS

So-called "miracles of the Sun" were observed, for instance, at Tilly-sur-Seuilles (France, 1901), Fátima (Portugal, 1917), Onkerzeele (Belgium, 1933), Bonate (Italy, 1944), Espis (France, 1946), Acquaviva Platani (Italy, 1950), Heroldsbach (Germany, 1949), Fehrbach (Germany, 1950), Kerezinen (France, 1953), San Damiano (Italy, 1965), Tre Fontane (Italy, 1982) and Kibeho (Rwanda, 1983). Many witnesses have described them and from their reports we can extract the following successively appearing characteristic features.

The witnesses are astonished that they can look straight into the Sun. Actually, they see *a gray disc*. It is perfectly centered, since the brilliant rim of the Sun is still apparent. Some persons have compared this phenomenon with an "annular eclipse."

Beautiful colors appear after a few minutes on the whole surface of the Sun and in the surrounding sky. They are different, and they change in the course of time. Whether they are blue, red, yellow, green, pink or violet, for instance, they are unusually vivid! A quite large part of the surrounding sky is colored, but its extension is irregular and changing. It was even mentioned that colored lights seemed to be *ejected* from the Sun. When the observers look away, they see that the landscape and all surrounding persons are also colored in a changing way.

At some particular moment, *the Sun starts to move*. First, the solar disk *rotates* about its center at a uniform and rather high velocity. Then the rotation stops, but it resumes in the opposite direction! The Sun is "dancing," but suddenly, the solar disk seems to detach itself from the sky. It *comes rapidly closer*, with increasing size and brilliance. This causes great panic, since people think that the end of the world has come. The Sun retreats, however, until it regains its initial appearance. These forward and backward motions can be combined with rotations and sometimes with lateral oscillations. All these motions are totally unexpected and very impressive.

Finally, after 10 or 15 minutes, the Sun is "normal" again; its luminosity is too strong to continue gazing at it. But after about another quarter of an hour, the prodigy can be *repeated* in the same way. The spectators are astonished that *their eyes did not hurt,* although they were looking straight into the Sun for a very long time during the "miracle."

Most observers have noted slight *local changes in the luminosity* of the solar disc, as if there were some kinds of images, but they were unable to recognize their meaning. Some persons were luckier, gifted or privileged, however. In Heroldsbach, for instance, the "seers" reported that they had *successive visions* of the Virgin Mary, with and without the Christ child. Then they saw the Holy Family, the Trinity and symbols, like a cross and the letters IHS. Some other persons reported also that they saw the Virgin Mary and/or religious symbols. Similar events occurred at Fátima.

Colored spheres, drifting slowly from the Sun towards the Earth, were mentioned at several places. They could appear during the "miracles of the Sun," but were more frequently noticed after them. It was mentioned, however, that when these spheres touched the vegetation or the ground, one never found any material trace.

The initial presence of a *gray disc,* covering nearly the whole Sun, led to the proposition that a UFO could have been interposed between the solar disc and the observers. It is conceivable, indeed, that such a craft came from far away and approached a selected place on Earth, by moving along a straight line that connects this place to the center of the Sun. We can also imagine that this craft had extraordinary technical capabilities, but is this sufficient to account for observed facts? At least, there should be no contradiction.

Although the disc was gray, at first, it had to be very luminous. Let's assume that it was a huge, semi-transparent filter of solar light. Then it would still be necessary to explain its subsequent coloring. The illumination of the surrounding sky and the ground, in daytime, would require tremendous amounts of energy. Even if this were possible, there would remain a geometric problem. An eclipse-like event produces *a cone of shadow,* intersecting the ground somewhat above its tip. This would define there a circular or elliptical surface, where a perfect or nearly perfect *annular eclipse* is seen, but near the border of this surface it should be possible to observe *a partial eclipse.* Nobody has ever reported such an appearance of the Sun. Moreover, the object would have to be very large.

Actually, there exist some reports, in Fátima as in Heroldsbach, about apparently simultaneous observations of the same phenomena at places that were separated from the main event by about five km and even more than 40 km. This was mentioned with some insistence, to exclude the possibility of "mass suggestion," but it excludes also the assumption of a screening craft. Its dimensions would have to be unacceptably large and there should have been many more reports from the whole region. The assumption of two more limited, but laterally displaced crafts, producing the same "show" at different places, as well as the assumption of a somewhat delayed repetition of the same performance by a single craft, are untenable, since these maneuvers would have been detectable from the side.

Searching for more and more witness reports concerning these astonishing "miracles of the Sun," I discovered some cases where very similar observations of extraordinary solar effects had been made *without* any apparitional context. It was thus necessary to find out what would happen if someone did look straight into the Sun for some time, although this is known to be dangerous. I found several reports by ophthalmologists, describing rather severe *retinopathies* resulting from sun gazing, but the specialists didn't describe what their patients had actually seen. I started then to study various kinds of *subjective effects*, generated by short or long observations of relatively intense light sources. There are colored after-images, but also motional after-effects. The Belgian physicist Joseph Plateau studied them in the middle of the 19th century and gathered all available accounts of relevant observations, from Aristotle to about 1875 (Mémoires de l'Académie Royale de Belgique). Plateau warned against sun gazing, but mentioned only that he lost his eyesight in this way, without saying *what* he saw. Nevertheless, his huge collection provided the first clues that favored a natural interpretation of these mysterious "miracles of the Sun."

At this stage, I engaged in a systematic study of *after-images* (produced at the retinal level) and *after-effects* (resulting from the neural processing in our brain). Experimenting with a large and powerful white electric light bulb, I saw vivid colors and noted their temporal changes. I also carefully scanned the medical and psychological literature to gather all kinds of useful indications, but my attention was mainly focused on *biochemical, physiological and neurological processes*. In November 2002, I looked directly into the Sun at about 4:00 p.m. The Sun was relatively low above the horizon and its light intensity was attenuated, although the sky was clear. I was amazed to see that the solar disk was nearly instantaneously converted into *a gray disc, surrounded by a brilliant ring*. The gray disc was practically uniform. The surrounding ring was somewhat irregular and flamboyant, but did not exceed the solar disk. It coincided with its rim. I stopped the experiment, since I wanted to be prudent, but I had observed myself the initial phase of a typical "miracle of the Sun." Moreover, I could explain it.

The Sun became gray, indeed, since my eyes responded to its great luminosity by an immediate and automatic reduction of their normal sensitivity. This *adaptation* did not simply result from the bleaching of pigments inside the color-sensitive cones of the fovea, on which the image of the Sun had been projected. There are very important secondary processes. Every activated molecule initiates biochemical reactions that are repeated over and over again. This yields a strongly amplified response, although it leads actually to a reduction of the normal concentration of a particular type of molecule, but this causes a disruption of the usual equilibrium for Na^+ ions passing through the photoreceptor membrane. The trans-membrane potential is modified and this constitutes the relevant neurological response to the incident light. That ingenious system provides *an automatic and highly efficient gain control,* allowing us to cope with very low and extremely high luminosities. Since this adaptation process is *completely unconscious,* the unexpected appearance of a gray disc in front of the Sun can give the impression, especially in the context of apparitions, that this was not a natural process.

The brilliant ring can also be explained. Since the number of nerve cells that carry information to the brain through the optic nerve is much smaller than the number of retinal photoreceptors, every cell of the optic nerve collects information from 1,000 to 10,000 receptors. They form a *receptor field,* but the intermediate connections are organized in such a way that photoreceptors situated in the central part of the receptor field provide *excitatory* responses, while photoreceptors situated in an about equally large surrounding ring yield *inhibitory* responses. The inverse arrangement is also possible, but the essential point is that the image of the solar disc that had been projected on the retinal fovea is not treated everywhere in the same way. To every spot that was situated inside the image of the solar disc, the brain associated a combination of excitatory and inhibitory responses, with a rather modest average value. But near the edge of the retinal image of the solar disc, the inhibitory part of a receptor field did cover a region where the light intensity was smaller. Inhibition was decreased, so that the average response was increased. *Visually, there had to appear a bright rim.* This mechanism is very useful to provide contrast enhancement, and it constitutes an efficient "edge detector," allowing us to represent an object by drawing only its contours. Since the averaging process is a statistical one, dependent on local and momentary fatigue, the brilliance of the rim had to be unsteady.

"Miracles of the Sun" are usually observed when the Sun is relatively low above the horizon, but at Fátima, the Sun was at its zenith on October 13, 1917. Nevertheless, the witnesses did look towards the Sun for a rather long time. How was this possible? Well, we know that it had been raining hard and that the low cloud layer was suddenly disrupted. There could thus still be a high degree of humidity in the air, so that the sunlight was sufficiently attenuated.

In a second experiment, performed at 3:00 p.m. in December 2002, I looked straight into the Sun for a much longer time. After several minutes, I saw impressive colors, up to two or three times the diameter of the Sun. They changed, but were mainly pink, deep blue, red and green. Further away, the sky became progressively more luminous. I stopped the possibly dangerous observation, since I understood that the colors resulted from the fact that *red, green and blue sensitive pigments* are bleached and regenerated at different rates. Moreover, it is well known that receptor fields combine the responses of cones to form blue-yellow, red-green and white-black *opponent pairs*. These neural responses are analyzed in the visual cortex, where information about form, color, and motion are extracted and analyzed at separate places. The brain functions like a parallel computer but is able to keep track of everything that belongs to the same perceptual entity by means of *synchronous oscillations*. Previously, I had already established a "brain-wave equation" that accounts for them. In spite of specialized analyses, performed in different cortical areas, the unity of perceptual entities is well preserved.

These highly efficient methods imply, however, that *illusions* are possible. Some of them are automatic and intrinsic to the "hard-wired" part of the brain, while other illusions result from modifiable processes. Recent experiments showed that fixed retinal images that have no precise meaning, according to previous learning, are *sequentially altered* by suppressing different parts, so that the remaining parts become identical to known perceptual entities. The brain simply tries to make sense of the enigmatic input by comparing it with stored knowledge of various types. Some features are eliminated and other features can eventually be added. Actually, we know that this is how reading errors occur.

For ambiguous situations, the brain tries various possibilities. These rapid and spontaneous attempts of identification allow us to select and retain the best fit. But that also explains why some "seers" experienced *successively changing visions* in the solar disc. The luminosity of the solar disc was not steady and uniform because of statistically changing fatigue processes in individual nerve cells. Some persons were then more "gifted" than others to make sense of ambiguous data. Under other circumstances, we might simply say that they are more creative.

What about the motions of the Sun? I didn't see them, because I didn't look at the Sun for a sufficiently long time, or perhaps my brain already knew too much. Once, after observing the passage of a long train, I saw for a short time that the background was moving in the opposite direction. This was an example of *motional after-effects*. Joseph Plateau discovered a very famous one, by looking at a spiral that was rotating at a given velocity about its center. When this motion was suddenly stopped, there appeared *a reversed rotation* lasting for several minutes, but that was merely an illusion. The mental perception of a rotating Sun had to be initiated, of course, by *a spontaneous generation of apparent motion*. This is possible since a particular group of neurons of the visual cortex can choose this possibility. This motion is then reversed, by changing the equilibrium of opposing excitatory and inhibitory activities. The same concept applies to oscillations and to forward or backward motions.

A very interesting study was recently devoted to this "zoom and loom effect." It tends to appear when the brain is confronted with the two-dimensional retinal image of an object that is situated at some unknown distance. The brain then considers the possibility that it could come closer by performing *an illusory mental zoom*, where the apparent size of the object is progressively increased. But when the "idea" of an approach does not lead to any real danger, the perceived object returns to its normal place. This inborn mechanism results from an evolutionary advantage: it could be beneficial for survival, to take into account the possibility of dangerous approach and to escape soon enough. In Heroldsbach, people were actually so frightened by the "descending Sun" that they fled into the adjacent fields and threw themselves on the wet and dirty ground. Subjective perceptions were obviously enforced by seeing the panic of others.

Even after such a dramatic collective experience, the Sun had to become finally too brilliant for continued gazing. After some 10 or 15 minutes, the bleached pigments had been regenerated and/or the secondary biochemical processes were not effective any more. J. B. Walz, a university professor of theology, collected over 70 eyewitness reports of the "miracle of the Sun" that occurred at Heroldsbach on December 8, 1949. These documents disclose some individual differences in perception, including the fact that one person saw the Sun approaching and receding *three times*, while most witnesses saw this only two times! The "colored spheres" that were usually perceived after the breathtaking "dance of the Sun" were simply *after-images*. They were not recognized as such, since the context of these observations suggested another interpretation. In Tilly-sur-Seules and Kerezinen, the colored spheres were mentioned on several occasions, but the witnesses did talk to one another. This favored reinforcements of the same interpretation.

That the sky and ground were perceived during "miracles of the Sun" as being colored is now understandable. These were after-effects, but I had to be concerned by the much more astonishing fact that some witnesses reported that colored lights seemed to be *ejected* from the Sun. They mentioned even "luminous fountains" and "fireworks." Trying to explain these facts, my attention was attracted by a peculiar observation of one scientist, who noted, in 1963, that after-images start to be blurred after about two minutes. He suggested that this could result from *a diffusion process* at the retinal level, but he could not identify its nature. More recent studies of the biochemistry of retinal photoreceptors allow me now to propose an explanation. Activated photoreceptors increase the density of Na^+ ions in their vicinity, which results in a facilitated activation of neighboring photoreceptors. A large part of the sky surrounding the solar disk can thus become colored and more luminous, as I saw myself.

The final result of this investigation is that "miracles of the Sun" can safely be interpreted without assuming an intervention of supernatural powers or extraterrestrial intelligences. Some people will claim that they knew this already, but they couldn't prove it. It should also be noted that there is no reason at all to be arrogant with respect to those who believed in a miracle or assumed the presence of a UFO. We were confronted, indeed, with *a highly remarkable illusion*, displaying sophisticated and totally unexpected features.

PROBLEMATIC MESSAGES

The seers who "communicated" with the Virgin Mary or Jesus are always stressing the importance of *prayer and penitence,* but a closer look at their messages reveals an underlying motivation: there are feelings of fear. They can be related to a concern with the awful prospect of damnation, but usually, they focus on *announcements of catastrophic events,* expressed in a conditional form: "If you don't… then…" Let's take an example.

On October 9, 1949, four girls, 10 to 11 years old, had collected colored leaves and were playing when they heard the clock of their village church. It was 5:00 p.m. Spontaneously, they started to pray, and at that moment, they saw in the sky, above a birchwood, an indistinct white silhouette. One of the children compared it to a nun, dressed in white, but then it seemed more plausible to say that it was *the Mother of God.* That's the usual German expression for the Virgin Mary. During the following days, the same white, statue-like person appeared again, and, according to the seers, became progressively more distinct. On October 14th, one of the children asked, "Dear Lady, who are you?" She answered, *"I am the Mother of God."* A few days later, the children asked the luminous Lady, now carrying a rosary, if she had a message for humanity. She simply said, *"Pray!"*

But Heroldsbach is a small village near Nuremberg, and World War II was still very present in the mind of everyone. On October 31, 1949, one of the children questioned the Being, *"Will there be war again?"* She replied, *"When you pray, there will be none."* She did not appear anymore, however, until December 8, 1949. That was the day where the "great miracle of the Sun" occurred in the presence of 8,000 to 10,000 persons! It started at 3 o'clock, during a procession, but the Virgin Mary had appeared already to the children at 2:30. For the first time, she was wearing a golden crown on her head. It was "brilliant like the Sun" and on her left arm, she carried the Christ child. After that event, the apparitions increased and became more explicit, with constant, heavy insistence on prayer and penitence!

The group of "seers" at Heroldsbach was now constituted of six girls, all about 11 years old. On May 15, 1950, Our Lady announced, *"The Russians will come and there will be a great famine!"* Over the birchwood, where the children had initially perceived the apparition, they saw an agitated war scene. Soldiers were shooting at one another. They fell on the ground and remained there, in blood and pain. That terrifying vision lasted for about 10 minutes, but during all of this time, the Virgin Mary covered the village of Heroldsbach with her protective veil. The following day, the children saw again a fierce battle in the sky, but now, there were brown and black soldiers. The brown ones had Mongolian eyes. They were winning and went into a village. They entered houses, dragged people into the street, and pushed them towards a place where they were savagely killed. The children recognized this village. It was their own. These visions were interpreted by N. Langhojer as follows: "When the request of the heavenly mother is fulfilled, the first vision of the Russians will be realized. The homeland will be saved, but when humanity does not listen, the second possibility occurs. Destruction will take its horrible course."

The next day, the Virgin Mary appeared with the Christ child, who said himself, *"Dear children, if you don't pray with diligence, the Russians will come and slay you!"* We have to recall that in 1949, the Russians had carried out their first experimental atomic explosion and in 1950 the U.S. announced the construction of a hydrogen bomb. In La Salette, in 1846, the seers reported that the weeping Lady told them, "When my people do not submit, *then I will be obliged to let go the arm of my son. It is so heavy that I am not able to hold it back anymore."* Does this depend on her? *Le Fait de La Salette*, published in 1873, presented the menace and the causes of culpability in a more explicit way.

The "third secret of Fátima," communicated on July 13, 1917 and written down by Lúcia in 1944, was finally disclosed in June 2000. Lúcia saw a very intense light and a bishop, clad in white, who she considered to be the Holy Father. With other bishops, priests, nuns and monks, he climbed a mountain towards a great cross, his face and stature being marked by sorrow and suffering. When he arrived at the cross, he knelt down, but was killed by a group of soldiers, using "fire weapons and arrows." His companions died in the same way. Lúcia suggested that this was a warning or a sign of imminent persecutions of the Church. Since this didn't happen, Cardinal Ratzinger established a connection with the attempted assassination of Pope John Paul II on May 13, 1981. Sister Lúcia had always insisted on a "consecration of Russia." This referred to the menace of atheistic communism, but why had such scourges as the Nazi regime, World War II, and the Nazi holocaust against the Jews not also been prophesized?

In Medjugorje, the seers reported that penitence should be more valued than charity. There are thus examples of basic theological problems, but in my view, the central difficulty stems from the fact that *the general trend of these messages conveys an inadequate image of God,* and Christian revelation tells us, "There exists a God, who loves us!" (see, e.g., John 17: 21 and 23). Most apparitions put forward a God of revenge and anger. This rather fundamental contradiction, as well as the emergence of a natural explanation of "miracles of the Sun," calls for prudence. It is necessary to examine the visionary experiences themselves, and this has to be done in the context of present-day psychology.

APPARITIONS AND ALTERED STATES OF CONSCIOUSNESS

For all apparitions that I studied in depth, I ended up with the conviction that the "seers" are *not lying or confabulating*. Whatever they saw and heard, it was real to them. This follows from numerous details and is coherent with their religious attitudes. They had to accept discomfort and even suffering, but they were living in a spirit of penance. In Heroldsbach, for instance, the Mother of God asked the children quite often to walk on bleeding knees. Moreover, they were not only attacked by some newspapers but also even officially excluded from the sacraments!

There were spiritual compensations, however, since these children were "allowed to touch" the garments, the hair, and the face of the Mother of God. They did "feel" it, they said, and when they carried the Christ child in their arms, they had the sensation of its weight. They could "smell" pleasant odors and they "tasted" the Holy Communion they got from an angel, in solid and liquid form. At Fátima, the three children also had mystical contact with an angel, before the more heralded apparitions of 1917. For the visionaries, all these sensations had *the same characteristics as real perceptions*, but this does not exclude purely mental processes.

Personal dispositions, the inducing power of special circumstances, and a customary cultural framework can favor the construction of a *virtual reality*. This expression should be considered in analogy with the "virtual image" that we can see behind a mirror. The eyes receive light that is reflected by the surface of the mirror, but this happens exactly in the same way as if it emerged from points that were situated behind the reflecting surface. This is an illusion, of course. *Could apparitions be a mental mirage?* Before we may eventually be able to answer this question, we have to gather facts and to define apparitional phenomena.

While "miracles of the Sun" result from real visual perceptions, involving many persons, *apparitions require no sensory input* and occur within a single individual or a small group of persons, interacting with one another. Apparitions are usually viewed as spiritual or mystical experiences, escaping any scientific scrutiny, but *at least some psychological processes have to be involved.*

There may be some exceptions, but in general, the seers are honestly experiencing what they report. In their mind and brain, they perceive things that have for them a supernatural, but nonetheless real, cause. Their mystical experiences are subjective but authentic.

Apparitions can involve different sense modalities. Most frequently, one does see and hear, but one can also feel, smell, and taste. This is also true for hallucinations. There is no evidence, however, that apparitions result from schizophrenia or some other mental pathology. Seers are not mentally sick, although their mental energy is strongly focused on their apparitional experiences.

Apparitions evolve through different stages. There are many well-documented cases, where the initial phase corresponds to becoming simply aware of the presence of some imprecise, relatively distant and usually silent, but more or less luminous, shape. *Ambiguous data is interpreted* by formulating the idea that it could be the Virgin Mary. This idea is shared when there are several "seers." Usually, this happens in an emotionally charged context and then kindles a sequence of reactions. The apparition is repeated and the initial interpretation is crystallized. Favorable echoes from valued sectors provide additional reinforcement. Even when the social context is partly hostile, this can contribute to consolidation, since the seers cannot admit anymore that they were wrong. Doubts are obliterated, while the apparitions become more precise and progressively more detailed. The seers get messages and even "secrets" that seem to be very important, since they should only be communicated to the highest authority.

The time course of these events is variable, but limited. Every particular "vision" can last from a few minutes to several hours. Sometimes, it ends by a stepwise vanishing of different parts, but usually, the luminous apparition disappears as a whole, through sudden extinction or progressive motion towards the sky, as if the supernatural being had to return to the place from where it was supposed to come. Identical or similar apparitions can be repeated during the same day, but the following apparition is usually fixed in advance, so that several seers and the whole assembly of attentive followers are synchronized. The total number of apparitions can be enormous for a particular group of seers. The apparitions of Heroldsbach, for instance, continued during three years, in spite of extremely harsh reactions from the bishop of Bamberg. Moreover, it happens that so-called "public apparitions" are followed by *private* ones, leading to further elaborations of the initial messages.

Previously, I assumed, like the responsible authorities of the Catholic Church, that some apparitions are true, while others are not. I simply thought that extraordinary interventions could be in *the power of God*. Why not? But what about the power of the human mind? We have to find out what could happen in this regard, even for pastoral reasons! When I studied the official documents that had been used for the evaluation of the apparitions at Beauraing in Belgium, I was somewhat disappointed by the lack of precision and clarity in the description of the basic events. Then I found a book by De Greeff, a professor of criminology at the Catholic University of Louvain. He was present during some of these apparitions. Moreover, he carefully studied the testimonies of the seers and other witnesses. His professional competence and his integrity are undeniable, but his conclusions were not in favor of an official recognition. Let's summarize what happened.

On the evening of November 29, 1932, when five children were near a statue of Our Lady of Lourdes, they saw a strange light, and the idea surfaced that it could be an apparition of the Virgin Mary. De Greeff shows that the children were quite emotional and that the light could come from a car, illuminating an object in an unexpected way. During the following evenings, the children again saw similar lights at about the same place and this strengthened their initial concept. The group of "seers" consisted of four girls and one boy, all between nine and 14 years old. They were interrogated, of course, but this happened at first in a very uncritical way. When the procedures were modified, partially because of De Greeff, it appeared that the seers did not have identical visions and that they did not "hear" the same words and sentences. There were even some contradictions.

Every evening, before the apparition started, the five children were standing in a row and praying the rosary with the surrounding assembly. Suddenly, they fell on their knees, in perfect *synchrony*. During the whole apparition, they prayed with a shrill voice and at an unusually rapid rate. This behavior astonished some witnesses, since it is atypical of apparitions, but most observers considered that it pleaded in favor of an authentic and simultaneous "mystical experience." The sudden and synchronous kneeling down could be explained, however, since they were waiting in tense expectation and could thus react as soon as one of them started to move, while the end of the apparition was easily synchronized by modified acoustic signals. Even when the "seers" were immediately separated from one another after the apparitions and subjected to separate interrogation, their declarations could still be relatively coherent, since they had ample opportunity to communicate during the day, and to prepare, in good faith, the questions they would ask the Our Lady in the evening.

Then I found the book by Ladon, a Belgian neurologist, who collected data on the series of apparitions that developed in several parts of Belgium after the events in Beauraing. In 1933, there were 47 persons who claimed that they saw the Virgin Mary! There were even two groups of over 100 persons who had apparently experienced common visions. Ladon's analysis led him to the conclusion that this was the result of contagion. He called it *"a mental epidemic."* The archbishop of Belgium, Cardinal van Roey, reacted very quickly. In agreement with his Study Commission, he denied the supernatural character of all these alleged apparitions with the possible exception of the initial ones, at Beauraing and Banneux. They were the subject of much longer examinations and negotiations but were finally recognized.

It is impossible to provide any *direct* evidence for or against the supernatural origin of apparitions, but it is reasonable and even necessary to study a large number of apparitions. Some of them are well-documented and particularly instructive. We also have to take into account what is known today about *various mental mechanisms* that could be related to apparitions. Moreover, we shouldn't be afraid of indirect methods, since they are customary in modern science. Nobody ever saw the internal structure of atoms and nuclei, for instance, but we learned a lot about these realities by means of *indirect observations and rigorous logical reasoning*. The convergence of all these arguments then becomes the decisive factor. In regard to apparitions, we have to consider the following observations and propositions.

During religious visions and locutions, those who experience them are in an *altered state of consciousness*. It is of limited duration and comparable to the state of a hypnotized person, but it can be reached by autosuggestion. The only essential requirement is that usually active control mechanisms are deactivated.

A false interpretation of an ambiguous perceptual experience can be sufficient to trigger a series of reactions, where the mind tries to make sense of unusual data and tries then to protect this interpretation.

Freud introduced the concept of the *subconscious,* considered as a part of our personality where some thoughts can be repressed by powerful control mechanisms and kept in quarantine. *Unconscious processes* can surely play an important role in apparitional phenomena. Selective filtering eliminates reasonable doubts. Special types of behavior are created and repeated, until they are autonomous.

Great progress was made during the last two decades in the study of a most remarkable psychological phenomenon, originally called "multiple personality disorder" (MPD), now called *dissociative identity disorder* (DID). It is characterized by the constitution of two or more distinct personalities living in the same body, with segregated memories, quite different ethical conceptions, and sometimes, with distinct manual and intellectual skills. Usually, this is an escape response to very traumatic and repeated childhood abuse, since it provides a way to cope with truly unbearable experiences, even when they recur. All associated memories are then isolated from those that are necessary to organize the tasks of daily life. Later on, it can happen that one of the hidden personalities "comes out" and *takes control of the actual behavior.* This breakthrough will last only for a limited time and the transitions are very abrupt. This "switching" is necessary, indeed, to ensure the mutual isolation of different memories. Psychotherapy can help one to become *aware* of other personalities, and eventually, achieve the interconnectivity in the brain that is normally characteristic of a person.

Apparitions are not identical to DID, but there are important similarities. In both cases, an altered state of consciousness appears during a limited time. It results from dissociation and requires switching. Visions can even culminate in "ecstasy," where external stimuli and pain are not perceived any more, but we know that hypnotic analgesia is also possible.

There are other states of altered consciousness, like drug-induced hallucinations, shamanic trances, automatic writing, out-of-body experiences, and possessions. The causes and symptoms are different, but the underlying mental mechanisms are not. It is essential to realize that the human mind *can* function in unusual ways.

Moreover, it is known that some persons are able to produce dream-like *hypnagogic images.* They are vivid and sometimes animated in a life-like way. Experimentation has also demonstrated that there are persons who can produce *eidetic images* in their mind. When they observe a picture, one can take it away, while they continue to "see" the same picture, as if it was still there! It stays in front of their eyes. This can last from several seconds to many minutes. The picture can get animated, as if it were three-dimensional. The

46

same kind of dynamic persistence is also possible for sounds, as well music and languages. This is not simply a more or less schematic reconstruction, due to memory, but *a continuation of the same neurological processes* that were activated in the brain during the initial perception. The ability to see real, eidetic images is more frequently encountered in children and adolescents than adults. It is remarkable that the same age bias exists also for apparitions.

Collections of data concerning apparitions of a non-religious type are now available. They prove that some persons are more "gifted" for visionary experiences than others. It does not require mental sickness or supernatural contacts.

The general conclusion is that *apparitions and miracles of the Sun should not be taken at face value.* There are natural mechanisms that could explain them. We can safely assert that "miracles of the Sun" do result from neurophysiologic processes in our eyes and visual cortex. It is more difficult to prove or disprove that all apparitions result from purely mental processes, but we have to at least face this possibility. Although the "seers" are honest, they can unconsciously put themselves in an *altered state of consciousness.* It is known, indeed, that the human brain allows for personality dissociation and for "switching" from one type of mental functioning to another without being aware of it. This view does not contradict, nor depreciate, the basic reasons of religious beliefs, but the phenomenon of Marian apparitions calls – perhaps even urgently – for *further scientific research.* This is not only a matter of truth, but also of great cultural and psychosocial importance.

References

ALTGOTT, C., *Heroldsbach, eine mütterliche Mahnung Mariens* [*Heroldsbach, an admonition of Mother Mary*], Altgott, Mönchengladbach, 1979.

ALONSO, J.M., *Histoire « Ancienne » et Histoire « Nouvelle » de Fátima* [*Ancient History and Modern History of Fátima*], in ALONSO, J.M. *et al.*, *Vraies et Fausses Apparitions dans l'Eglise* [*True and False Apparitions in the Church*], Lethielleux-Bellarmin, 1973.

ANGELIER, F. and LANGLOIS, C. (eds.), *La Salette: Apocalypse, Pèlerinage et Littérature* [*La Salette: Apocalypse, Pilgrimage, and Literature*], Grenoble, Éditions Jérôme Millon, 2000.

AUCLAIR, R., *Kerizinen: Apparitions en Bretagne* [*Kerizinen: Apparitions in Brittany*], Paris, Nouvelles Éditions Latines, 1970.

BARNAY, S., *Le Ciel sur la Terre: Les Apparitions de la Vierge au Moyen-Âge* [*Heaven on Earth: Apparitions of the Virgin in the Middle Ages*], Paris, Les Éditions du Cerf, 1999.

BARTHAS, C. and da FONSECA, G., *Fátima, Merveille Inouïe* [*Fátima, Marvel Unheard*], Toulouse, Fátima-Editions, 1943.

BARTHAS, C., *Fátima, Merveille du 20ᵉ Siècle d'après les Témoins et Documents* [*Fátima, Marvel of the 20th Century according to the Witnesses and Documents*], Toulouse, Fátima-Editions, 1951.

BASSETTE, L., *Le Fait de La Salette, 1846-1854* [*The Fact of La Salette, 1846-1854*], Paris, Les Éditions du Cerf, 1955.

BIANCHI, L., *Fátima – Medjugorje*, Hauteville, Éditions du Parvis, 1987.

BONCAMPAGNI, S., "Un secolo di "soli rotondi" nelle visione mariane" ["A century of 'only round' in Marian vision"], UFO, CUN, 50-55, March 2002.

BOUFFLET, J. and BOUTRY, P., *Un Signe dans le Ciel: Les Apparitions de la Vièrge* [*A Sign in the Sky: Apparitions of the Virgin*], Paris, Grasset, 1997.

BOUFFLET, J., *Medjugorje ou la Fabrication du Surnaturel* [*Medjugorje or the Supernatural Fabrication*], Paris, Salvator, 1999.

BOUFFLET, J., *Faussaires de Dieu* [*Forgeries of God*], Paris, Presses de la Renaissance, 2000.

BRINDLEY, G.S., "Two new properties of foveal after-images and two photochemical hypotheses to explain them," *Journal of Physiology* 164, 168-179, 1962; "Afterimages," *Scientific American*, October 1963, 84-93.

CAROL, M.P., "Visions of the Virgin Mary: The effect of family structure," *Journal of the Scholarly Study of Religion*, 22, 205-21, 1983.

CASEY, J.F. and WILSON, L., *Joan: L'Autobiographie d'une Personnalité Multiple* [*Joan: The Autobiography of a Multiple Personality*], Paris, Éditions Presses de la Cité, 1992.

CASTELBRANCO, J., *Le Prodige Inouï de Fátima* [*The Unheard Prodigy of Fátima*], Brussels, Centre Marial de Fátima, 1972.

CASTELLA, A., *San Damiano: Le Messager de Notre-Dame des Roses* [*San Damiano: The Messenger of Our Lady of Roses*], Hauteville, Éditions du Parvis, 1989.

CENTINI, M., "Les guérisons miraculeuses – les miracles" ["The miraculous healings – the miracles"], in *Le Grand Livre des Miracles* [*The Ledger of Miracles*], Paris, Éditions de Vecchi, 2000.

CHIRON, Y., *Enquête sur les Apparitions de la Vièrge* [*Survey of Apparitions of the Virgin*], Paris, Perrin-Mame, 1995.

COLIN-SIMARD, A., *Les Apparitions de la Vièrge: Leur Histoire* [*Apparitions of the Virgin: Their History*], Paris, Fayard-Mame, 1981.

Comité international d'informations et d'études historiques, *L'Étoile dans la Montagne* [*The Star in the Mountain*], Garabandal, 1966.

CROSS, L.M. and OLPHE-GAILLARD, M., *Lourdes, 1958: Témoins de l'Evènement* [*Lourdes, 1958: Witnesses to the Event*], Paris, Lethielleux, 1957.

De GREEFF, E., *Notes sur les Faits de Beauraing: Rectifications, Compléments, Confirmations Concernant les Documents Contenus dans les Notes (Les Faits Mystérieux de Beauraing)* [*Notes on the Facts of Beauraing: Corrections, Complements, Confirmations Regarding Documents Contained within the Notes*

(*The Mysterious Facts of Beauraing*)], Desclée DB, 1933; *Beauraing: Conclusions Médico-Psychologiques* [*Beauraing: Medical-Psychological Conclusions*], Paris, Ètudes Camélitaines, October 1934.

De MARCHI, R.P., *Témoignages sur les Apparitions de Fátima* [*Testimonies on the Apparitions of Fátima*], Fátima, Edité par Imprime a Leiria, 1966.

De SÈDE, G., *Fátima, Enquête sur une Imposture* [*Fátima, Investigation of an Imposter*], Paris, A. Moreau, 1977.

DHANIS, P., *Bij de verschijningen en het geheim van Fátima* [*The apparitions and the secret of Fátima*]; Brugge, Kinkhoren, 1945; À propos de "Fátima et la critique" [À propos of "Fátima and the critic"], *Nouv. Rev. Theol.*, 64, 580-606, 1952.

DINZELBACHER, P., *Vision und Visionsliteratur im Mittelalter* [*Vision and Vision Literature in the Middle Ages*], Hiersemann, *Monogr. Gesch. Mittelalt*, 23, 1981.

DIRKENS, A. (ed)., *Apparitions et Miracles: Problèmes d'Histoire des Religions* [*Apparitions and Miracles: Problems of the History of Religions*], Brussels, ULB, 1991.

DOWLING, J.E., "Retinal Processing of Vision," in GREGOR, R. and WINDHORST, U., *Comprehensive Human Physiology*, Berlin, Springer-Verlag, 1996.

EIZEREIF, H., *Das Zeichen des Lebendigen Gottes – Marienfried* [*The Sign of the Living God – Marienfried*], Stein am Rhein, Christiana-Verlag, 1976.

ENGLEBERT, O., *Dix Apparitions de la Vièrge* [*Ten Apparitions of the Virgin*], Paris, Éditions Albin Michel, 1960.

EPARVIER, J. and HÉRISSÉ, M., *Fátima aux Soleils Dansants* [*The Dancing of the Sun at Fátima*], in *Les Miracles* [*Miracles*], Paris, Historia, 394, 1979.

ERNST, R., *Maria redet zu uns – Marienerscheinungen seit 1830* [*Mary speaks to us – Marian apparitions since 1830*], Marquain, Belgium, Editions Hovine, 1983, 1993; *Lexikon der Marienerscheinungen* [*Lexicon of Marian apparitions*], Altötting, Ruhland, 1983, 1989; *Zum Problem des Person-Seins* [*On the Problem of Personal Being*], Eupen, MG and Eupen, 1999.

Erzbischöfliche Kommission, *Was ist von den Heroldsbacher Visionen zu halten?* [*What is to keep of the vision of Heroldsbach?*], Bamberg, 1950.

EVANS, H., *Visions, Apparitions, Alien Visitors: A Comparative Study of the Entity Enigma*, Wellingborough, England, Aquarian Press, 1984.

EWALD, R.E. et al., "Sun gazing as the cause of foveamacular retinitis," *American Journal of Ophthalmology*, 70, 491-7, 1970.

FAULHABER, L., "Die Visionen von Heroldsbach," ["The vision of Heroldsbach"], *Münchener Theologische Zschr.*, 1, 98-104, 1950.

FELICI, I., *Fátima*, 1952, translated by FERRY, E., Fátima, Apostolat de la Presse, 1963.

d'ARMADA, F. and FERNANDES, J., *Intervenção Extraterrestre em Fátima – as aparições e o fenómeno OVNI* [*Extraterrestrial Intervention at Fátima: The Apparitions and the UFO Phenomenon*], Amadora, Livraria Bertrand, 1982.

FIEBAG, P. and FIEBAG, G., *Zeichen am Himmel: UFOs und Marienerscheinungen* [*Signs in the Sky: UFOs and Marian Apparitions*], Berlin, Ullstein, 1995.

FINKE, R.A., "Theories relating Mental Imagery to Perception," *Psychological*

Bulletin, 98, 236-9, 1985.

GABRIEL, J., *Présence de la très Sainte Vièrge à San Damiano* [*The Presence of the Very Virgin Mary at San Damiano*], Paris, Nouvelles Éditions Latines, 1968, 1975.

GETRY, G., *Kibeho ou la face cachée de la tragédie Rwandaise* [*Kibeho or the hidden face of the Rwandan tragedy*], Paris, Éditions François-Xavier de Guibert, 1998.

GLADSTONE, G.J. and TASMAN, W., "Solar retinitis after minimal exposure," *Archives of Ophthalmology*, 96, 1368-9, 1978.

GÖKSU, C., *Heroldsbach – Eine Verboten Wallfahrt* [*Heroldsbach – A Forbidden Pilgrimage*], Würzburg, Echter, 1991.

GRABINSKI, B., *Flammende Zeichen der Zeit – Offenbarungen, Prophezeiungen, Erscheinungen* [*Blazing Sign of the Times – Revelations, Prophecies, Phenomena*], Gröbenzell, Hacker, 1972.

GREEN, C., *Lucid Dreams and Out-of-the-Body Experiences*, London, Hamish Hamilton, 1968.

GREEN, C. and McCREERY, C., *Apparitions*, Oxford, Oxford Institute of Psychophysical Research, 1975.

HABER, R.N., "Eidetic images," *Scientific American*, April 1969, 36-44.

HACKING, I., *Rewriting the Soul: Multiple Personality and the Science of Memory*, Princeton, Princeton University Press, 1995.

HALLET, M., *Que Penser des Apparitions de la Vièrge?* [*What to Think of the Apparitions of the Virgin?*], Paris, Éditions Favre, 1985.

HERSHENSON, M., "Moon illusion and spiral after-effect: Illusions due to Loom-Zoom System?," *Journal of Experimental Psychology*, 111, 423-40, 1982; "Directional Symmetry in the spiral after-effect," *Perceptual and Motor Skills*, 55, 1203-8, 1982.

HESEMANN, M., *Das Fátima Geheimnis* [*The Secret of Fátima*], Rottenburg, Kopp-Verlag, 2002.

HOFFMANN, H., *Die Wahrheit über die Botschaft von Fátima* [*The Truth about the Message of Fátima*], Bietigheim, Rohm, 1984.

HOPE-ROSS, M. *et al.*, "Solar retinopathy following religious rituals," *British Journal of Ophthalmology*, 72, 931-4, 1988.

HUBER, M., *Multiple Persönlichkeiten* [*Multiple Personalities*], Frankfurt, Fischer, 1995.

HUNT, H.T., "A cognitive psychology of mystical and altered-state experience," *Perceptual and Motor Skills*, 58, 467-513, 1984; "Relations between the phenomena of religious mysticism (altered states of consciousness) and the psychology of thought," *Perceptual and Motor Skills*, 61, 911-961, 1985.

JANSSENS, A., "L'absence de surnaturel dans les faits de Beauraing" ["The absence of the supernatural in the facts of Beauraing"], in B. de Jésus-Marie, *Les Faits Mystérieux de Beauraing: Ètudes, Documents, Réponses* [*The Mysterious Facts of Beauraing, Studies, Documents, Answers*], Desclée De Brouwer, Bruges-Paris, 1933.

JEAN-NESMY, C., *Lucie raconte Fátima* [*Lúcia recounts Fátima*], Desclée De

Brouwer, Bruges-Paris, 1976.

JOSET, C.J., S.J., *Dossiers de Beauraing, vol. 1- 5* [*Dossiers of Beauraing, vol. 1- 5*], Beauraing, Pro Maria, Research University of Namur, 1981-84.

JOYEUX, H. and LAURENTIN, R., *Ètudes Médicales et Scientifiques sur les Apparitions de Medjugorje* [*Medical and Scientific Studies of the Apparitions of Medjugorje*], Paris, Editora O.E.I.L., 1985.

KLÜWER, H., "An experimental study of the eidetic type," *Genetic Psychology Monographs*, 1, 71-230, 1926, "Mescal visions and eidetic visions," *American Journal of Psychology*, 37, 502-515, 1926.

KOLERS, P.A., "Perception and representation," *Annual Review of Psychology*, 34, 129-66, 1983.

KOSSLYN, S.M. *et al.*, "The cognitive neuroscience of mental imagery," *Neuropsychologia*, 33, 1335-44, 1995.

LADON, A., *Une épidémie mentale contemporaine – Les apparitions de Belgique* [*A contemporary mental epidemic – The Belgian apparitions*], Paris, Doin, 1937.

LANGHOJER, N., *Reich der Mystik: Die Botschaft von Heroldsbach* [*Kingdom of Mysticism: The Embassy of Heroldsbach*], Heroldsbach, Arche Joseph, 1971.

LAURENTIN, R., *Lourdes : Histoire authentique des apparitions, 6 vol.* [*Lourdes : An authentic history of the apparitions, 6 vol.*], Paris, Lethielleux, 1961.

LAURENTIN, R., *Multiplication des apparitions de la Vièrge aujourd'hui* [*Multiplication of the apparitions of the Virgin today*], Paris, Éditions Fayard, 1988, 1995.

LEESER, J. *et al.*, "What is a delusion?: Epistemological dimensions," *Journal of Abnormal Psychology*, 108, 687-94, 1999.

Le HIDEC, M., *Les Secrets de La Salette* [*The Secrets of La Salette*], Paris, Nouvelles Éditions Latines, 1969.

LESSERTEUR, R.P. and Marquis de L'ESPINASSE-LANGEAC, *Notre-Dame de Tilly* [*Our Lady of Tilly*], Tilly, Les amis de Tilly [The friends of Tilly], 1966.

LYNN, S.J. *et al.*, "The fantasy-prone person," *Journal of Personality and Social Psychology*, 51, 404-8, 1986.

MAES, R.P., *Beauraing, Observations sur L'Étude de M. De Greeff* [*Beauraing, Observations on the Study of M. De Greeff*], Louvain, St. Alphonse, 1934.

MAINDRON, G., *Les Apparitions de Kibeho Annonce de Marie au Cœur de l'Afrique* [*The Apparitions of Kibeho Announce Mary to the Heart of Africa*], Paris, Editora O.E.I.L., 1984.

MAISONNEUVE, R. and M. de BELSUNCE, *San Damiano – Histoire et Documents* [*San Damiano – History and Documents*], Paris, Tequi, 1983.

MAXENCE, J.L., *Le Secret des Apparitions et des Prophéties Mariales* [*The Secret of the Apparitions and the Marian Prophecies*], Paris, de Falois, 2000.

McCONKEY, K.M. *et al.*, "Trance logic in hypnosis and imagination," *Journal of Abnormal Psychology*, 100, 464-72, 1991.

McCLURE, K., *The evidence for visions of the Virgin Mary*, Wellingborough, Aquarian Press, 1983.

MICHAEL, C.R., "Retinal processing of visual images," *Scientific American*, May

1969, 104-14.

MICHEL de la SAINTE TRINITÉ (frère), *Toute la Vérité sur Fátima* [*The Whole Truth about Fátima*], Édition de La Contre-Réforme Catholique, Saint-Parres-lès-Vaudes, France, 1984; *The Whole Truth about Fátima*, 3 vol., Immaculate Heart Publishing, 1989-90.

MISRAKI, P., *Des Signes dans Le Ciel* [*Of Signs in the Sky*], Paris, Éditions Labergerie, 1968.

MONROE, R.A., *Journeys Out of the Body*, New York, Doubleday, 1972.

O'BRIAN, D.F., "The chemistry of vision," *Science*, 218, 961-966, 1982.

ORAISON, M. and CHAUFFEN, Y., *Le tribunal du merveilleux* [*The court of the marvelous*], Paris, Plon, 1976.

OTTAVIANI, A., "Chrétiens, ne vous excitez pas si vite" ["Christians, do not get excited so fast"], *Documentation Catholique*, 48, 345-55, 1951.

PANNET, R., *Les Apparitions Aujourd'hui* [*The Apparitions Today*], Chambray, C.L.D., 1888.

PENNER, R. and McNAIT, J.N., "Eclipse blindness," *American Journal of Ophthalmology*, 61, 1452-7, 1966.

PINON, G., *Fátima: Un ovni pas comme les autres?* [*Fátima: A UFO like no other?*], Paris, Éditions Osmondes, 2001.

PLATEAU, J., *Bibliographie Analytique des Principaux Phénomènes Subjectifs de la Vision* [*An Analytical Bibliography of the Principal Subjective Phenomena of the Vision*], Brussels, Mém. Acad. Roy. Belg. XLII, 1°(1-59), 2°(1-59), 3°(1-26.), 4°(1-44.), 5°(1-35), 6°(1-45), Suppl. 1877, 1880 and 1882.

PRITCHARD, R.M., "Stabilized images on the retina," *Scientific American*, June 1961, 72-8.

PYLYSHYN, Z.W., "What the mind's eye tells the mind's brain," *Psychology Bulletin*, 80, 1-24, 1973.

RAHNER, K., *Visionen und Prophezeiungen* [*Vision and Prophecy*], Freiburg, Herder, 1958, 60, 89.

RAMON GARCIA de la RIVA, J., *Maria erscheint in Garabandal* [*Mary appears in Garabandal*], Meersburg, Weto-Verlag, 1983.

RATZINGER, J., "Comprendre le sens du message de Fátima" ["Understanding the meaning of Fátima"], *La Documentation Catholique*, 2230, 677-83, 2000, dossier.

REGAN, D., "Visual processing of four kinds of relative motion," *Vision Research*, 26, 127-145, 1986.

REGAN, D. and BEVERLEY, K.I., "Looming detectors in the human visual pathway," *Vision Research*, 19, 415-21, 1978.

RUSHTON, W.A.H., "Visual pigments in man," *Scientific American*, November 1962, 120-132; "The Ferrier Lecture: Visual adaptation," *Proceedings of the Royal Society*, London B, 162, 20-46, 1965.

RUSHTON, W.A.H. and MacLEOD, D., "The equivalent background bleaching," *Perception*, 15, 689-703, 1986.

SANCHEZ-VENTURA and PASCUAL, F., *La Vièrge est-elle apparue à Garabandal?* [*Is the Virgin appearing at Garabandal?*], Paris, Nouvelles Éditions

Latines, 1966.

SCHACHTER, D.L., "The hypnagogic state: A critical review of the literature," *Psychology Bulletin*, 83, 452-81, 1976.

SCHEFFCZYK, L., *Die theologischen Grundlagen von Erscheinungen und Prophezeihungen* [*The theological foundations of apparitions and prophecies*], Leutesdorf, Johannes, 1981.

SCHELLINCK, G., *Het wonderbare leven van Leonie van den Dijck* [*The wonderful life of Leonie van den Dijck*], Onkerzele, 1994.

SIVRIC, I., *La face cachée de Medjugorje* [*The dark side of Medjugorje*], Saint-François-du-Lac, Quebec, Canada, Editions Psilog, 1988.

STAMM, H., *Im Bann der Apokalypse: Endzeitvorstellungen in Kirchen, Sekten, und Kulten* [*In Captivity of the Apocalypse: End Time Performances in Churches, Sects, and Cults*], Zurich, Pendo, 1998.

STERN, J., *La Salette Documents Authentiques: Dossier Chronologique Intégral* [*Authentic Documents of La Salette: Integral Chronological Dossier*], Desclée De Brouwer, Bruges-Paris, 1980, 1984.

THURSTON, H., *Les Phénomènes Physiques du Mysticisme* [*The Physical Phenomena of Mysticism*], Paris, Gallimard, 1961.

TIZANÉ, E., *Les Apparitions de la Vièrge; un Enquêteur S'Interroge* [*Apparitions of the Virgin; an Investigator Interrogates*], Paris, Éditions Tchou, 1977.

TRICLOT, A., *Le Livre d'Or de Kerizinen* [*The Golden Book of Kerizinen*], Sainte Anne, 1977.

TURI, A.M., *Pourquoi la Vièrge apparaît aujourd'hui* [*Why the Virgin appears today*], Paris, Éditions du Felin, 1988.

TOUSSAINT, Monsignor and JOSET, C.J., S.J., *Beauraing, les Apparitions, le Livre du Cinquantenaire* [*Beauraing, the Apparitions, the Book of Cinquantenaire*], Desclée De Brouwer, Bruges-Paris, 1981.

VAUZELLE, Marquis de la, *Le Secret de La Salette Devant l'Episcopat Français* [*The Secret of La Salette Before the French Episcopate*], Tours, Salmon, 1917.

VERGOTE, A., "Visions et apparitions: Approche psychologique" ["Visions and apparitions: Psychological approach"], *Revue Théologie de Louvain*, 22, 202-225, 1991.

VILLEPELÉE, J.F., *Marie Martel, I et II* [*Marie Martel, I and II*], Tilly, The Friends of Our Lady of Tilly, 1982, 1983.

von DÄNIKEN, E., *Le Livre des Apparitions* [*The Book of Apparitions*], 1975.

von DÄNIKEN, E., *Die Götter waren Astronauten!* [*God was an Astronaut!*], Gütersloh, Bertelsmann, 2001.

von LICHTENFELS, K., *Lexikon der Prophezeihungen: 350 Voraussagen* [*Lexicon of Prophechy: 350 Forecasts*], Herbig, 2000.

von REISSWITZ, C.K., *Das letzte Geheimnis von Fátima* [*The Last Secret of Fátima*], Pattloch, 2000.

von URBANTSCHITSCH, V., *Über Subjektive Optische Anschauungsbilder* [*About Subjective Visual Images*], Deuticke, 1907; *Über Subjektive Hörerscheinungen und subjektive optische Anschauungsbilder* [*About Subjective Auditory and Visual Images*],

Vienna, Deuticke, 1908.

WADE, N.J., "A selective history of the study of visual motion aftereffects," *Perception*, 23, 1111-34, 1994.

WAGNER, H., *Mystische Erlebnisse: Licht über Eisenberg* [*Mystical Experiences: Light on Eisenberg*], St. Andrä Wördern, Mediatrix-Verlag, 1986.

WALZ, J.B., *Die Muttergottes-Erscheinungen von Heroldsbach-Thurn, I: 9.10.1949-13.8.1950, II: bis 25.7.1951, III: Augenzeugenberichte vom Sonnenwunder... Wichtige Antworten auf häufige Fragen um Heroldsbach im Lichte der theologischen Forschung*, als Manuskript gedrukt [*The Mother of God Apparitions of Heroldsbach-Thurn, I: 9.10.1949- 13.8.1950, II: bis 25.7.1951, III: Eyewitness Accounts of the Miracle of the Sun... Important answers to common questions to Heroldsbach in light of theological research,* manuscript form], Frensdorf, Bamberg, 1958.

WETZEL, F., "Die Phänomene von Heroldsbach-Thurn" ["The Phenomena of Heroldsbach-Thurn"], *Natur und Kultur*, 130-145, 1950.

WILMET, L., *Beauraing – Banneux – Onkerzeele*, Dupuis, 1933.

MIND CONTROL AND MARIAN VISIONS — A THEORETICAL AND EXPERIMENTAL APPROACH

— Raul Berenguel —

Several researchers have disclosed the possibility of mind control and of the induction of voices in the human auditory system. The techniques involved are essentially based upon the utilization of microwaves and electromagnetic fields. This paper presents an historical synthesis of the problem, explains several relevant experimental and theoretical approaches, and compares similar laboratory results that have also been described in the analysis of "Marian visions." This text, in an abbreviated form, was presented at the 2nd International Science Frontiers Symposium, at Porto, Portugal, in 2001.

INTRODUCTION

According to several authors [see Valerian, 2001], many projects seeking mind control with recourse to a vast array of technologies, including electromagnetic fields, microwaves and hallucinogens, have taken place in the past and continue today, mainly in the United States.

Some of the projects that were launched by the U.S. intelligence community have included:

- *Project Moonstruck*, 1952, CIA:

Emphasis: electronic implants in the brain and teeth
Targets: long-range targets
Range: HF - ELF
Goals: location, behavioral control, conditioning
Method: electronic brain stimulation

55

- *Project MK-Ultra*, 1953, CIA:

Emphasis: drugs, electronic and electromagnetic devices
Targets: short-range targets
Range: VHF, HF, and UHF with ELF modulation
Goal: programmed behavior
Effects: narcoleptic trance, programming by suggestion
Method: memory dissolution by electronic means

- *Project Orion*, 1958, CIA:

Emphasis: drugs, hypnosis, and electronic brain stimulation
Targets: long-distance targets
Range: modulated ELF
Goals: behavioral programming, induction of loyalty

- *Project MK-Delta*, 1960, CIA:

Emphasis: subliminal programming by electromagnetic means
Targets: long-distance targets
Range: VHF, HF and UHF with ELF modulation
Goals: exhaustion, mood changes, behavioral dysfunction, criminality
Method: transmission and reception via TV and radio antennas, power lines, magnetic fields modulated at 60 Hz

- *Project Phoenix II*, 1983, USAF, NSA:

Emphasis: multidirectional targets in selected population groups
Targets: medium-range targets
Range: radar, microwaves, EHF and modulated UHF
Potencies: from GW to TW
Goals: population programming, location-specific earthquake propagation

- *Project Trident*, 1989, NSA:

Emphasis: direct action upon individuals or populations by electronic means
Range: UHF
Potency: 10 GW
Goals: behavioral control of large population groups, riot control
Method: black helicopters flying in triad formation

- *Project RFMedia*, 1990, CIA:

Emphasis: subliminal, multi-directional programming and suggestion
Target: United States population
Range: ULF, VHF, HF with phase modulation
Potency: GW
Goals: programming and stimulation of desires, subversion of the population's psychic capacities, preparation for mass behavioral control via EM means
Method: mass transmission via TV and radio

- *Project Tower*, 1990, CIA:

Emphasis: programming and subliminal suggestion throughout the country
Target: United States population
Range: microwaves, EHF, SHF
Goals: neural degeneration, DNA modification by resonance, psychic suppression
Method: cellular telephone system, ELF modulation

- *Project HAARP*, 1995, CIA, NSA:

Emphasis: induction of electromagnetic resonance
Range: UHF and VHF, phase resonance with the atmosphere
Potency: GW and TW
Goals: behavior modification, DNA alteration

- *Project Clean Sweep*, 1997, 1998, CIA, NSA

Emphasis: induction of electromagnetic resonance
Goal: behavior modification
Potency: unknown, with the possibility of retransmission use in the cellular telephone frequencies

It would be exhausting to continue, but we would still like to point out the existence of many other projects with the same objectives, namely MK-Chaos, COINTELPRO, etc.

As one would expect, other countries have developed similar projects in this area, the most important probably being those that were launched by the former Soviet Union. An interesting treatment of this subject can be found in the article "Amplified Mind Power Research in the Former Soviet

Union" (Ebon, 2001). As for the main investigation centers, we can mention the following:

- Institute of Scientific Research in General and Educational Psychology;

- Baumann Institute of Advanced Technology;

- State University of Moscow, laboratory of Professor Kholodov;

- Institute of the Energy, laboratory of Professor Sokolov.

Twenty-four other research centers were allegedly involved in this kind of investigation, as well as related research.

APPLICABLE TECHNOLOGIES

That very high frequencies of short wavelength, like those used by radar, can alter the potentiation gradient in nerve cells was demonstrated by Allan Frey at Cornell University in 1962. In fact, the waves in the radio and television emissions cannot penetrate the potentiation gradient through the walls of the nerve cells. When the radar signals are pulsed, however, they can surpass that barrier. Differences in the osmosis of the ions produce a small potential difference along the walls of the cells. When a small voltage appears in a small distance, that potential change is called "steep" and its gradient is what prevents normal electromagnetic signals from causing us to have convulsions (White, 2000).

The first successful transmission of the human voice, directly to a living person's cranium, was achieved by Dr. Joseph C. Sharp at the Army Institute of Research at Walter Reed in 1974 (White, 2000). The method used was the conversion of a hypnotist's voice into an ultrasonic frequency. This methodology can be analyzed in Figure 1.[1]

Extracting the most pertinent information from these studies, we can conclude that powerful pulses of short wavelength and high-frequency can penetrate through the walls of the nerve cells and alter its potentiation gradient, as Frey demonstrated.

Using this same source, we can see in detail how the experiment works via the production of a stable tone within the limits of human hearing, starting

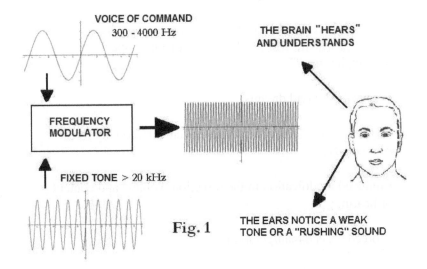

Fig. 1

from 15 KHz. Simultaneously, another device receives the induction voice command in the range between 300 Hz and 4 KHz. These two sources are mixed in a frequency modulator, where the command voice executes the modulation functions.

The result is a tone that is not very perceptible by the test subject's hearing but that his brain still understands as a command. The sense of hearing can only slightly perceive a vague tone or "buzzing" sound. This method can be applied to other emitting sources, such as microwaves or electromagnetic fields of diverse typology.

Frey's article (1962) is worthy of attentive study. One passage in particular deserves scrutiny:

> The closest match occurred when the acoustic amplifier was driven by the RF transmitter's modulator. Peak power density is a critical factor and, with acoustic noise of approximately 80 db, the peak power density of approximately 275 mw/rf is needed *to induce perception* at the carrier frequencies 125 Mc and 1,310 Mc. The average power density can be at RF as low as 400 μW/cm^2 [emphasis added].

To induce perception! This passage suggests that experiences like the apparitions perceived by the "seers" at Fátima can be propagated via contemporary mind control technologies. Among the relevant physiologic effects at the level of the brain are the following:

• flawed memories, inducing erroneous actions;

59

• seemingly *telepathic* communication, as when the children of Fátima asked, "Mother, how does that lady speak without moving her lips?";

• controlled, vivid dreams;

• forced visions, some including movements, equally forced, of the body;

• induced modification in the direction, volume and content of hearing;

• forced speech manipulation;

• hearing via microwave transmission.

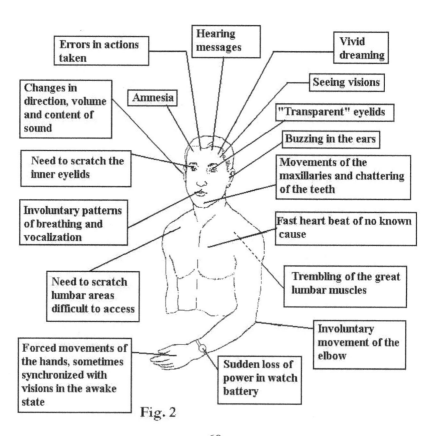

Errors in actions taken

Hearing messages

Vivid dreaming

Changes in direction, volume and content of sound

Amnesia

Seeing visions

"Transparent" eyelids

Buzzing in the ears

Need to scratch the inner eyelids

Movements of the maxillaries and chattering of the teeth

Involuntary patterns of breathing and vocalization

Fast heart beat of no known cause

Need to scratch lumbar areas difficult to access

Trembling of the great lumbar muscles

Forced movements of the hands, sometimes synchronized with visions in the awake state

Sudden loss of power in watch battery

Involuntary movement of the elbow

Fig. 2

Other effects at the bodily level that are of interest in the context of this presentation include irresistible command orders such as "go there," "do this," and "do that."

In order to thoroughly examine the experimental and theoretical results, we suggest that the reader consult the findings of Persinger (1995) and Lin (1989) at Laurentian and Illinois Universities, respectively.

One of the possibilities brought forward by Frey for the receiving mechanism, and confirmed by his experiments, is that a kind of electrical capacitor effect exists between the tympanic membrane and the oval window of the ear. Frey points out some aspects that could contradict such a possibility, namely, rotation movements of the subject's head that would result in a variation of the capacitor according to its location in space. Another possibility was the involvement of the cochlea as a detecting device. To date, efforts to explain the reception mechanism have proven inconclusive.

The probability that more than one receiving center is involved remains an option. Work done by some authors (see Jones, Steven, and Laurie, 1940), involving placing electrodes in the ear and stimulating it electrically, suggest the possibility that there is more than one detection area.

The hearing and bodily sensations that have been evinced during so-called "Marian apparitions" have included the following:

• sound effects, involving "voices" inside the cranium;

• forced speech, not belonging to the subject;

• "rush" effects in the skin;

• sudden bodily heating;

• a decrease in sleep duration, with increase in the vigilant periods;

• vivid dreams seemingly controlled by an "intelligence";

• hearing of a "buzzing" sound.

According to Frey, the sound sensation is located in the anterior part of the cranium, although the spatial position of the head in relation to the source is not important. Based on experiments done by Persinger, and cited by Fernandes and d'Armada (1995), the emission of microwaves directed to the nape of a subject's head makes him or her hear a sound similar to "the buzzing of bees."

COMMENTS

In all likelihood, these types of technologies have already been directly applied in open warfare. According to the news service of British ITV, in March 1991, during the first Gulf War, an ultrasound system was used via a commercial channel of FM to prompt a sense of despondency and desperation in Iraqi troops by direct stimulation of the brain.

Furthermore, regarding the same conflict, *The Guardian* referred to the possibility of a modified C-130 airplane emitting high potency microwave pulses in order to transport an acoustic frequency between 5 and 15 KHz that

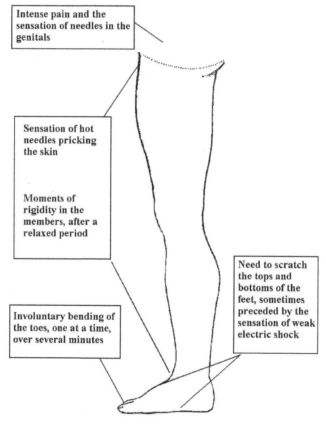

Fig. 3

induced the Iraqis to believe that "they were hearing the voice of God." This project was coupled with another one that emitted holographic images.

SIMILARITIES WITH MARIAN VISIONS

On the frontier of scientific investigation, we see that there are phenomenological correlations to be found between the experiences of individuals "contacted" during "Marian apparitions" and the altered states found in individuals exposed to electronic mind control technologies.

In the case of Fátima, we find some disturbing similarities between physical effects reported at that time and the effects of microwaves.

Nevertheless, as we have always done, we recommend the abandonment of passionate discussions, and insist that only the *facts* related *at that time* by the *clairvoyants* themselves and by *reliable eyewitnesses* prevail.

The best collection of transcriptions of documents from that time is, in our opinion, those investigated and published by Fernandes and d'Armada (see FERNANDES, J. and d'ARMADA, F., *Heavenly Lights: The Apparitions of Fátima and the UFO Phenomenon*, San Antonio, TX, Anomalist Books, 2006 and FERNANDES, J. and d'ARMADA, F., *Celestial Secrets: The Hidden History of the Fátima Incident*, San Antonio, TX, Anomalist Books, 2006.) Among the important facts found in those volumes, we emphasize the following:

• The Being apparently "spoke" without moving her lips;

• On multiple occasions, her speech was not perceptible, instead, only a noise similar to "the buzzing of bees" was heard; [2]

• Heat was felt by the witness; and,

• The fast drying of clothes resulted.

The hearing in the "interior of the cranium," without any movement of the Being's lips, is *identical* to what is felt by individuals subjected to mind control technologies that use microwaves. Let us note the fact that in the case of Marian apparitions, this seems to be a common factor. Father Cros, who described the visions in Lourdes, France, mentions that the children received messages in the brain without knowing where they came from.

Those individuals who are subjected to mind control technologies also mention hearing inside their cranium a buzzing sound similar to that of a bee.

Another physical factor that attracts our attention is the rapid drying of clothes. After the so-called "Miracle of the Sun," a number of eyewitnesses at Fátima mentioned that the clothes that were wet from the rain that had just fallen suddenly dried in a very short time. In their investigation, Fernandes

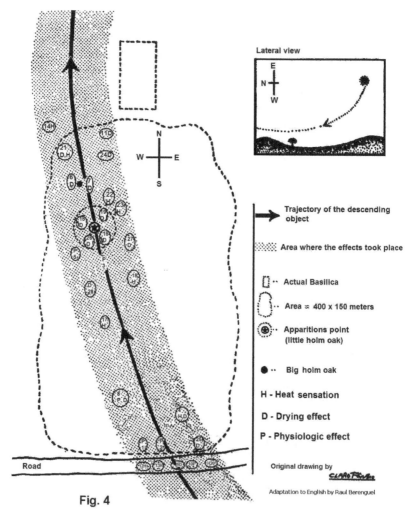

Lateral view

Fig. 4

→ **Trajectory of the descending object**

▒ **Area where the effects took place**

⬚ ·· **Actual Basilica**

⬭ ·· **Area ≈ 400 x 150 meters**

◉ ·· **Apparitions point (little holm oak)**

● ·· **Big holm oak**

H - Heat sensation

D - Drying effect

P - Physiologic effect

Original drawing by CLARO FELIX

Adaptation to English by Raul Berenguel

and d'Armada mapped the location of the eyewitnesses that had mentioned the phenomenon of heat, drying, and related physiologic effects. This verified that, in terms of area, these effects took place in a perfectly outlined, rectangular area of approximately 65 meters by 290 meters. In Figure 4, we can observe the same map.[3]

This map was drawn by Fernandes and d'Armada based on the location of individuals who were present, who later made statements to John Haffert and who were quoted by him in his work.

Based on this map, we executed a transcription for an axis of Cartesian coordinates, where the origin (x = 0; y = 0) is located at the little holm oak over which the apparitions took place. By analyzing the coordinates, we have the location of the several eyewitnesses x; y and the described effect (D = drying; H = heat; P = physiologic):

-181.5	-41.3	H
-181.5	-54.8	H
-180.0	-68.3	D
-178.5	-78.2	P
-178.2	-92.3	H
-166.5	-42.0	P
-166.2	-82.0	D
-165.0	-55.5	P
-142.1	-72.2	H, D
-127.5	-24.8	P, D
-72.2	-8.3	H
-45.9	2.3	D
-38.4	-30.8	H
-27.1	-8.3	P
-20.3	15.0	P
-12.0	3.0	D
-9.8	-28.6	D
-6.8	-10.5	D
4.5	9.8	D
7.5	-8.3	D
15.0	-20.3	H
21.1	-11.3	H
31.6	0.8	D
33.1	11.3	D
56.4	-9.8	D
57.9	24.8	D, H
73.7	-10.5	D
76.7	36.1	H

As one can readily see, the values of the coordinates also have a metric value. Based on the values, we can execute a linear correlation among the points and a line that best satisfies the sample, of the type: $Y = a + bx$ (1), thus $y = -6.22 + 0.32x$ (2).

From statistics, we find that n = 28, the standard deviation for x and y, Sx = 92.12, Sy = 34.04, and the coefficient of correlation is r = 0.85. The

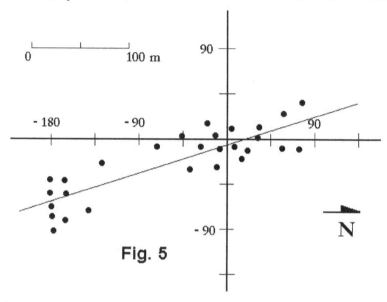

Fig. 5

projected line corresponds, as clearly shown, to the trajectory of the "Sun" during the "miracle," and its distance to the origin (the holm oak) determines a positioning error of just 6.2 meters, which is quite satisfactory for an analysis in these conditions. We can observe the 2D position of the witnesses and the effects in Figure 5.

The height at which one could locate the "Sun" is estimated to be 30 meters, according to eyewitness reports [see Fernandes and d'Armada, 2006]. The energy involved in the process requires more precise calculations, and should include the humidity of the atmosphere after the rain that fell. Consulting the "*Observações Metereológicas, Magnéticas e Sísmicas*" of the Meteorological Observatory of Coimbra, vol. LVI, 1918, we verified that the precipitation between 12 noon and 2 o'clock, was 9.5 mm, with a relative humidity of 87.04%.

DRYING BY MICROWAVES

Currently, the most efficient drying process is the one that uses microwaves (see *www.meac.com*). Microwave dryers generate heat through magnetron tubes like those used in microwave ovens. In the magnetrons, electrostatic and magnetic fields are used to move electrons, accelerating them in a spiral course. The electrons in movement enter in resonance in the cavities of the device, producing microwaves of determined wavelengths.

In the dryers, these beams of microwaves sweep the molecules of water out of wet clothes, causing its alignment in one direction and in another alternately, at rates as high as 2.5 thousand million times per second (see *www.see.it*). These fast changes produce heat, which evaporates the water. The energy of the microwaves reaches the water directly, heating it up and leaving the fabrics untouched. The key resides in the molecular structure. It determines how fast the vibration induced by the microwaves will be in that molecule, which means that the heating of different types of molecules has different speeds.

A form of measuring this difference is to use the coefficient of dielectric loss of each material. Water has a coefficient loss that is much superior to the one in common fabrics, and for this reason it seems "to attract" the microwaves, leaving the fabrics cold. This coefficient assumes the value of 12 to 25° C for water, while cotton and polyester are close to zero. Mixed wool fiber reaches 0.29 and the nylon 0.038.[4]

RECOMMENDATIONS

It is not our intent to alter conscience or to discount acts of faith. We just believe that a more thorough investigation should be imposed in the area of physiologic results of the exposition of individuals to microwaves, in parallel with the emergence of physical and psychological effects observed in the Marian visions. Expurgating the acts of faith and belief, these cases should be analyzed under the light of present knowledge regarding certain phenomena, remembering again, that from a strictly analytical point-of-view, for this study, only the facts and the eyewitness reports at that time have any interest to us. This is due to the fact, that with time, facts, statements, and memories related to the events are often distorted and falsified.

The correlation of the physical and physiologic effects from microwaves and those that are revealed in some Marian visions is clearly obvious, though far from supplying answers, they seem, at the moment, simply to raise more questions.

Notes

[1] Some information presented in this article was inspired by the diligent work of Eleanor White. See *www.raven.net*.

[2] The father of two of the clairvoyants, Manuel Pedro Marto, stated, "Then, I started to hear like a rumor, a hum, the way of a blowfly in an empty pitcher..." The priest Humberto Pasquale affirmed, "I heard like a buzzing of a fly in an empty barrel, but without articulation of words." We could cite additional testimonies, which are numerous, but the most interesting can be found in the works referenced.

[3] Used with the authors' permission.

[4] Of course, for that time period, we can only consider the cotton and wool in the examples.

References

EBON, M., "Amplified Mind Power Research in the Former Soviet Union," on the internet: *www.biomindsuperpowers.com/Pages/Ebon1.html*.

FERNANDES, J. and d'ARMADA, F., *As Aparições de Fátima e o Fenómeno OVNI [The Apparitions of Fátima and the UFO Phenomenon]*, Lisbon, Estampa, 1995.

FREY, A.H., "Human Auditory System Response to Modulated Electromagnetic Energy," *Journal of Applied Physiology*, 689-692, 1962, and on the internet: *www.raven1.net/frey.htm*.

JONES, R.C., STEVENS, M.H., and LAURIE, J., "Acoustics," *Scientific American*, December 1940, p. 281.

Leading Edge International Research Group [LEIRG], "Major Electromagnetic Mind Control Projects," on the internet: *www.angelfire.com/or/mctrl/projects.html*.

LIN, J.C., "Biological Structures which can Amplify Pulsed Microwave 'Voice-to-Skull' Signals," Proceedings of the Joint Symposium on Interactions of Electromagnetic Waves with Biological Systems, August 25 to September 2, 1987, Tel-Aviv.

PERSINGER, M.A., "Possibility of Direct Access to Every Human Brain," *Rumor Mill News* Forum, 1995.

VALERIAN, V., "Mind Control Projects – Major Electromagnetic Mind Control Projects," on the internet: *www.geocities.com/Area51/Shadowlands/6583/project027.html*.

"Steaming and Drying of Yarns and Threads," on the internet: *www.flecher.de/flecherengl/html/garne.html*, 2003.

"Microwave Drying Principles" on the internet: *www.meac.be/Application/Drying/drying.htm*, May 4, 2003.

GEOMAGNETISM AND VISIONARY MANIFESTATIONS

— Fernando Fernandes, Ph.D. —

This paper takes as its point-of-departure the episode known as the pre-announcement of the Fátima apparitions of 1917. Several speculative approaches are presented, mainly resulting from a wide range of experimental and theoretical research conducted from a multi-disciplinary perspective wherein Physics, Parapsychology, and Consciousness Studies figure prominently. With regard to the emergence of modified states of consciousness, namely, those of a geophysical nature, the possible influence of environmental variables is debated.

INTRODUCTION

Lisbon, February 7, 1917. Gathered around the medium, Carlos Calderon, a prominent figure in the esoteric milieu of the Portuguese capital, a group of spiritualists awaits the precious communications sent from the distant astral.

Suddenly, somebody asks for paper and pencil and, automatically, from the right to the left, in mirror-like fashion, the following psychographic message appears:

> Judge ye not. He who would judge you would not be pleased with your prejudice. Have ye faith and be ye patient. It is not our custom to predict the future. The mystery of the future is impenetrable, though at times God permits a corner of the veil to be lifted over that which it covers. Have ye confidence in our prophecy. The day of May 13th will be one of great happiness for the good souls of the world. Have ye faith and be ye good. *Ego Sum Charitas* ("I am Love"). Always at your side shall ye have your friends, who will guide your steps and who will assist ye in your work. *Ego Sum Charitas*. The brilliant light of the Morning Star will illuminate the path.
> ~ Stella Matutina [The Morning Star]

69

Undoubtedly, an enigmatic message, one made even more so by the fact that the events at Cova da Iria, on May 13, 1917, belonged, at the time of the message, to a future not yet manifested. On the other hand, no doubt exists regarding the authenticity of this pre-announcement. According to Furtado de Mendonça, who included the message above in his booklet entitled *Raio de Luz Sobre Fátima* [*Ray of Light over Fátima*], "so that no doubts would remain about the truthfulness of the facts," the group of mediums decided to publish an announcement in the daily newspaper, *Jornal de Notícias*. So, in that newspaper, with the date of March 10, 1917, we find an announcement entitled "135917" (May 13, 1917), where the following can be read (1):

> "Don't forget the happy day when our martyrdom will finish. The war they rage against us will finish. A. and C."

Following this miniscule announcement, the event happened that we all know of today: two months later, on May 13th, the apparitions began at Fátima, which has transformed it into the largest Marian shrine of the 20th century.

SPECULATIVE MODELS OF PRECOGNITION

For some, this whole episode doesn't rise above a mere coincidence, an insignificant detail lost in the tumult of the events that followed. From an historical perspective, however, the precedents are enlightening. As we know, the Old Testament contains countless cases of prophecies. While regarding classical antiquity, E. R. Dodds reminds us that the gift of precognition, among alleged paranormal phenomena, was accepted, in spite of the inherent logical difficulties (2):

> The paradox of the situation was recognized in antiquity: Aristotle opens his discussion of the subject with the remark that it is difficult either to ignore the evidence or to believe it. Ostensible precognitions formed part of the accepted matter of history: the pages of nearly all ancient historians, from Herodotus to Ammianus Marcellinus, are full of omens, oracles, or precognitive dreams or visions. Yet how can an event in an as yet non-existent future causally determine an event in the present? This was already for Cicero, and even for his credulous brother, Quintus, the *magna quaestio*, as it still is today.

On the actual positioning of the physical sciences relative to this problem, we could consider several quite speculative, but also quite intriguing, proposals. For instance, as noted by the physicist Gerald Feinberg of Columbia University (3), in general terms, the mathematical equations that describe the time evolution of a given phenomenon present symmetry between the past and the future. In other words, the reason for the exclusion of phenomena involving a reversed time order of cause and effect are because they have not been observed experimentally and not because the underlying theory forbids them.

For example, if there was experimental evidence of time symmetry, then a solar eruption, let us say, would be observed twice: once, corresponding to the arrival of the advanced wave, and then later, corresponding to the arrival of the retarded wave. Because this does not happen in practice, we may conclude the physical improbability of such solutions. According to Feinberg, however, this situation may imply that advanced waves are not as strongly produced as retarded waves. This would also be in consonance with the paucity of the precognition phenomenon. As for the mechanism associated with precognition, it would necessarily involve the observer's own consciousness:

> A plausible analogy between information about the past and future would suggest that if information about the future is available to a person at all, the main source of it might well be observations that he, or others, will make in the future and which will then be stored in his brain. It might be expected that whatever the mechanism of precognition, it could work more easily upon the future state of the percipient's own brain than on the world outside. In other words, I am suggesting that precognition, if it exists, is basically a remembrance of things future, an analogy to sense perceptions of the very recent past... By a process similar to memory of the past, it could be possible for the advanced pattern to be brought into consciousness, so that the person involved would "remember" the future stimulus connected with the advanced pattern.

In the area of speculative models involving multidimensional metrics, there are also interesting contributions, such as the one proposed by Rauscher and Targ (4, 5). In this case, a geometrical model of space-time with an eight-dimensional metric is proposed. This model is consistent with the paranormal phenomena and the structure of modern physics. According to the authors, these phenomena "are not a result of an energetic transmission, but rather they are an interaction of our awareness with a non-local hyper-dimensional space-time in which we live. Although we have demonstrated that this model does not contradict physics, we cannot explain why these phenomena manifest in consciousness and apparently not in the rest of physics. Nor can we presently describe the mechanism by which consciousness has access to the complex space."

It is in the field of quantum theory, however, that speculation and controversy proliferate. The proposal of Penrose and Hameroff (6-12) – that underlying the workings of the human brain and human consciousness we may find the macroscopic expression of quantum processes – opens a vast horizon of possibilities. In quantum theory, the "principle of non-locality" (the production of effects in the absence of any local cause) constitutes one of the fundamental concepts of the theory. Related to this, the EPR paradox, initially proposed by Einstein, Podolsky, and Rosen in 1935, involves the basic formulation that exists between two quanta of light, emitted from the same source, travelling in opposite directions. The paradox predicts, and experiments have confirmed (13), that they maintain their connection to one another, independently of the distance among them. That is, the measurement of, say, the polarization of one photon determines the polarization of the other photon at their respective measurement sites. This "action-at-a-distance," expressed as coherence between distant entities, is what is called non-locality. This property includes both time and space. The physicist Olivier Costa de Beauregard, drawing out the implications of such situations, goes on to say: (14)

> The distant correlation, which is at stake, seemed unacceptable: to Einstein as implying "telepathy;" to Schrödinger as being "magic;" and to de Broglie as "upsetting our accepted ideas pertaining to space and time." Even now that there is plenty of experimental evidence of the distant Einstein correlations, some distinguished physicists, who have helped in clarifying the problem, are somewhat upset that quantum mechanics is once more right at this point!... There is no *a priori* reason why antiphysics is intrinsically symmetrical to physics... And one need not say that antiphysics looks extremely like parapsychology.

> The point is that microphysics, that is, quantum mechanics, is neutral between physics and antiphysics. It has essentially, and symmetrically, one foot in physics and one in antiphysics, just as it has one hand in particles and one in antiparticles.

As for the EPR paradox that Beauregard simply calls the Einstein paradox, the implications for our common conceptions of space and time are thus explained:

The predictive Einstein paradox consists in a correlation between outcomes of distant measurements connected through their past, while the retrodictive Einstein paradox consists in a correlation between distant preparations connected through their future. In neither case is there a "present" interaction (which, indeed, would raise relativistic problems). Therefore, paradoxical as they look to common sense, these relations are fully consistent with relativistic covariance and the limited velocity of signals. The common sense belief that they violate is Einstein's prohibition against telegraphing into the past, thus showing that this prohibition is of a fact-like, or macroscopic, nature, rather than a strictly law-like one.

This hypothetical connecting bridge between quantum mechanics and psi phenomena, precognition included, conjugated with the possible correlation between consciousness/memory and quantum brain processes, opens countless possibilities for the elaboration of surprising and fantastic theories. We will just take a brief note of the proposals of Evans Harris Walker (15-18) and Jon Taylor (19). The work of Walker is based on the orthodox interpretation of quantum theory. Physical phenomena are thus described by statistical laws (wave function) and it is the act of measurement (perception) itself that determines what is measured (the collapse of the wave function). In a certain way, consciousness is responsible for the world as we know it by virtue of its role in actualizing a particular possibility. The alternative proposed by Taylor is centered in David Bohm's interpretation (20) of quantum theory and the so-called "hidden variables."

In fact, the actual mechanisms, if they exist at all, linking human consciousness and the paranormal and quantum domain, must be seen, at this stage, as purely conjectural. The same can be said regarding the eventual exogenous factors influencing this type of phenomena. About this last point, however, some interesting insights have recently surfaced. We mean the correlations detected between psi phenomena and global geomagnetic activity (21-25). According to Krippner and Persinger (26-28), analyses have shown an association between certain psi phenomena involving minimal temporal displacement between the event and the experience (e.g., "telepathy" and "clairvoyance") and relatively quieter geomagnetic activity. Psi that involved significant temporal displacement between the experience and the event (e.g., "precognition") does not appear to display the same effect. In fact, "visual" (primarily "post-mortem") apparitional experiences occur more frequently on days or months with enhanced geomagnetic activity" (29).

THE PRE-ANNOUNCEMENT OF FEBRUARY 1917

Surprisingly, and returning to the pre-announcement of Fátima on February 7, 1917, on that date the Meteorological Observatory of Coimbra, consigned in its official publication (30) a measurement of an episode of magnetic disturbances. Also, the average values of the aa index (31) that measures planetary geomagnetic activity, confirm, for that date, the variations detected locally by the Observatory of Coimbra. The data from the aa index also reveals peaks of geomagnetic activity on the 15th and 20th of the same month, whereas the Observatory of Coimbra only detected a local magnetic disturbance on the 20th. Coincidence or not, this finding is also in concordance with the spontaneous cases and experimental evidence reported in several studies.

Regarding this issue, neuroscientist Michael Persinger has long maintained that geomagnetic activity is able to affect the brain's receptivity to phenomena of this nature by a specific action on certain neural pathways, thus facilitating the consolidation and conscious access to this information. The investigation of religious and mystic/paranormal experiences has led Persinger to develop a protocol for magnetic stimulation of the temporal lobes. In his laboratory, at the Laurentian University of Sudbury, Ontario, more than a thousand volunteers have already submitted themselves to the use of a motorcycle helmet adapted with a set of solenoids capable of generating weak electromagnetic fields directed to the temporal lobes of the brain (32, 33). In this way, an induction of altered states of consciousness is possible, namely the "sense of presence" and also spatial and visual distortions.

In 1994, Susan Blackmore, a senior lecturer in Psychology at the University of the West of England, Bristol, agreed to participate as a volunteer in one such trial (34):

> I was wide-awake throughout. Nothing seemed to happen for the first 10 minutes or so. Instructed to describe aloud anything that happened, I felt under pressure to say something, anything. Then suddenly my doubts vanished. "I'm swaying. It's like being on a hammock." Then it felt for all the world as though two hands had grabbed my shoulders and were bodily yanking me upright. I knew I was still lying in the reclining chair, but someone, or something, was pulling me up.
>
> Something seemed to get hold of my leg and pull it, distort it, and drag it up the wall. It felt as though I had been stretched half-way up to the ceiling. Then came the emotions. Totally out of the blue, but intensely and vividly, I suddenly felt angry – not just mildly cross but that clear-minded anger out of which you act – but there was nothing and no one to act on. After perhaps 10 seconds, it was gone. Later, it

was replaced by an equally sudden attack of fear. I was terrified – of nothing in particular. The long-term medical effects of applying strong magnetic fields to the brain are largely unknown, but I felt weak and disoriented for a couple of hours after coming out of the chamber.

Persinger has always maintained that mystical, apparitional and psi experiences are interlinked, somehow, to sudden endogenous peaks of electrical activity in the temporal lobes (35). As a consequence of this, people with highly "unstable" temporal lobes would be more inclined to report mystical and psychic experiences. In addition, also according to Persinger, natural magnetic fields, as those resulting from earthquakes, could be strong enough to produce this kind of temporal lobe "instability."

To test this hypothesis, considerable research as been conducted (36) in order to try to correlate the dates of seismic incidents and the dates of occurrence of several modalities of anomalies and psi/apparitional phenomena, with particular emphasis on the so-called Anomalous Luminous Phenomena (ALP). In the ALP case (37), a significant correlation was obtained, in a given area, between the number of earthquakes in a given time-slot (six months) and the number of ALP occurrences during the six months immediately previous. This supports the idea that a significant part of the ALP was motivated by a temporal evolutive phenomenon (tectonic stress) that precedes and originates the seismic disturbances.

Following a similar approach, Persinger also suggested an identical mechanism for the apparitional cases of Fátima and Zeitoun. Hundreds of people reported seeing apparitions of the Virgin Mary in Zeitoun, near Cairo, Egypt, between April 1968 and May 1971. The incidents were characterized by intense luminous displays as well as "visions" of diverse nature. The temporal analysis (38) showed a moderate correlation between increases in the seismicity of the area and the occurrence of the luminous/apparitional phenomena during the same or previous month. Persinger's view of Fátima is similar, albeit more qualitative than quantitative (39).

So the notion that environmental geomagnetic factors may influence a wide range of paranormal phenomena seems to gain, more and more, a certain factual consistency. Naturally, the debate remains open, mainly in the more controversial ramifications, including those of Persinger (40), pioneer of so-called "Neurotheology" and a strong advocate of the geophysical approach to the paranormal.

CONCLUSION

To conclude, I don't want to leave out a small and curious detail. As I was writing this, I noticed that the search for answers concerning the episode of the pre-announcement of Fátima had led us quickly to the mysteries of the landscape and the local geography, as well as to the synergies with the surrounding community – in other words, to an unexpected and, to me, surprising face-to-face encounter with the problem of the "places of power."

If, as Mircea Eliade says (41), "a world entirely profane, a totally sacredless Cosmos, constitutes a recent discovery in the history of the human mind," it doesn't seem less evident that, even today, as before, the "forces in motion" speak to us through the atmosphere and the geology, by "miracles" and celestial prodigies, coincidences and visions, in an apparent and foreseeable communion not only between mind and body, but also, and mostly, between matter and spirit.

Notes

[1] d'ARMADA, F., and FERNANDES, J., *Fátima – Nos Bastidores do Segredo* [*Fátima – Behind the Secret*], Lisbon, Âncora Editora, 2002.

[2] MACKENZIE, A., *Riddle of the Future: A Modern Study of Precognition*, London, Arthur Baker, 1974.

[3] FEINBERG, G., "Precognition: a Memory of Future Things," in OTERI, L. (ed.), *Quantum Physics and Parapsychology, Proceedings of an International Conference held in Geneva, Switzerland, August 26-27, 1974*, New York, Parapsychology Foundation, Inc., 1975.

[4] RAUSCHER, E.A., "Some Physical Models Potentially Applicable to Remote Reception," in PUHARICH, A. (ed.), *The Iceland Papers: Select Papers on Experimental and Theoretical Research on the Physics of Consciousness*, Southern Pines, Full Sky Publishing, 1994.

[5] RAUSCHER, E.A. and TARG, R., "The Speed of Thought: Investigation of a Complex Space-Time Metric to Describe Psychic Phenomena," *The Journal of Scientific Exploration*, 15(3), Fall 2001.

[6] PENROSE, R., *The Emperor's New Mind: Concerning Computers, Minds, and the Laws of Physics*, Oxford, Oxford University Press, 1989.

[7] PENROSE, R., *Shadows of the Mind: A Search for the Missing Science of Consciousness*, London, Vintage, 1995.

[8] PENROSE, R., *The Large, the Small, and the Human Mind*, Cambridge, Cambridge University Press, 1997.

[9] HAMEROFF, S., "Quantum Coherence in Microtubules: A Neural Basis for

Emergent Consciousness?," *Journal of Consciousness Studies*, 1(1), 1994.

[10] PENROSE, R., "Mechanisms, Microtubules, and the Mind," *Journal of Consciousness Studies*, 1(2), 1994.

[11] PENROSE, R. and HAMEROFF, S., "What 'Gaps'? Reply to Grush and Churchland," *Journal of Consciousness Studies*, 2(2), 1995.

[12] HAMEROFF, S. and PENROSE, R., "Conscious Events as Orchestrated Space-Time Selections," *Journal of Consciousness Studies*, 3(1), 1996.

[13] ZOHAR, D., *Through the Time Barrier: A Study in Precognition and Modern Physics*, London, Paladin, 1983.

[14] COSTA DE BEAUREGARD, O., "The Expanding Paradigm of the Einstein Paradox," PUHARICH, A. (ed.), *The Iceland Papers: Select Papers on Experimental and Theoretical Research on the Physics of Consciousness*, Full Sky Publishing, Southern Pines, 1994.

[15] WALKER, E.H., "Foundations of Paraphysical and Parapsychological Phenomena," in OTERI, L. (ed.), *Quantum Physics and Parapsychology: Proceedings of an International Conference held in Geneva, Switzerland, August 26-27, 1974*, Parapsychology Foundation, Inc., New York, 1975.

[16] MATTUCK, R.D., WALKER, E.H., "The Action of Consciousness on Matter: A Quantum Mechanical Theory of Psychokinesis," PUHARICH, A. (ed.), *The Iceland Papers: Select Papers on Experimental and Theoretical Research on the Physics of Consciousness*, Full Sky Publishing, Southern Pines, 1994.

[17] EYSENCK, H.J. and SARGENT, C., *Explaining the Unexplained: Mysteries of the Paranormal*, London, Book Club Associates, 1982.

[18] WALKER, E.H., *The Physics of Consciousness*, Cambridge, Perseus Books, 2000.

[19] TAYLOR, J., "Information Transfer in Space-Time," *Journal of the Society for Psychical Research*, London, 64(4), 861, October 2000.

[20] BOHM, D., *Wholeness and the Implicate Order*, London, Routledge, 2000.

[21] PERSINGER, M.A., "Geophysical Variables and Behavior: XXII. The Tectonogenic Strain Continuum of Unusual Events," *Perceptual and Motor Skills*, 60(1), February 1985.

[22] PERSINGER, M.A., "Geophysical Variables and Behavior: XXXIII. Onsets of Historical and Contemporary Poltergeist Episodes Occurred with Sudden Increases in Geomagnetic Activity," *Perceptual and Motor Skills*, 62(2), April 1986.

[23] SPOTTISWOODE, S.J.P., "Geomagnetic Activity and Anomalous Cognition: A Preliminary Report of New Evidence," *Subtle Energies*, 1, 1990.

[24] KRIPPNER, S., VAUGHAN, A., and SPOTTISWOODE, S.J.P., "Geomagnetic Factors in Subjective Precognitive Dream Experiences," *Journal of the Society for Psychical Research*, 64(2), 859, April 2000.

[25] RADIN, D., "A dog that seems to know when his owner is coming home: Effect of environmental variables," *Journal of Scientific Exploration*, 16(4), Winter 2002.

[26] PERSINGER, M.A., "Geophysical Variables and Behavior: XXX. Intense Paranormal Experiences Occur during Days of Quiet, Global, Geomagnetic Activity," *Perceptual and Motor Skills*, 61(1), August 1985.

[27] PERSINGER, M.A. and KRIPPNER, S., "Dream ESP Experiments and Geomagnetic Activity," *The Journal of the American Society for Psychical Research*, 83, April 1989.

[28] KRIPPNER, S. and PERSINGER, M.A., "Evidence for Enhanced Congruence between Dreams and Distant Target Material during Periods of Decreased Geomagnetic Activity," *Journal of Scientific Exploration*, 10(4), Winter 1996.

[29] PERSINGER, M.A., "Geophysical Variables and Behavior: XXXI. Global Geomagnetic Activity during Spontaneous Paranormal Experiences: A Replication," *Perceptual and Motor Skills*, 61(2), October 1985.

[30] OBSERVATÓRIO METEOROLÓGICO DE COIMBRA [METEOROLOGICAL OBSERVATORY OF COIMBRA], Observações Meteorológicas, Magnéticas e Sísmicas Feitas No Ano de 1917 [Meteorological, Geomagnetic and Seismic Observations for the Year 1917], Coimbra, Vol. LVI, Imprensa da Universidade, 1918.

[31] SERVICE INTERNATIONAL DES INDICES GEOMAGNETIQUES [INTERNATIONAL SERVICE OF GEOMAGNETIC INDICES], "aa Index," on the internet: *www.cetp.ipsl.fr/~isgi/des_aa.htm*.

[32] DE SANO, C.F. and PERSINGER, M.A., "Geophysical Variables and Behavior: XXXIX. Alterations in Imaginings and Suggestibility during Brief Magnetic Field Exposures," *Perceptual and Motor Skills*, 64(3), Part 1, June 1987

[33] COOK, C. M. and PERSINGER, M.A., "Experimental Induction of the 'Sensed Presence' in Normal Subjects and an Exceptional Subject," *Perceptual and Motor Skills*, 85(2), October 1997.

[34] BLACKMORE, S., "Alien Abduction – The Inside Story," *New Scientist*, 1952, November 19, 1994.

[35] PERSINGER, M.A., "People Who Report Religious Experiences May Also Display Enhanced Temporal-Lobe Signs," *Perceptual and Motor Skills*, 58(3), June 1984.

[36] PERSINGER, M.A. and LAFRENIÈRE, G.F., *Space-Time Transients and Unusual Events*, Chicago, Nelson-Hall, 1977.

[37] PERSINGER, M.A., "The Tectonic Strain Theory as an Explanation for UFO Phenomena: A Non-Technical Review of the Research, 1970-1990," *Journal of UFO Studies*, Chicago, New Series, 2, 1990.

[38] DERR, J.S. and PERSINGER, M.A., "Geophysical Variables and Behavior: LIV. Zeitoun (Egypt) Apparitions of the Virgin Mary as Tectonic Strain-Induced Luminosities," *Perceptual and Motor Skills*, 68(1), February 1989.

[39] PERSINGER, M.A., "The Fátima Phenomena," 1984, *infra*.

[40] PERSINGER, M.A., "Experimental Simulation of the God Experiences: Implications for Religious Beliefs and the Future of the Human Species," JOSEPH, R (ed.), *Neurotheology: Brain, Science, Spirituality, Religious Experience*, Berkeley, University of California Press, 2002.

[41] ELIADE, M., *Le Sacré et le Profane* [*The Sacred and the Profane*], Paris, Gallimard, 1965.

EVIDENCE FOR ENHANCED CONGRUENCE BETWEEN DREAMS AND DISTANT TARGET MATERIAL DURING PERIODS OF DECREASED GEOMAGNETIC ACTIVITY

— Stanley Krippner, Ph.D. and Michael Persinger, Ph.D. —

The determination of eventual correlation between deeper human psychism with the dream state and the neuro-cerebral network that underlies it, and the non-controllable external stimulus, are here dissected in detail. This paper attempts, overall, to articulate the information perceived by the oneiric activity and environmental factors at the level of earthly geomagnetism, distinguishing itself here by the fluctuations of that geophysical component. It explores new clues and correlations that could be statistically relevant, in the wake of the approach made here in pre-text of the conditions of "reception" of the predictive messages of May 13, 1917.

The accuracy of concordance between dream content and target pictures over 20 nonconsecutive nights (1964-1967) for a single percipient was correlated with global geomagnetic activity. Spearman p correlations demonstrated a significant association between geomagnetic activity and accuracy (greater accuracy/less geomagnetic activity) for the 24-hour periods that corresponded to the dream nights. These results support the hypothesis that the geomagnetic effect is most evident when anomalous effects obtained under psi task conditions is present.

INTRODUCTION

Phenomena obtained under psi task conditions can be regarded as anomalous because they appear to preclude the constraints of time, space, and force. Over the past century, considerable research has been conducted in an attempt to understand psi phenomena and to determine whether they are worthy of continued attention and investigation (Edge, Morris, Palmer and Rush, 1986; Rao and Palmer, 1987). The understanding of the mechanism by which psi phenomena occur would facilitate acceptance of these phenomena as legitimate areas of investigation by mainstream science.

Several analyses of spontaneous cases of presumptive telepathy and/or clairvoyance (i.e., *general extrasensory perception* or GESP) have shown that these reported experiences are more likely to occur when the global geomagnetic activity is significantly quieter than the days before or the days after the experience (e.g., Churchill, Persinger, and Thomas, 1994; Persinger, 1987, 1989, 1993; Persinger and Schaut, 1988; Schaut and Persinger, 1985). The effect sizes are equivalent to correlation coefficients of between *0.35* and *0.45*.

An independent analysis of the reported spontaneous cases of clairvoyance and telepathy appearing in the *Journal of the Society for Psychical Research,* and subsequently used by Persinger (1987), detected a weak but persistent statistical relationship between low absolute levels of geomagnetic activity and the spontaneous cases. A small tendency also was reported for days of poltergeist and haunting onsets to have greater than usual geomagnetic activity (Wilkinson and Gauld, 1993).

Spottiswoode (1991), who evaluated the presence of correlation between tri-hourly geomagnetic activity and accuracy during remote viewing (anomalous cognition), reported that the significant association between geomagnetic measures and psi scores was most evident when psi was operative. Stated alternatively, if there was no evidence of anomalous cognition, the significant negative correlation between the intensity of the geomagnetic activity and the magnitude of anomalous cognition was absent.

The history of science has repeatedly demonstrated that the understanding of a process is most successful when the experimental conditions closely simulate the natural context. Because classic, spontaneous GESP experiences often occur at night and at least one-half of these reported experiences are associated with dreams (e.g., Rhine, 1977), it can be conjectured that the pursuit of psi during dream periods should have the highest probability of success. It can also be argued that if some factor (environmental or neuro-chemical) associated with geomagnetic activity is relevant to psi, then the association should be stronger during nighttime dream periods. Two hypotheses were designed on the bases of these conjectures:

• Nights on which the strongest experimental GESP occurred would also be nights that displayed the quietest geomagnetic activity compared to the days before and after.

• Nights that demonstrated weak or questionable GESP would not demonstrate this effect.

PROCEDURE

To test these hypotheses, data were retrieved from the experimental sessions conducted at Maimonides Medical Center in Brooklyn during the 1960s and 1970s (e.g., Krippner and Ullman, 1970; Ullman and Krippner with Vaughan, 1989). A total of 20 separate, nonconsecutive nights (with at least five days between any two sessions) were obtained from a single subject, William E., a New York psychoanalyst; these sessions involved 10 different months over four successive years (Ullman and Krippner, 1969; Ullman and Krippner, 1970). It was assumed that the utilization of scores from a single subject (especially one like William E. who frequently manifested anomalous results under psi task conditions) should enhance the discrimination of any geomagnetic effect because of the elimination of individual differences – the largest source of variance in these studies. Indeed, William E.'s first night as a laboratory subject was included in our initial investigation of anomalous dreams and geomagnetic activity (Persinger and Krippner, 1989). The typical procedure followed at Maimonides was for the percipient to arrive at the dream laboratory in time to meet and interact with the agent. The percipient would then spend much of the night focusing upon the contents of a randomly selected art print, after requesting to attempt dreaming about the art print. After electrodes were attached to the percipient's head for the monitoring of brain waves, eye movements, and muscle tonus, the percipient parted company with the agent and entered a soundproof sleep room. An experimenter threw dice that, in combination with a random number table, provided a number that corresponded to a numeral on a sealed envelope that contained a smaller sealed envelope in which there was an art print. The agent was dispatched to a distant room, opened the envelopes, and focused on this target picture during the course of the night.

Two experimenters took turns monitoring the percipient's sleep. Toward the end of each period of rapid eye movement (REM) sleep, the percipient was awakened by an experimenter via intercom and was asked to describe any dream content that could be recalled. The percipient's comments and the experimenter's questions were tape recorded, as was a morning interview in which the percipient gave associations to his or her dream report. The interviews were conducted double blind; neither the percipient nor the experimenters knew the identity of the target or the pool of art prints from which the target had been randomly selected.

To determine the possibility of chance correspondences, the Maimonides team obtained judgments of similarity between the dream content and each of the other potential targets in the pool from three judges who worked blind and independently with materials (i.e., typed transcripts of the dream reports and copies of the target pool never handled by the agent or experimenters) that had been mailed to them. Any extra chance difference between targets and non-targets in their congruence to dream transcripts was considered an apparent anomaly.

For William E., the judges' ranks of the 20 protocols and the numbers of comparison targets were obtained from the records. An accuracy ratio was calculated by dividing the rank (e.g., 1 = greatest compatibility between dream content and target picture) by the number of reference pictures (range six to 12). The mean and standard deviation for this ratio were 0.31 (range 0.13 to 1.00) and 0.25, respectively. Because a rank of 1 indicated the greatest concordance between dream content and target, the smaller ratios are inferred to reflect a larger magnitude of psi. From a dichotomous perspective, 10 of the nights were "high hits" with maximum concordance, while the remaining 10 were outside of this range.

The daily average aa (antipodal) index (Mayaud, 1973) was selected as the most appropriate measure of planetary geomagnetic activity. The aa index is the oldest continuous geomagnetic index, initiated in 1868. Although the aa values are based upon data from only two stations (one in each of the hemispheres), the daily aa index is highly correlated with better-known daily global measures that utilize the magnetic activity from several geomagnetic observatories. Although local variations in the amplitude of geomagnetic activity do occur, the average daily temporal pattern of the changes in

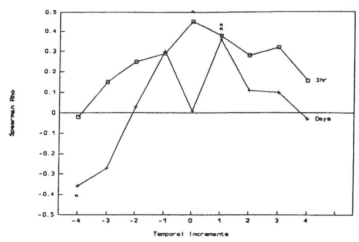

Spearman r correlation coefficients between (absence of) concordance scores between target and content for daily (pluses) and 3-hour (squares) intervals of geomagnetic activity for 20 sessions with William E. [* r < 0.05].

amplitude are relatively similar everywhere, the only exception being those areas subject to transient geomagnetic storms in which the effects of stronger static components emerge.

The aa index was used as the measure of global geomagnetic activity in Persinger's (1987) study of spontaneous case material reported in Great Britain between 1868 and 1886 (e.g., Gurney, Myers, and Podmore, 1886). By using this same index, direct comparisons could be made between the experimental data from the Maimonides studies and the spontaneous telepathic experiences a century earlier. For the collection of 20 sessions, daily average aa values were collected each of the four days before and each of the four days after each session began. In addition, aa values for successive three-hour intervals, time adjusted for the discrepancy between UT and Eastern Standard Time (Brooklyn), were also obtained from a computer database (Boulder, Colorado). Because the accuracy ratio did not necessarily imply equal intervals, and because the data were rank ordered, we selected a non-parametric correlation (Spearman p) to test our hypotheses. All analysis involved SPSS software.

RESULTS

Spearman p correlations between the nightly accuracy scores are shown in Figure 1 (daily aa averages) for daily increments (pluses) and for three-hour increments (squares). During the 24-hour period that corresponded with the local night (midnight to 6:00 AM), there was a significant positive correlation between geomagnetic activity and the score ($p = +0.36, p < 0.05$). Since *smaller* accuracy ratios indicate a closer correspondence between the dream content and the target, these positive coefficients indicate a *negative* relationship between geomagnetic activity and psi functioning.

When the three-hour aa averages (squares) are examined, the maximum correlations occurred during the same time intervals as the analyzed dreams ($p = +0.45, p < 0.05$) and in the next time intervals of the same mornings ($p = +0.38, p < 0.05$). Again, *larger* accuracy ratios, implying *poorer* psi performance, were associated with periods of more intense geomagnetic activity.

The strongest and most significant correlation between the score and the geomagnetic activity occurred with the day of the experiment and the next day. This is not surprising, because the actual time of the experiment would involve the following day. Figure 1 indicates that the greatest effect upon accuracy occurred between psi scores and geomagnetic activity between 0600-0859 hours, 0900-1159 hours, and 1200-1459 hours the day the experiment ended. Because Eastern Standard Time is five hours behind UT, this period would be 0100-0359 hours, 0400-0659 hours, and 0700-0959 hours local time. Thus, the concordance was highest during the time when most of the dream reports were collected, that is, during the later part of the night.

DISCUSSION

These findings are in accord with the earlier analysis of the Maimonides experimental GESP sessions as well as analyses of other psi experiments (e.g., Berger and Persinger, 1991), and of spontaneous cases of reported GESP (e.g., Persinger, 1987, 1993). These analyses have shown an association between relatively quieter geomagnetic activity and this class of anomalous cognition.

These results are also commensurate with a study in which Spottiswoode (1991) reported that a geomagnetic effect was only evident when psi was evident within the database. We also noted an association between the remote viewing scores by one subject who displayed anomalous cognition (data kindly supplied by Ed May) and the concomitant (three-hour increment) geomagnetic activity. There was no association between geomagnetic activity and accuracy when scores (from another subject) did not display anomalous effects.

"Telepathy" and "clairvoyance" have been inferred as manifestations of psi that involve minimal temporal displacement between the event and the experience. This class of phenomena appears to occur more frequently or with greater intensity during periods of decreased geomagnetic activity. Analysis of experimental studies by Berger and Persinger (1991), dream experiments by Persinger and Krippner (1989), and spontaneous cases (Persinger, 1993) has demonstrated an association between relatively quieter geomagnetic activity and this class of anomalous cognition. The effect size is equivalent to a correlation coefficient between 0.35 and 0.45.

Psi that involved significant temporal displacement between the experience and the event, e.g., "precognition," does not appear to display the same geomagnetic effect. In fact, visual (primarily "postmortem") apparition experiences occur more frequently on days (Persinger, 1988) or months (Randall and Randall, 1988) with enhanced geomagnetic activity. Consequently, over-inclusion of cases that involve "precognition" and "postmortem" apparitions with "telepathy" within the same analyses could mask or confuse primary effects.

In his wide-ranging book, *The Future of the Body*, Michael Murphy (1992) claims that "we live only part of the life we are given" (p. 3) and catalogs dozens of anecdotal and research reports to demonstrate his point. Parapsychological data are placed side-by-side with data from medicine, sports, the martial arts, and the behavioral and social sciences. The examples he gives of voluntary control, self-regulation, transformative practice, and extraordinary human experience indicate not only that many human potentials are overlooked by Western science but also that these capacities can provide practical avenues for an acceleration and betterment of human life. The anecdotal and experimental material on anomalous dreams is one of several examples of data that mainstream science ignores at its peril.

References

BERGER, R.E. and PERSINGER, M.A., "Geophysical variables and behavior: LXVII. Quieter annual geomagnetic activity and larger effect size for experimental *psi* (ESP) studies over six decades," *Perceptual and Motor Skills,* 73, 1219, 1991.

CHURCHILL, D.R., PERSINGER, M.A. and THOMAS, A.W., "Geophysical variables and behavior: LXXVII. Increased geomagnetic activity and decreased pleasantness of spontaneous narratives for percipients but not for agents," *Perceptual and Motor Skills,* 79, 387, 1994.

EDGE, H.L., MORRIS, R.L., PALMER, I. and RUSH, J.H., *Foundations of Parapsychology,* London, Routledge & Paul Kegan, 1986.

GURNEY, E., MYERS, F.W.H. and PODMORE, F., *Phantasms of the Living* (2 vols.), London, Trubner, 1886.

KRIPPNER, S. and ULIMAN, M., "Telepathy and dreams: A controlled experiment with electroencephalogram-electro-oculogram monitoring," *Journal of Nervous and Mental Disease,* 151, 394, 1970.

MAYAUD, P.M., "A hundred-year series of geomagnetic data, 1868-1967," *JAGA Bulletin,* 33, 1973.

MURPHY, M., *The Future of the Body: Explorations into the Future Evolution of Human Nature,* Los Angeles, Jeremy P. Tarcher, 1992.

PERSINGER, M.A., "Spontaneous telepathic experiences from phantasms of the living and low global geomagnetic activity," *Journal of the American Society for Psychical Research,* 81, 23, 1987.

PERSINGER, M.A., "Increased geomagnetic activity and the occurrence of bereavement hallucinations: Evidence of melatonin-mediated microseizuring in the temporal lobe?," *Neuroscience Letters,* 88, 271, 1988.

PERSINGER, M.A., "*Psi* phenomena and temporal lobe activity: The geomagnetic factor," in HENKEL, L.A. and BERGER, R.E. (eds.), *Research in Parapsychology, 1988,* Metuchen, NJ, Scarecrow Press, 1989, p. 121.

PERSINGER, M.A., "Geophysical variables and behavior: LXXI. Differential contributions of geomagnetic activity to paranormal experiences concerning death and crisis: An alternative to the ESP hypothesis," *Perceptual and Motor Skills,* 76,

555, 1993.

PERSINGER, M.A. and KRIPPNER, S., "Dream ESP experiments and geomagnetic activity," *Journal of the American Society for Psychical Research*, 83, 101, 1989.

PERSINGER, M.A. and SCHAUT, G.B., "Geomagnetic factors in subjective telepathic, precognitive, and postmortem experiences," *Journal of the American Society for Psychical Research*, 82, 217, 1988.

RANDALL, W. and RANDALL, S., "The solar wind and hallucinations – a possible relation due to magnetic disturbances," *Bioelectromagnetics*, 12, 67, 1991.

RAO, K.R. and PALMER, J., "The anomaly called psi: Recent research and criticism," *Behavioral and Brain Sciences*, 10, 539, 1987.

RHINE, L.E., "Research methods with spontaneous cases," in WOLMAN, B.B. (ed.), *Handbook of Parapsychology*, 59, New York, Van Nostrand Reinhold, 1977.

SCHAUT, G.B. and PERSINGER, M.A., "Subjective telepathic experiences, geomagnetic activity and the ELF hypothesis," Part I, data analysis, *Psi Research*, 4, 1, 4, 1985.

SPOTTISWOODE, S.J.P., "Geomagnetic activity and anomalous cognition: A preliminary report of new evidence, *Subtle Energies*, 1, 91, 1991.

ULIMAN, M. and KRIPPNER, S., "An experimental approach to dreams and telepathy: II. A report of three studies," *American Journal of Psychiatry*, 126, 1282, 1969.

ULIMAN, M. and KRIPPNER, S., "A laboratory approach to the nocturnal dimension of paranormal experience: Report of a confirmatory study using the REM monitoring technique," *Biological Psychiatry*, 1, 259, 1970.

ULIMAN, M. and KRIPPNER, S., with VAUGHAN, A., *Dream Telepathy: Experiments in Nocturnal ESP*, Jefferson, NC, McFarland, 1989.

WILKINSON, H. and GAULD, A., "Geomagnetism and anomalous experiences, 1868-1980," *Proceedings of the Society for Psychical Research*, 57, 275, 1993.

ALTERED STATES OF CONSCIOUSNESS IN FÁTIMA

— Vitor Rodrigues, Ph.D. —

The possibility that the phenomenology of Fátima could have a communicational nature leads the author to several considerations. The first of these suggests that it is a matter of a phenomenology with points of contact and divergence in relation to modified states of consciousness that have been studied by Transpersonal Psychology – which we would rather call, out of our concern for accuracy, the Psychology of Consciousness.

INTRODUCTION

The states that are usually studied by Transpersonal Psychology can arise both spontaneously, in the seeming absence of any definite context "outside" the person, or within the context of specific practices (meditation, breathing practices, dance, bodily expression, intense physical effort, prayer, etc.). Usually, they imply some sort of *expansion* of consciousness, although sometimes this will happen in the sense of a sharper "internal" perception, allowing psychological insights that are relevant to the subject and to other people, or amount to experiences of a wider perception of the social and physical world and their functioning. In some events, this wider perception seems to refer to the whole world or even the Universe, and the person feels that he is part of what he perceives: he feels "united" or "fused" with this ample object of perception.[1] Therefore, such states of consciousness are not at all typically mentioned as being the product of a more or less enforced external induction by outside beings.

DISCUSSION

In the case we are considering, it seems rather unlikely that the experience of the visionaries of Fátima can be equated with the experience of "expansion" more frequently studied by the Psychology of Consciousness. Everything hints at a clear outside interference with the subject, which this

87

one describes as something that is modifying him. Apparently, no mystical experiences, like the subjective sensation of seeming to fuse with the perceived object, are mentioned, and the subjects only describe what they see and hear. So it seems that no definite consciousness expansion is going on, but instead, we have a perceptive alteration and even a shrinking of the field of consciousness, therefore getting closer to Psychiatry's classical descriptions of pathological alterations of consciousness than to descriptions of healthy changes in it. The enforcing character of outside commands over Fátima's "contactees" once more seems closer to pathology than to the experiences of higher freedom, wider vision, and increasing field for options that are so familiar in descriptions of "transpersonal" states. One should emphasize the fact, however, that Fátima's observers did undergo a shrinking of their field of consciousness in what concerns the outside, but at the same time, they could be opening windows of inner perception in very precise directions that correspond to the information being conveyed to them. In this sense, one can say that simultaneously taking place is both a narrowing of the field of consciousness and a partial expansion in a clearly delineated "inner" direction.

I believe the phenomenology described is closer to the descriptions made by persons who claim to be "contacted" by "spirits" than to those made by persons undergoing modified states of consciousness, arising spontaneously or through "transformative practices."[2] The "sophrologic" state Joaquim Fernandes refers to seems to parallel the trance state of mediums and the experiences of persons who claim to be in relationship with "discarnate entities." As a matter of fact, mediums in trance seem to become alienated from the environment they are in and to focus entirely, as if they were hypnotized, on the "communicating entity" and the contents he or she is conveying. They are listening to, or somehow grasping, inwardly, the thoughts and images that he or she is transmitting. Sometimes, they can even act on the communicating Being's commands, which is quite obvious in the trance of mediums.[3] In this sense, it is rather interesting to verify, as Fernandes points out, the specific character of the Being's communication with Fátima's witnesses (as with other "contactees"). Within the Spiritist movement's tradition and the texts of its codifier, Allan Kardec,[4] we can find a clear assertion that "spirits," as they are trying to communicate with the "living" through mediums, use the "materials" their brains provide in such a way that what can be transmitted through a certain medium is limited and makes for a necessary adaptation of the communicating Being or of the communicated content. In what concerns Fátima's percipients, the hypothesis Fernandes is raising, about a communication that could be directly "transferred" to the brain, would entail the need for adapting it to each percipient's neurological architecture and cognitive structure, since this would amount to a better understanding of the message he would receive. Going a little bit further, if an intelligible message for a larger audience was intended, then the personal decoding/interpreting style of the little shepherds should be taken into account, thus preventing it from becoming adulterated by early poor decoding. The question of adequately transmitting messages is a well-known one for people in contact with traditional, non-technological societies, even when their language is known and spoken, because their members tend to "read" technical contents in the light of their tribal myths. Moreover, the possibility of direct communication to a receptive subject's nervous system is not strange to contemporary science, although apparently the experiments done in this field have been conducted in rather spooky contexts implying remote manipulation and destruction of human targets' nervous systems.[5]

CONCLUSION

In summary, it would appear that the phenomenology described at Fátima is closer to the one arising when subjects describe experiences of contact with spiritual beings than to "transpersonal" experiences. It is also true, however, that in Shamanic societies, the ingestion of psychedelic drugs by neophytes in appropriate ceremonies is frequent and aims at facilitating contact with spiritual realms.[6] Furthermore, the fact that such drugs can change brain electrical patterns to a high degree is compatible with the facilitation of its receptivity to a direct information transfer into the nervous system.[7] So, I believe that the idea of a possible contact by entities that were exterior to Fátima's subjects, a contact that could have been enforced by technical means with some intent, does find some echo both in what we know from current research about modified states of consciousness and classical literature about mediumship.

Notes

[1] See, e.g., WEIL, P., *A Consciência Cósmica* [*Cosmic Consciousness*], Petrópolis, Brazil, Editora Vozes, Ltd., 1976.

[2] MURPHY, M., *The Future of the Body*, New York, Jeremy P. Tarcher/Putnam, 1992.

[3] See, e.g., CASTELLAN, Y., *Le Spiritisme* [*Spiritism*], Paris, Presses Universitaires de France, 1982.

[4] KARDEC, A., *O Livro dos Médiuns* [*The Book of Mediums*], Translation from a French printing of the 19th century, Brazil, Federação Espírita Brasileira, Departamento Editorial, 1944.

[5] OSTRANDER, S. and SCHROEDER, L., *Psychic Discoveries*, New York, Marlowe & Company, 1997.

[6] POVEDA, J.M.D., *Chamanismo: El Arte Natural de Curar* [*Shamanism: The Natural Art of Healing*], Madrid, Ediciones Temas de Hoy, 1997.

[7] See DON, N.S., *et al.*, Effects of Ayahuasca on the human EEG, *Photomedicine*, 5(2), 87-96, 1998; DON, N.S., and MOURA, G., "Topographic brain mapping of UFO experiencers," *Journal of Scientific Exploration*, 11(4), 1997.

TRANCE(S) IN FÁTIMA

— Mario Simões, Ph.D. —

While the phenomenology of Fátima evokes an ideological reaction in almost everyone and prompts explanations that run the gamut of ufology, psychology, and science, it is best to maintain an attitude of openness regarding precisely what happened there. In the opinion of the author, the apparitions of Fátima can be explained in terms of what anthropology, psychology, and psychiatry tell us about trance states, specifically, the known characteristics of trance states, altered states of consciousness, and dissociative states. A review of the evidence on the apparitions of Fátima suggests that the percipients experienced an "eclectic trance" with characteristics of other types of trances, namely, possession/fascination, auto and hetero-hypnotic, mediumistic, shamanic, transpersonal, psychedelic, creative, and dream-like trances.

INTRODUCTION

Fátima phenomena do not let most people remain indifferent. These are, however, far fewer in number compared with the naïves, fanatics, and rationalists who are against it, or simply curious. An open attitude towards others' explanations, beyond those already known, is difficult on the moving ground of the passions, which, normally, in most individuals, only considers matters of religion, sex, and politics. The contribution by Joaquim Fernandes in this book, advances, without fear, other theories about the experiences, and tries to understand the phenomena from the psychological and anthropological point-of-view.

THREE TYPES OF ALTERED STATES

In my opinion, the kind of phenomena reported fits the anthropological, psychological and psychiatric definitions of *trance, modified states of conscience (sometimes and traditionally known as altered states of consciousness) and dissociative states*, respectively:

- *Trance* is a transitory modified state of consciousness, in

91

some way or another appearing as a transcendence of the individual, a liberation resulting from an intensification of a mental or physical predisposition, and finally, like an exhalation – sometimes as a discontinuity – from the *self* (Rouget, 1980). Physiological *trances* are hypnotic or hypnopompic phenomena.

• *Modified State of Consciousness (MSC)* exists as long as it occurs as a modified subjective experience or in the psychological functioning that is recognized by the individual or by an observer, regarding some ordinary rules for a certain individual (Kokoszka, 1987). Physical states are *sleeping* and *dreaming*.

• *Dissociative State* is observed as a "dissociation" of cognitive functions, namely in logic and time perception, with magical and paradoxical thinking patterns, and greater absorption of suggested ideas (Jacobson and Jacobson, 1996). Examples of dissociative states include driving while thinking of other things or sensing that time passes more rapidly while reading a novel.

ALTERED STATES AT FÁTIMA

In a way germane to this discussion, I think that those phenomena, however different, in this case encompass a *vast* definition of *trance* that includes other aspects. This first consideration refers simultaneously to the anthropological, psychological, and psychiatric aspects, although not minimizing any of them, indicating an interpretation atypical in terms of nosology.

There also appears in this context other terminology different from psychiatric "jargon," namely, "locutions," "visions," and "apparitions," in contradistinction to auditory, visual and pseudo-hallucinations, respectively. There is support for this difference, when hallucinations and pseudo-hallucinations are considered in a *normal vigilant state* (without trance, MSC, or dissociation), when there exists no outside critic, and when there is no presence of a person/ object perceived by oneself or by others present. In such instances, from a psychological point-of-view, "locutions" mean that a person is talking to himself, and receiving a message from "something or someone" from the "sacred" ambit, which is different from hallucinatory content and presentation – auditory and visual – as is typical in pathology. "Visions" and "apparitions" are initially objects of doubt and "natural" images or sensations of a real presence, a *presence* that can be felt and described by the person and other witnesses.

The person senses a presence that is *somewhat* objective, in the sense that the presence is perceived as outside the person. At its absolute, it is a distorted perception and one not without object (Valla, 1992). It is considered an experience, *in a state of trance*, with the sensation of a presence (not an image or a statue), as if it were real, transmitting messages to the person and giving him a mission to spread them (Murad, 1997). Even psychopathologists establish this difference, calling it *metachoric experience*. The whole visual field is substituted, with superposition, through a *unique* hallucination, and the percipient also loses the perception of the environment (Green and Leslie, 1987). These authors even describe three kinds of "apparition" – "in the middle of the air," "projected on a flat surface," and "inside a sort of painting."

Therefore, "apparitions" (as already defined above) exist – that is, there are people who can see "something," but describe it according to their understanding. One example of this is the incongruence manifested in the case of Fátima. Lúcia says, in one of her messages, that "in October Our Lord, Our Lady of the Pains and Our Lady of Carmo, Saint Joseph and Little Jesus shall come to bless the world." As we can see, there are three Mary's and two Jesus' – which would hardly be transmitted by a psychic acquainted with the unity of Mary and Jesus. This is strongly related to rural devotion at the beginning of the century and with associations of the image of the protective mother (Murad, 1997), which Fátima's "little shepherds" could not escape. It is, therefore, also a subjective experience in a cultural context, in which the subject is immersed.

Murad (1997) added, regarding this matter, an anecdotal observation that it would be "impossible the Divine appears naked," as long as we understand that a glorified body does not need clothes. Therefore, it is important to distinguish the personal from the essential part of the message. This refers, almost always, to conversion, prayer, cataclysm, and secrets. What does this really mean, even more so, since it is repeated in other Marian's apparitions? It seems it works like a "press release" for the entire world (Murad, 1997). A search for the *sacred* and the *wonderful* does not explain the vision but only their social importance (Torbado, 2000). One author (Torbado, 2000) presents a devastating report, by means of the social perspective of Marian apparitions. That the search for the sacred begins with the collective unconscious – autonomous from the *self* of the seer, however convoluted with personal elements – or from the knowledge obtained paranormally by the seer.

The word *seer* also remits to concepts of parapsychology, namely, *clairvoyance* – to be aware of distant facts occurring at the present moment, *telepathy* – communication between people, and *precognition* – prior knowledge of future events. All these psychic abilities are present without the help of any physical device known as a transmitter of information.

In the context of the sacred, precognition is denominated as *prophecy*. These phenomena are also present in this case, but as is nowadays known, they derive from a natural and human source, although they can be accompanied by an advanced spirituality. It is St. John of the Cross who warns about the ambiguity of these manifestations and insists that one should not be concerned about these "extraordinary phenomena."

It is acknowledged that seers are usually people with extra-sensory capacities (facilitated by adolescence or a physical-psychic constitution). For that reason, they would be more susceptible to emotive stimuli (Marcozzi, 1993), and in modified states of consciousness (real trance), *extra-sensory perception would be increased* (Simões, 1996). What is referred to above is not reducible, therefore, to pure divine communication, or to a production of the human mind, or to ecstatic psychophysiology.

The *ecstatic states* are usually attained after a long practice in spiritual or other disciplines (for instance, autogenous training, yoga, meditation, Zen, Cabala, Sufism, and so on). These states manifest through a fixation/ concentration on an object, with a reduction of the field of *consciousness, an exclusion of other mental functions, and an emergence of a huge internal peace*, feeling as if one "has been overwhelmed by something," "trespassed," in "fusion," remaining afterwards in a state of energetic deficit.

Murad (1997) observes that the state of "fusion," being "overtaken by something" or "trespassed," doesn't occur from action, but from a passive receptivity by surrendering oneself. They are not considered *states of possession* (anthropological and/or mediumistic trances), because subjectivity and reason are not switched off. In sum, the *reflexive self* remains. *Possession* is a belief, a way to interpret, in some societies, states of trance (modification of behavior and subjective experience of oneself and the world) attributed to the presence of a god or a spirit, temporarily animating the subject (Bourguignon, 1976). They can implicate a *personification of identity* (*impersonation*) addressed to spirits (voice, gestures and social behavior), a mediumistic activity (alteration of diction), or language modification (glossolalia).

In the case of Fátima, there would have been only a modification of verbal behavior, which would remit, according to Bourguignon (1976), to a particular kind of "belief" in possession. That belief would be neither ritual nor collective, spontaneous nor recognized by the subject before its own subjective experience, although occurring in trance. This fact distinguishes it from what a disease, even in cultures used to dealing with states of trance, in which possession without trance is considered a malady. In the case of Fátima, it is not a possession, but an *exclusive contact with a spirit* (Hardy, 1996) because there exists no discontinuity of identity.

It is emphasized that *possession* is an explanation, or a cultural understanding, because, from a psychological point-of-view, it is a dissociative state in which a separate part of the personality "possesses" temporarily the field of consciousness and behavior, as if one has to deal with secondary sub-personalities of the subject. From a psychiatric point-of-view, this would be a pathological dissociative state, classified in the same way as epilepsy, somnambulism and personality identity disorder (multiple personalities) (Prince, 1968). Psychologists and psychiatrists with no anthropological specialization or sensitivity to these aspects usually interpret these states as hysterical or epileptic manifestations, ignoring the context of their appearance. In reality, such states would only be pathological if they occurred when they were not desired, and simultaneously, if they dominated, causing avoidance of suitable solutions in daily life, and when there are no personal cognitive or social structures to deal with MSC (Crombach, 1974). They are not psychotic experiences, however, although they can have some characteristics in common, such as how they often "relate back" to the social environment and adaptivity of the person. For more information about this differentiation, see Simões (1991).

States of ecstasy are *trances* in which the temporary perception of reality is radically different from the usual *vigilant state*. It can be via *learned practices or techniques*, and normally exists in those who already possess a *favorable predisposition*. In Lúcia's case, there was no practice. It can be substituted occasionally, however, by the use of drinks with specific chemically composed substances (*mescaline, Ayahuasca, and so on*) or to other stimuli – *powerful lights*, which could have been the case.

It was thus *an ethnological trance*, same as that of the *shaman*, in which he or she contacts "spirits" and vice-versa, in *ecstasy*, which is different than *hypnotic and mediumistic trances*. It is also not an *auto or hetero-hypnotic trance*, as there are neither *inductions*, nor *particular suggestions* (at most, *an autosuggestion of mental preparation*). It is not mediumistic, as there is no *possession by spirit* (*or by spirits*) and these do not dialogue with the *assistants* through the "*medium.*" Naturally, there are other *modified states of consciousness* without *trance* and because of their nature these are excluded, like *dream, meditation, hypnagogic and hypnopompic trances*, "*reverie,*" *daydream*, or *dissociative and psychotic pathological states*.

In terms of *trance differentiation*, especially the characterization of what was experienced at Fátima, the dimension of *identity* and *subjectivity* (its presence or its absence) is fundamental. Therefore, according to Hardy (1996), it should also be referred to as concepts like *supra* and *subconscious*, in order to explain the direction taken by the *modification of the identity sense* (always changed to a higher or lower degree in states of trance) and the concept of *discontinuity* (already mentioned as the purpose of possession and ethnic trance, e.g., voodoo). This discontinuity stops subjectivity and reason – *the reflexive self* – its means *of its identity and unity*. In *mediumistic trance*, it is the same process, where the *"entering entity"* is, at least, partially lived as strange to the *self* and, sometimes, does not *apprehend* reflexively what is going on. Therefore, these two types of *trance* do not explain what could have happened at Fátima.

As to the question of whether an identity alteration seems to exist, in the sense of a *subconscious self*, during the trance – e.g., *hypnotic trance* – that seems to be the case, but with some nuances. This is not a *hetero-induction*, but, at most, a suggestion of *auto-preparation* for the event; in hypnosis, there usually exists the achievement of a highly personalized purpose, which was not the case here. On the other hand, recall *of the experience* is maintained, and it is clear in the interrogatory to which they were submitted, what is more frequent in *trances* in which a *supra conscious identity* is present. This is meant to be the case of *trances* of the *shamanic* type already mentioned or *transpersonal experiences* (peak, mystical, satori, and so on).

It is known, however, that hypnotic trances can facilitate the presence of a supra-conscious self. The same happens in psychedelic trances (with narcotics), in which the sense of the *presence of identity* remains *subconscious* or can develop to *supra-conscious*, both with spiritual content (Krippner and Sulla, 2000), and this should not be left out of our analysis of the present case.

In shamanic trance *(supra-consciousness)*, there exists *"travel outside of the body,"* but that didn't happen at Fátima.

Supra-consciousness (from the point-of-view of the identity of the self during the trance) *implies a sense of transcendence of self, an amplified identity, globalization – integration in a whole –* and *the potential for self-actualization*. These are more frequently considered as *cosmic experiences* and are mainly characterized by the sense of *responsibility and responsivity* (i.e., the need to answer questions posed by the experience). This means that there exists an *auto-consciousness of the experience* and of its previous preparation and a return to society where he or she belongs, with answers about daily and social life, concurrently from what has been learned in trance. These aspects are also found at Fátima.

There is a unity in this *complex trance* – continuity of the self of the individual that experiences simultaneously an *"imaginary" that is apprehended as a presence or real*, and at the same time, keeps an attention to life. This is a characteristic of vigil states (Lapassade, 1987).

CONCLUSION

To summarize, in Fátima were realized several *trances* simultaneously, or better, an *eclectic trance*, with partial characteristics of the several discussed – *possession/fascination, auto* and *hetero-hypnotic, mediumistic, shamanic, transpersonal, psychedelic, creative*, and *dream-like* – but not reducible to any one of them.

Notes

[1] BOURGUIGNON, E., "Spirit possession and altered states of consciousness: the evolution of an enquiry," in CHANDLER and SHARP, *Possession*, Corte Madera, CA, 1976.

[2] CROMBACH, G., "Psychopathologie aus der Sicht veränderter Bewusstseinzustände" ["Psychopathology from the perspective of modified states of awareness"], *Confinia Psychiatrica*, 17, 184-191, 1974.

[3] GREEN, C. and LESLIE, W., "The imagery of totally hallucinatory or "metachoric" experiences," *Journal of Mental Imagery*, 2, 67-74, 1987.

[4] HARDY, C., *La Connaissance de L'Invisible* [*Knowledge of the Invisible*], Paris, Philippe Lebaud Editeur, 1996.

[5] JACOBSON, J. and JACOBSON, A., *Psychiatric Secrets*, Philadelphia, Hanley & Belfus, 1996.

[6] KOKOSZKA, A., "An integrated model of the main states of consciousness occurrence," *Imagination, Cognition, and Personality* 3, 285-294, 1987.

[7] KRIPPNER, S. and SULLA, J., "Identifying Spiritual Content in Reports from Ayahuasca Sessions," *The International Journal of Transpersonal Studies* 19, 59-76, 2000.

[8] LAPASADE, G., *Les États Modifiés de Conscience* [*Altered States of Consciousness*], Paris, PUF, 1987

[9] MARCOZZI, V., *Fenómenos paranormais e dons místicos* [*Paranormal phenomena and mystical gifts*], São Paulo, Edições Paulinas, 1993.

[10] MURAD, A., *Visões e Aparições* [*Visions and Apparitions*], Petrópolis, Editora Vozes, 1997.

[11] PRINCE, R., "Can the EEG be used in the study of possession states?," in PRINCE, R., *Trance and Possession States*, Montreal, University of Montreal Press, 1968.

[12] ROUGET, G., *La Musique et La Transe* [*Music and Trance*], Paris, Gallimard, 1980.

[13] SIMÕES, M., "São as experiências místicas e psicóticas, estados alterados de consciência?" ["Are mystical and psychotic experiences altered states of consciousness?"], *Psiquiatria Clínica* 3, 117-125, 1991.

[14] SIMÕES, M., "Estados alterados de consciência e fenómenos parapsicológicos" ["Altered states of consciousness and parapsychological phenomena"], in *Aquém e Além do Cérebro -1º Simpósio da Fundação Bial*, 107-125, Porto, Fundação Bial, 1996.

[15] TORBADO, J., *Milagro, Milagro!* [*Miracle, Miracle!*], Barcelona, Plaza & Janes, 2000.

[16] VALLA, J.P., *Les États Étranges de la conscience* [*Strange States of Consciousness*], Paris, PUF, 1992.

FÁTIMA —
A MULTIDIMENSIONAL PERSPECTIVE

— Gilda Moura —

In light of new scientific studies and ancient philosophical interpretations, it is proposed that apparitional phenomena, such as the one at Fátima in 1917, may have heralded the return to an old/new special state of consciousness that would facilitate the interaction of our consciousness with other "realities" or higher planes of existence. Beginning in the 20th century, with the apparitions of Fátima, this state of human consciousness – the ecstasy before only accessible to enlightened mystics – seems to indicate the beginning of a new order of sacred manifestation in our reality. This work also discusses, based on the new discipline of "neurotheology," the telluric influences that might facilitate cerebral activity corresponding to states of ecstasy in different categories of phenomena.

INTRODUCTION

May 13, 1917 – Three children: Lúcia, 10 years old, Jacinta, seven years old, and Francisco, nine years old. As all three were caring for their herd, a beautiful Being showed up, "and the sheep remained quiet while the children saw the Lady..." (d'Armada and Fernandes, 1995).

Why was this event so striking in Portuguese life, so that even today, scientific explanations, at all levels, are advanced, with the goal of demystifying the apparition and transforming it into a natural event? And why does the possibility of communication with the "supernatural," or other levels of reality, disturb the Western mind so much?

Since ancient times, similar events have taken place on our planet. Even today, the explanations have been either mystic/religious or scientific/ skeptical in nature. Why do we not study the possible causes that facilitate or propitiate "openings" for the occurrence of phenomena of this magnitude, in a scientific and multi-disciplinary way, with current resources, and from the evidence gathered, try to understand what facilitates or promotes such manifestations?

Why not search for comprehension of the phenomenon at a multi-

99

dimensional level as well, utilizing ancestral and mythological/philosophical knowledge as helpers in our interpretations? Why not consider the possibility that our brains and, more deeply, our minds, and their psycho-physiological relationships, as well as the alteration of this same consciousness, lead us to perceive, intuit, remember, and live uncommon events that are not accepted by the scientific world?

How many theories, almost all restrictive, abound on these phenomena, not because of their correctness, but because they approximate a small aspect of the phenomena? Oureana, Fátima, the occult Imam, the Virgin Mary, the Mother of the World, or an alien being, who manifested or brought about the phenomenon? (d'Armada and Fernandes, 2002; Espírito Santo, 1995).

What altered state of consciousness (ASC) were these children in? What conditions could have provoked this state? Was this state an anomaly or was it a familiar one in other types of apparitions, as those found in connection with para-religious and unidentified flying phenomena? Does one of these explanations invalidate the others, or are all these theories complementary and needed for the comprehension of a new order of manifestations?

Is it possible that Fátima was important because it heralded a return of an ancient/new interference of the "sacred" in our planet? Is Fátima possibly important because it is related to the return of a state of consciousness that will lead us to the understanding of other realities and the acceptance of a new world order and prove the existence of a World Center? This concept of a World Center, or Onphalus, has been known since antiquity. Delphi is one of the oldest representations of this special place for communication with the Divine. This same hope to reach it guided the Portuguese explorers in their maritime quest that resulted in the Era of Discovery. Could Fátima be a sign of the return of the dream of re-encountering the Divine or the Center? A Center that may be symbolic, that signifies a journey inside ourselves and, from there, to another reality, more Divine, towards Unity?

We may correlate this return to the Center with the possibility of communication with invisible yet present powers that have always guided and taught the human species. And by this it is meant that we may be led, by way of an expanded state of consciousness, to an awakening that would enable us to access information from extra-natural realities that lie beyond our normal perception, and integrate this information in an organized fashion. These realities are always present but are not perceived in our ordinary state of consciousness.

What is important is to think about the possibility that Fátima may have been a watershed and to create a working hypothesis, based on our current state of scientific knowledge, that may lead us to further understanding, rising, even, to the Source from where these realities and their corresponding phenomena emanate.

THE FACTS

Cova da Iria, 1917. An anonymous gathering of people awaited the announced miracle:

> I looked continually at the star. It seemed to me pale and deprived of its flaring clarity. It could be compared to a spinning globe of snow. Then, suddenly, it seemed to descend in a zigzag pattern, threatening to fall to Earth.

> During the lengthy minutes of the solar phenomenon, the objects located close to us reflected all the colors of the rainbow. Our faces turned sometimes red, sometimes blue, sometimes yellow ...

> After 10 minutes, the Sun returned to its place in the same manner that it had descended. The Sun began to shine and at some point it seemed to dislodge itself from the firmament and, in circles of fire, precipitate over us (Ferreira, 1985).

The middle of Asia, 1927. "Nicholas Roerich and his group sight a shining spheroid oval cruising, at high speed, the clear skies, suddenly change direction. The Tibetan lamas present said to Roerich that the flying object was the sign of Shambala and its blessing" (Le Page, 1999).

Baturité, Ceará, Brazil, 1994: Repeated apparitions of the Lady before a crowd. The moment the seer goes into an ASC and speaks to the Lady, he is the only one capable of seeing a change that takes place in the Sun and in the atmosphere that lasts for only five minutes. A research team records a change in the electric field and photographs unidentified lights in the skies at the same time that the Lady appears (Moura, 2003).

Is it possible that there is a relationship? Are apparitions of the Virgin Mary intrinsically connected with UFO-type phenomena on our planet? And if they are, what does it mean? Are they also signs of Shambala? If so, what is Shambala?

Shambala is an ancestral myth that possesses an archetypal power to unify and transform the psyche. It represents the belief in the possibility of the existence, in our planet, of a perfect society, inhabited by spiritually advanced sages. It would be the habitat of the minds that drive us at an unconscious level. This belief is very old and can be found in many traditions and cultures. Why is it that, at this time, this myth is re-emerging, now associated with a phenomenon that evokes the image of the "extraterrestrial," a civilization extra-human, harbinger of messages and energetic stimuli with the potential to create a large planetary transformation (Le Page, 1999)?

In the Tibetan literature, this myth is represented by the Mandala. The Mandala (meaning "magic circle") is a symbol of the inner search for a center of unity and transcendence. Carl G. Jung, in his work *Flying Saucers: A Modern Myth of Things Seen in the Sky* (1957), about the UFO phenomenon, ventures the possibility that these strange celestial objects exhibit the symbolism of a Mandala projected by us in the skies, as if we were searching for equilibrium and the totality of the psyche. In this way, Shambala, and its symbolic, Mandala-like, representation, would be teaching us the path for returning to the sacred, to what transcends us.

Mircea Eliade wrote:

> [T]he myth tells a sacred history, it relates an event that took place at a primordial time... [I]t tells how, due to supernatural beings, a reality was created, be it a complete reality – the Cosmos – or a fragment, an island, a behavior. It is always the narrative of a "creation." The myth does not speak of what really took place; instead, it describes eruptions of the sacred (or supernatural) into the world that are diverse and at times dramatic. This eruption of the sacred is what in reality provides the foundations of the world and makes it the way it is today.

According to this view, parallel with the facts of history, there is a super-history that is always driving our reality (Evola, 1994).

What is the meaning of these "dancing suns" or the brilliant globe that shows up simultaneously with apparitions of Mary, not only in Fátima but also in Medjugorje, in Hriushiu and Hoshiu, in Svata Hora, and in Garabandal, among other places (Le Page, 1999)? Did the solar phenomenon impact the state of consciousness of those present?

At Hoshiu, the apparition was preceded by sightings of radiant celestial spheres. Are these sightings of disks of light, concomitant with the apparitions and messages of the Being, the vehicle chosen by invisible powers (like those from Shambala or some other high level of reality, Divine or Celestial) to transmit superior energies and guidance, creating "fields" that impact our consciousness? Could it be that the continuous presence at these telluric places might eventually activate "openings" and access to this other knowledge, through the expansion of our consciousness? At our present state of knowledge, we don't know enough to answer these questions, but we allow ourselves to speculate along these lines.

THE APPARITIONS OF FÁTIMA

Let us move on to the study of the facts at Fátima and focus on the reports of the seers and the type of trance and shift in consciousness that took place. What could have triggered it? How can we define the visions and associated phenomena? The explanations, described in the writings about these apparitions, are varied and cover a broad body of literature and many dimensions of analysis.

The Fátima seers experienced two different types of effects in the following sequence of visions:

- After the meeting with the "angel," described as a "crystal statue crossed by sun rays," that approaches the children from the air, as if floating;
- After the meeting with the "Virgin."

After these meetings, the children felt paralysis and went into a mental state similar to hypnosis. They had the following symptoms:

- Extreme fatigue;
- Difficulty sleeping;
- Amnesia;
- Lowering of consciousness;
- Irresistible attraction towards the phenomenon.

However, according to Joaquim Fernandes and Fina d'Armada in their work *Fátima, Nos Bastidores do Segredo* [*Fátima, Behind the Secret*] (2002), the children experienced different symptoms while in the presence of the "angel" and the "Lady."

In the presence of the angel, the children felt:

- Muscle pain;
- General fatigue;
- Trauma;
- Immobility;
- Hypnosis;
- Mental induction;
- Loss of the sense of time and space.

In the presence of the Lady, they experienced:

- Optical disturbances;
- Allure;
- Apathy;
- Amnesia;
- "Deafness";
- Euphoria;
- Mental, telepathic contact.

Seomara de Veiga Ferreira would have us add to the list the following: "The main difference between the effects after the angel and after the Lady can be attributed to the fact that in the former there was preparation, and in this sense, possibly abduction, with the eventual loss of a sense of time and space, thus ensuring the later prostration." In the case of the apparition of the Lady, the psychological and physiological effects are different.

It does not seem to us that there was an abduction phenomenon. It could have been that the children were taken and prepared for meeting with the Lady. However, there is the report of the ingestion of a liquid served by the angel (d'Armada and Fernandes, 2002). In my experiences with abductees, there are descriptions of a "liquid" that the beings offer them that causes some sort of paralysis and sleep; the substance seems to have a taste not unlike that of the radioactive substances used in neurological tests. Despite the similarities in the reports, there is no evidence that an abduction episode took place. Even though the children were not submitted to hypnotic regression, there are no memories of "examinations" typical in abductee narratives. It is possible to accept the hypothesis of contact and preparation for the later meeting.

In their 2002 work, d'Armada and Fernandes give a detailed comparison of the after-effects experienced by the seers and those experienced by contactees. In this article, however, the focus is more on the analysis of the ASC of the seers and on the hypothesis that this state might be similar to the mystical ecstasy that is characterized mainly by such manifestations as:

- Absorption in a vision of God;
- Intense emotional state (happiness or anguish);
- Immobility or speechlessness;
- Possible insensitivity to pain (Catala, 2003).

There is, in this state, a disconnection from the exterior world, similar to some cases of hypnosis. The apparition probably desensitizes the sensorial-motor system of the experiencer, as happens to contactees and abductees.

According to Pascale Catala (2003), in Medjugorje this disconnection from the environment was gradual. Something similar took place at Fátima. Lúcia, initially, talked with the crowd. Later, little by little, the seers were totally absorbed by the vision.

D'Armada and J. Fernandes (2002) report that in the beginning, lighting was seen and, then, the Being manifested herself over a holm oak, while the children were enclosed in halos of light. "The light is probably what initiates the induction of the ASC" (d'Armada and Fernandes, 2002). It is interesting to note that, in the ancient descriptions of the communications with the thunder gods, there were always loud noises and communication was frequently in the vicinity of oaks. In the Bible, many of the communications with God also took place near an oak, e.g., Abraham's Oak of Mambre. "There goes the lightning, now comes the Lady." The children's first reaction to the phenomenon was fear and then the Being talks to them and calms them down. The seers entered a different state of consciousness and calmed themselves down.

If there was ecstasy, what was its cause? What was the factor, internal or external, that facilitated the children to enter an ASC? Regardless of the nature of the source that stimulated the phenomenon at Fátima, it is necessary to consider some factors in order to better understand the state in which the children found themselves. The source that generated the ecstasy could have been a light, the sound of the thunder, or the typical "buzzing of bees," so peculiar to contemporary "close encounters" and to those with the "gods" in the past.

Could it have been induction by electromagnetic (EM) stimuli? Higher or lower frequency EM fields? Many recent studies have tried to uncover the effects of EM fields in the brain. The region's telluric force could also have been a facilitator of such states.

If there was induction by some force, provoking an anomalous brain frequency, the experience probably would be registered in the state of consciousness induced by this new frequency as a "state dependent memory." Roland Fischer (1971) calls meditative and ecstasy states "dependent states." When the brain switches from a state of hypo-cerebral excitation to a state of hyper-cerebral excitation, amnesia can result.

Rossi and Cheek (1988, p.7) report that a hormonal information substance secreted during stressful life events acts as a neuromodulator. These informational substances can modulate the behavior of the brain's neural systems in order to codify memories and learning in a special way.

According to the state-dependent memory concept, we would only recover, completely, a memory from a stressful or extraordinary event if we could return to the same state of consciousness in which the event took place and, probably, to the same brain frequency experienced during the event. Unfortunately, it is not possible to have access to Fátima's children seers anymore. If it were, we would be able to access the memory of those events uncontaminated. Because an event that takes place during a state of ecstasy is different from one that takes place during the normal waking state, the memory of such an event can only be totally recovered if the person is returned to the same state naturally or by directed induction.

In this way, it might be possible to recover memories still intact, without distortions added by belief and dogma acquired later on. In order to prove this hypothesis, however, we would need to investigate other seers, still alive, like those from Medjugorje, when there are enough resources and interest for pursuing this research. I believe that no Marian seer has been submitted to hypnotic regression. If they were subjected to this type of evaluation alongside EEG measurements (as was the case in Medjugorje), maybe such a study would generate clues and information about brain function that would be of value to humanity.

Based on the reports from some researchers, after the apparitions the children felt as if they were paralyzed. "The force of God's presence was so intense that it completely absorbed and annihilated us. It seemed as if it deprived us even from the use of our corporeal senses for a lengthy period of time" (Ferreira, 1985). This physical "annihilation" is commonplace among those who encounter beings of a higher order, as was the case of the prophets Ezekiel and Daniel in the Bible, among others. We believe that this state is the result of the lack of human preparedness for interacting with these manifestations. During these events, the brain alters its functioning and starts working at a higher frequency, focused on the frontal lobe and adjacent loci. As a result, activity in other areas of the brain is significantly reduced, and total muscular relaxation can follow (Don and Moura, 1997).

Rouget (1989) defines this state as a mental state characterized by profound contemplation followed by loss of mobility and sensitivity. Vallée (1988) calls this state of profound attraction to the contacting power "cosmic seduction."

It is necessary to consider the differences between these states, what I call here "ecstasy," and those of medium-related and shamanic trances, where usually there is a lowering of consciousness towards a more "nebulous" consciousness (Ey, n.d.), leading, in many cases, to amnesia. In this state of ecstasy, human consciousness becomes more awake and alert, focused, with loss of mobility and time sense. It is not hypnotic, medium-related, or shamanic. It is a new/old state of consciousness, previously only reached by mystics and other enlightened people, and now accessible to ordinary people through extraordinary experiences propitiated by the new "eruption" of the sacred in our everyday reality.

Observing that the children, like some contactees but in contrast with mystics in prayer, were not in a contemplative state, the state of ecstasy ought to have been triggered by some factor external to the children. It could have been something intrinsically connected to the external aspects of the phenomenon, such as light or sound, or some peculiarity in the characteristics of the terrain. It could also have been a combination of both.

This expanded consciousness, and, as such, state of awareness stemming from the enormous cerebral activity that it induces, has significant neurophysiologic consequences. It requires special physical preparation by the mystic in order to avoid painful side effects, like those reported in so many cases.

The contact with realities of another Order, or the Numinous, as described by Carl G. Jung in his work *Symbols of Transformation*, takes us to a different state of consciousness. This contact impacts and transforms the consciousness.

The differences in the consequences point to differences in the causes. The contact with a superior or divine level of reality modifies, permanently, the consciousness and not only at the moment of the event (Moura, 2002). It is possible to measure the results in the brain, but it is not possible to reduce it to the neurons alone. It is not possible to reproduce the subsequent effects on the consciousness in laboratories, only the neurological changes. In the laboratory, it is also possible to stimulate a subject's memories by activating the regions of the brain where amnesic events are stored. In this case, when the brain is activated in certain places and at specific frequencies, memories can surface with the force and emotional expression with which they were lived. In this way, it is also possible to recover ancestral or racial memories stored in the Collective Unconscious.

Telluric forces, acting on the brain, can also promote an ASC. They do not have the impact, however, of the ecstatic state. Artificial activation of the temporal lobes can provoke visions, hallucinations, and the retrieval of memories of events, but they do not later create permanent changes in consciousness.

In innumerable reports in the mystic/religious literature of many cultures, encounters with God, or the Numinous, always trigger similar reactions. As a result, it is not surprising that the higher frequencies and real ecstasy states have only been described and measured in mystic and religious communications or in the Samadhi and yogi ecstasies (Das and Gastaut, 1957). The issue is not whether Fátima involved an encounter with an ET rather than with Mary, Mother of Jesus. It is to what extent an encounter with a real phenomenon of the UFO type and alleged extraterrestrial beings is also another way that the superior entities and evolved spiritual masters, described in the spiritual traditions, guide our evolution, warning us through an awakening of our consciousness. Fátima would then be an important milestone, not only of a divine encounter, but also of an encounter with other evolved forms of civilization.

THE RESEARCH

This section reviews the results of recent studies by us and others that attempt to answer some of the questions and hypotheses discussed above. These investigations were undertaken to improve our understanding of the different trance states, including those we call "ecstasy" here. The review examines the many ways to produce the different forms of brain activity resulting from these states.

Maybe if we could understand in detail the consequences of these states on our brains, we would be able to separate the different causes that produce the different effects, or even similar ones resulting from diverse origins.

Even though the current techniques to obtain scientific measurements are quite advanced, it is still difficult to obtain significant results from analyses in this area that go beyond inferences and correlation.

A laudable body of work in this area has been developed by the group of investigators at Laurentian University in Canada led by Michael A. Persinger. This group has studied the propagation of luminous phenomena by telluric forces, and its concomitant effect on the human brain, as the source of the majority of anomalous aerial manifestations and apparitions. These forces would also be responsible for the increase in human sensitivity leading to the perception of spiritual entities as well as other beings usually found in phenomena of the UFO type.

For example, Persinger indicates that within a behaviorist perspective, a persistent correlation between UFO sightings and seismic events might suggest that anomalous human behavior (in the form of strange perceptions) can precede earthquake activity in a given region. The rise in UFO sightings may be considered a type of epidemiological phenomenon analogous to other uncommon forms of animal behavior that precede earthquakes.

His theory, Tectonic Strain Theory (TST), although already developed and applied on a larger scale, is believed not to be applicable to the case of

Fátima, even though there were Earth movements after the first apparition or vision of the Being. It could not explain the other apparitions and, even less, the last event, the "Miracle of the Sun," with set day and time. Besides, Brazil, one of the countries with the highest incidence of sightings of phenomena like UFOs and Marian apparitions, is not subject to significant seismic activity. The theory could much less explain many luminous sightings, such as the natural telluric phenomena that also manifests in many locations in Brazil, in which luminous balls surge as fire and roll down the hills, and are identified as UFOs. It does not seem to us, then, that Persinger's TST is a theory capable of explaining all of the things that occurred during the Fátima incident.

Persinger and his group also developed a helmet to emit electromagnetic waves to stimulate an individual's temporal lobes in the laboratory and, at the same time, measure the electrical activity in the brain. The central idea is based on the experiencer's perceptions of a "visitation" and the "presence" felt is one of these experiences (Persinger, 1989). In an initial phase, the person would feel a presence and then perceive sounds, smells, tastes and bodily sensations. As the experience deepens and more areas of the brain are involved, visions and sensations of "flight" and "falling" occur, as well as stings, whistles, or "energy" throughout the body.

When the experience intensifies, it is possible to acquire, as well, a visual component, when the temporal lobe activity reaches the occipital areas (Murphy, Todd, 1999). At this time, the sensation of a "presence" becomes a figure – an angel, a ghost, a deceased loved one, a spirit guide, or even God.

According to Todd, "[I]f the experience includes the lower area of the temporal lobes, where the old memories are saved (Squire, 1991), it could include repressed memories of sexual abuse (Gardner, 1994), memories of a 'past life,' or memories of an encounter with aliens" (Schrabal, 1994). These memories can seem "real" for the individual, but they are often explainable in terms of "false memory syndrome," since they do not correspond to actual events.

In regard to recovered memories, Persinger refers to the concept of dissociation as a mechanism used by individuals to protect themselves from uncomfortable memories. In his words:

> If a specific stimulus was associated with the dissociation, then a later presentation of that stimulus or something similar to it can activate these alterations in memory. Because these "altered memories" are often odd or personally acceptable, their revelation generates anxiety; consequently, there are strong psychological forces that prevent their emergence... During periods of personal stress, these dissociated memories, modified by beliefs and expectancies, occur

as experiences that are perceived as originating "outside" of the self. These experiences are perceived as real and are frequently ascribed to religious or mystical interventions...

According to our observations in our clinical work, Persinger is right to utilize the concept of dissociation as a mechanism that occurs in these cases. Human beings, however, don't exclude from consciousness solely uncomfortable, repressed memories as unacceptable. The new studies of abductees demonstrate that memories of situations that trigger significant impact on consciousness can remain in amnesia, dissociated, by some mechanism associated with them. In a concept of "state-dependent memory" (see Cheek and Rossi, Fischer), we only retrieve them when we return to the same state of consciousness in which the episode occurred.

In the case of alien contacts and abductions and, probably, mystical ecstasies as well, this premise could be true. In such instances, it may be that the total or partial memory remains in amnesia until it is possible to reach that same state of consciousness, by induction of some natural stimulus or artificially, as was the case in Persinger's experiments. In this way, the memories retrieved at the moment of an experience during the stimulation of an area of the brain, e.g., the temporal lobe, could already exist and not merely be external visions caused by the stimulus of a determined area. Clinically, in hypnotic regressions, these are perceived as present events that are external to the person. This is verified, repeatedly, in studies with abductees. Thus, perceiving a presence, at a given time, does not mean that it is the stimulus of a cerebral area that triggered it, but the memory stored there. Memories are not only facts, but also symbolic expressions of emotions and feelings experienced during the original event.

Such memories retrieved by hypnotic regression are constantly referred to under the rubric of the "false memory syndrome." But a memory is never false, even if it doesn't represent reality. It is always a symbolic representation of some reality experienced in the space-time continuum. Specifically, in the case of the young seers from Fátima, some type of induction external to the shepherds was used and triggered an ASC similar to ecstasy. In this situation, in which the consciousness is momentarily centered on the phenomenon stimulus, it is possible to verify an environmental abstraction, muscular relaxation, while probably a more elevated activation of the brain occurs by induction of different frequencies. Since it is a state not familiar to our physical body, it triggers a later physical imbalance. We don't believe there is a lessening of consciousness at the time of the experience; to the contrary, the mind expands in order to interact with the source of the phenomenon at another, higher level of reality. Abstraction and low response to the environment is registered given the fact that this activation is found in the frontal lobes, while suppressing, in general, the activities in other areas of the brain.

The experience of London neurologist James Austin clarifies what could occur in our brain in these instances. When, suddenly, it loses the sensation of separation – I plus object – time ceases to exist and the mind embodies the notion of eternity (Begley, *Newsweek*). By investigating, *a posteriori*, the possible cerebral areas involved, Austin concluded that the parietal lobe circuits, which give direct time plus space, should be blocked. This episode led to the study of the cerebral functions involved in some mystical ecstasies.

According to Joaquim Fernandes, following the example of Fátima – the contactee (via humanoid or mystical-religious Being) does not develop, as far as is known, his aptitudes immediately, at the moment of "revelation." The symptoms of the contactee, in general, are insinuated in infancy, even if no contact is established for some years.

We understand, however, that this preparation is necessary and do not believe that it is for the purpose of establishing a "mental manipulation" – as Fernandes infers – but rather to have the possibility of communication between two different cognitive universes and realities. The seduction or fixation by the stimulus/phenomenon will be a consequence of this development and not one of its causes.

Still, according to Fernandes, the following are common to the preparation of the individual who is contacted:

• A trance state, involving physical immobility;
• General muscular weakness after the first contact;
• A communication process through "mystical illumination" (via a contemplative, transformative, or metanoic state);
• The precocity or predisposition of this state as receptor or "contactee" that often manifests itself at a young age.

These characteristics, found during the "preparation of the contacted," are also found in states described by investigators in the seers from Fátima and, probably, in other seers whose experiences are real.

Before we move on to the results from our study and that of d'Aquili and Newberg, which better explores our inferences, we will finish the correlation between Persinger's experiments relative to the contactees' state of ecstasy and those of seers, such as the ones at Fátima.

Murphy Todd, describing one of the experiences Persinger affirms, writes, "[A]s the experience becomes more intense, it might acquire a visual component. When the activity in the temporal lobes reaches the occipital lobes, the presence becomes a figure, an angel, a ghost... or God."

It is interesting to note that, in our study of the cerebral map in approximately 100 people from four different groups experiencing ASC in Brazil, we found this description of perception of figures only in the study of Ayahuasca ingestion in which, under the effect of the substance, it would activate, initially, the temporal lobes and, following that, the occipital.

The ingestion of Ayahuasca (*Banisteriopsis caapi* vs. *Psydrotriviridis*) triggers greater activity in the visual cortex found in the occipital region, producing an increase in internal visions. For more technical details, see the published literature (Don *et al.*, 1998).

The mediums studied by us also presented greater activity in the temporal lobes (Moura, 2003). These results are on par with the analyses by Persinger and Ramachandra. In the studies of epileptic and non-epileptic patients, the bodies of the former, when looking at religious images, had a great change in galvanic skin resistance. Ramachandra concluded that there are certain circuits in the temporal lobes that are selectively activated in these subjects. In some way, the specific activity of these neuronal circuits allows us a greater relationship with religious beliefs. Therefore, it would seem that the neuronal base of religious experience is the temporal lobes.

Despite these studies being on par with our results with the Ayahuasca ingestion group and mediums, the same cannot be said of the results obtained by us with contactees/abductees or by d'Aquili and Newberg with Tibetan monks in meditation.

In our study, we found a rare activation of the beta waves of high frequency, above 40 Hz, in the frontal, pre-frontal, and adjacent areas of the individuals from the contactee/abductee group. In our investigation, contrary to Persinger's experiments, as the trance would intensify, the existing temporal activity would diminish, and the activity would start localizing in the frontal lobes. Only three individuals, after an intense period, showed a distribution of activity among other cerebral areas that previously had been found very inactive (Don and Moura, 1997).

In many studies (Damasio, 1994; Newberg and d'Aquili, 2000), it has been demonstrated that the frontal lobe is related to the emotions and has a connection with the limbic system. This area is also important to the superior functions and in consciousness studies.

It was also in this frontal area that Newberg and d'Aquili (2002) found an increase of blood flow in their study of nine Tibetan monks in meditation, or yogi ecstasy, the Samadhi.

These results tend to reduce religious experiences to simple neuronal activations, independent of the real external factors. In the case of the experiences of the young seers of Fátima, we believe that they had more in common with our notion of ecstasy and shared characteristics similar to those of contemporary contactees.

It is suggested, as well, that these areas are connected to the Divine and Unity experiences, and to the more ineffable states of consciousness. Newberg presents the hypothesis that there is a pre-program in our brain for the experience of God. We do not know if this is true, but we are certain that the contactees/abductees in our group, not only those from the cerebral map study, but all of those who were investigated through hypnotism, seem to have been subjected to previous conditioning, to special and profound ASC. At this level of consciousness, the subjects are relaxed, completely immobile, almost without voluntary movement, and in a deep hypnotic state that they access with much ease, which suggests a pre-conditioning in the brain.

CONCLUSION

Newberg (2000) writes:

> The neurology of transcendence can, at the very least, provide a biological framework within which all religions can be reconciled. But if the unitary states that the brain makes possible are glimpses of an actual higher reality, then religions are the reflections not only of neurological unity, but also of a deeper absolute reality. There is nothing that we have found in science or reason to refute the concept of a higher mystic reality.

This superior mystic reality manifests itself or is apprehended by us at the moment that our brain enters a specific state of cerebral activity. Probably, it reflects a specific state of consciousness, in which we come to interact and perceive other realities and to communicate with beings, be they God, the Virgin Mary, the occult Imam, or the Totality. These mystic states are already considered, at least, as a different possibility in our brain and not only as a psychopathic detour of some kind or an illusion (Murphy; Newberg.)

We say that Fátima was a sign because it was a precursor of many other extraordinary experiences that, given the pressure of their enormous incidence, be they in the mystical realm or the realm of contemporary UFO phenomena, have brought science closer to these manifestations that exist at the margin of established knowledge, and with greater attention and seriousness.

We are about to conduct the studies that are needed to achieve a profound understanding of these phenomena, but we can already infer something and with a somewhat greater precision. We can even perceive the existence of a Superior Reality to our own, one that coexists with us, and that we can access from certain specialized states of consciousness; or, it can come to us. The eruption or reemergence of the "sacred" in our reality provokes, today, precious phenomena that shake our reasoning, as in the case of the "solar" phenomenon at Fátima and many other occurrences, be they mystical/religious, or connected to unidentified aerial manifestations.

We do not possess the pretense to interpret the Fátima phenomena in a way so as to reduce them to a cultural reading of the contemporary technological flying machines, since this would be excessively limiting and would diminish the power and the expression of the manifestation of this other Superior Reality.

We are, however, raising the possibility of an existence of a reality system that manifests itself to guide and help us develop and expand our consciousness. According to Jacques Vallée, there is probably a control system of human spiritual consciousness, of which the present Unidentified Flying Objects are a part.

Kenneth Ring, organizer of the Omega Project, says that Near-Death Experiences (NDEs) and UFO contacts might reflect the psychophysical changes that humanity and Earth are going through. Something profound is happening to us as a species. These extraordinary contacts and their effects show us this. There are a great variety of contacts and an enormous variety of reactions to them. The strong emotions these contacts unleash, and the consciousness impacts they make, bring about a drastic rupture in our reality, and with that ontological shock.

When speaking with the three children, the luminous Being of Fátima said she was from Heaven. In Christianity, we have many descriptions of Heaven. Saint Paul was taken to Heaven on the third day. Enoch was raised to Heaven; thus, there must exist many heavens. In different philosophical and religious systems, there are reports of seven heavens. The Vedic literature reveals seven superior planetary systems and seven inferior ones. From the perspective of consciousness studies, we can consider them as levels of consciousness. From the Vedic point-of-view, it is perfectly possible that the revelations of Fátima would emanate from one of these "heavens" (Thompson, 2002). Could these old descriptions of *heavens* refer to other *universes*? Do not some astrophysicists today suggest the existence of "multiple universes?" (Rees, 2002).

Be it the Virgin Mary, the Being that visited Fátima, or some other archetype, transcending from a divine power or coming from another Universe or Reality, this fact caused and continues to provoke a shock to our consciousness. Fátima became a great center radiating energies of transformation and healing. A place of Marian apparitions, like Fátima, would not continue for so many years to stimulate our consciousness and increase the feeling of faith in its visitors if it was not intrinsically connected to some superior center and power that transcends us.

As we have already noted, in the case of the children, seismic activity or magnetic fields could have stimulated their temporal lobes, facilitating their entry into a special state of consciousness – ecstasy – capable of allowing them to interact with this other reality, and not only to create the illusion of a presence felt, culturally interpreted as the Lady and, later, the Virgin Mary.

To this day, few clinical and physiological studies have been performed with Marian seers. Only one medical study is known, one that was performed on the seers of Medjugorje. In this investigation, during the apparitions, a state of alpha (with some beta waves) was registered, similar to a hypnagogic state (Joyeux and Laurentin, 1995). Since we don't know which cerebral frequency limits were evaluated, we can't compare these data with our own results. We verified that the extraordinary phenomena, mainly ecstasy, occur in frequencies above 40Hz. The measurements with clinical electroencephalograms usually register only up to 30Hz; therefore, they are not capable of measuring the full range of these phenomena (Moura, 2002).

Among the contactees/abductees that we have studied, only one state of deep relaxation, the cerebral waves in alpha, progressing to theta, brought about a sudden activation of the brain, with a great flow of energy. In our study, we found beta waves above 40 Hz in the frontal lobes of individuals reporting previous contact experiences. Similarly, in his studies, Newberg found a sudden rise in blood flow to the frontal lobes following a deep meditative state.

In the case of Marian seers, we believe that there has never been any study combining hypnotic regression with electrophysiological measurements. Could we learn more, in terms of revelations and important information for all of us, if this were done? Maybe use of the Electroencephalograph, and even the PET Scan, as was done by Newberg, with Christian mystics, who would have had, in fact, ecstasy experiences, with other extraordinary experiences, could constitute a significant step toward a better understanding of these transcendent states and the existence of the "pre-programming" that enables them to happen. We may be on the verge of these discoveries.

References

BEGLEY, S., Religion and the Brain – In the field of "Neurotheology," scientists seek the biological basis of spirituality. Is God in our heads?, *Newsweek* e-commerce, V.S. Edition, p. 50.

CATALA, P., "Apparitions and Hallucinations," on the internet: *gerp.free.fr/apparitions/hall2.htm.2003.*

DAMASIO, A., "The Feeling of What Happens," New York, Harwest Books, Harcourt, Inc., 1999.

DAS, N. and GASTAUT, H., "Variations de l'activité électrique du cerveaux, du coeur et des muscles squelettiques au course de la méditation et de l'extase yogique" ["Variations in the electrical activity of the brain, heart, and skeletal muscles during yogic meditation and trance"], *Electroencephalography and Clinical Neurophysiology,* Supplement 6, 211-219, 1955.

DON, N.S. and MOURA, G., "Topographic brain mapping of UFO experiencers," *Journal of Scientific Exploration,* 11(4), 435-453, 1997.

DON, N.S. *et al.,* "Effects of Ayahuasca on the human EEG," *Phytomedicine,* 5(2), 87-96, 1998.

ELIADE, M., *Shamanism: Archaic Techniques of Ecstasy*, Princeton and New York, Princeton University Press, 1964.

ESPIRITO SANTO, M., *Os Mouros, Fatimidas e as Aparições de Fátima [The Moors, the Fatimides, and the Apparitions of Fátima]*, Lisbon, Institute of Sociology and the Ethnology of Religion, New University of Lisbon, 1995.

ESTRADE, J.B., *As Aparições de Lourdes [The Apparitions of Lourdes]*, Coimbra, Coimbricense, 1926.

EY, H., BERNARD, P., and BRISSET, C., *Manual de Psiquiatria [Manual of Psychiatry]*, Editora Masson do Brasil, Ltd., n/d.

EVOLA, J., *The Mystery of the Grail*, Vermont, Inner Traditions International, 1997.

FENWICK, P., "The Neurophysiology of the Brain: Its relationship to altered states of consciousness, with emphasis on mystical experience," on the internet: *www.scienceandreligion.com/b_myst-2html.*

FERREIRA, S. da Veiga, *As Aparições em Portugal dos Século XIV a XX [The Apparitions in Portugal from the 14ᵗʰ to the 20ᵗʰ Century]*, Lisbon, Editora Relógio d'Água, 1985.

FISCHER, R., "Transformations of consciousness – a cartography," Proceedings of the American Academy of Psychoanalysis Conference, May 1974.

FISCHER, R., "A cartography of the ecstatic and meditative states," *Science*, 174, 897-904, 1971.

d'ARMADA, F. and FERNANDES, J., *As Aparições de Fátima e o Fenómeno OVNI [The Apparitions of Fátima and the UFO Phenomenon]*, Lisbon, Editorial Estampa, 1995.

d'ARMADA, F. and FERNANDES, J., *Fátima – Nos Bastidores do Segredo [Fátima – Behind the Secret]*, Editora Âncora, Portugal, 2002.

JOYEUX, H. and LAURENTIN, R., *Estudes Medicales et Scientifiques sur the Apparitions de Medjugorje* [*Medical and Scientific Studies about the Apparitions of Medjugorje*], Paris, Editora O.E.I.L., 1985.

Le PAGE, V., *Shambala – A Fascinante Verdade Oculta no Mito de Shangri-lá* [*Shambala – The Fascinating Truth Hides in the Myth of Shangri-lá*], São Paulo, Editora Cultrix, 1999.

MOURA, G., "A expansão da consciência e alta freqüência cerebral – um estudo do êxtase" ["The expansion of consciousness and higher brain frequency – a study of ecstasy], Proceedings of the Symposium on the International Frontiers of Science, University Fernando Pessoa, *Cons-Ciências*, vol. I, Porto, 2002.

MOURA, G., "Evolução e expansão da consciência: uma nova abordagem transpessoal na pesquisa de experiência extraordinárias" ["The development and expansion of consciousness: a new transpersonal approach in the investigation of extraordinary experience"], in *Psicologia da Consciência* [*The Psychology of Consciousness*], 2003.

MOURA, G., *Transformadores de Consciência – UFO Contato Alienígena* [*Transformations of Consciousness – UFO Alien Contact*], Rio de Janeiro, Editora Nova Era, 1996.

MURPHY, M.D., "Marian apparitions – an anthropological perspective," on the internet: *www.skeptica.dk/artiv-us/030-murphy.htm*.

NEWBERG, A.B., d'AQUILI, E., and RAUSE, V., *Why God Won't Go Away*, New York, Ballantine Books, 2001.

PERSINGER, M.A., "The Tectonic Strain Theory – as an explanation for UFO Phenomena," on the internet: *www.laurentian.com/neurosci/tectonic.htm*.

REES, M.J., "Life in our Universe and others: A cosmological perspective," *Many Worlds*, New York, John Templeton Foundation, 2000, pp. 61-78.

RING, K. and ROSING, C., "The Omega Project: a psychological survey of persons reporting abductions and other UFO encounters," *Journal of UFO Studies*, 2, 59-58, 1990.

RING, K., "The Omega Project," New York, William Morrow and Co., 1992.

ROSSI, E.L. and CHEEK, D.B., *Mind-Body Therapy*, New York, W.W. Norton, 1988.

ROUGET, G., *Music and Trance*, Chicago, University of Chicago Press, 1985.

THOMPSON, L.R., *Identidade Alienígenas – O Fenómeno Ufológico Moderno sob a Ótica da Sabedoria Antiga* [*Alien Identity – The Modern UFO Phenomenon under the Lens of Ancient Wisdom*], Rio de Janeiro, Editora Nova Era, 2002.

TODD, M., "The sensed presence and vectorial hemispherity," on the internet: *www.innerworlds.50megs.com/sp.htm*.

TRUCKER, L., "God on the brain," *BBC News*, Science and Nature, April 17, 2003.

VALLÉE, J.F., *Dimensions*, Chicago, Contemporary Books, 1988.

NATURAL ORIGINS OF THE SUPERNATURAL

— Scott Atran —

Religion in general and awareness of the supernatural in particular are converging by-products of several cognitive and emotional mechanisms that evolved under natural selection for mundane adaptive tasks. As human beings routinely interact, they naturally tend to exploit these by-products to solve inescapable, existential problems that have no apparent factual or logical solution, such as the inevitability of death and the ever-present threat of deception by others.

THE SUPERNATURAL AGENT:
HAIR-TRIGGERED FOLK PSYCHOLOGY

A growing number of converging cross-cultural experiments on "domain-specific cognition" emanating from developmental psychology, cognitive psychology, and cognitive anthropology indicate that human minds are innately endowed with core cognitive faculties,[1] or "modules," for understanding the everyday world of readily perceptible substances and events (for overviews, see Atran, 1989; Hirschfeld and Gelman, 1994; Sperber *et al.*, 1995; Pinker, 1997). These core faculties are activated by stimuli that fall into a few intuitive knowledge domains, including folk mechanics (object boundaries and movements), folk biology (biological species configurations and relationships), and folk psychology (interactive agents and goal-directed behavior). Sometimes operation of the structural principles that govern the ordinary and "automatic" cognitive construction of these core domains are interrupted or violated, as in poetry and religion. In these instances, counter-intuitions result that form the basis for the construction of special sorts of counterfactual worlds, including the supernatural, e.g., a world that includes self-propelled, perceiving, or thinking mineral substances (e.g., Maya *sastun*, crystal ball, Arab *tilsam* or talisman), or beings that can pass through solid objects (angels, ghosts, ancestral spirits) (cf. Atran and Sperber, 1991; Boyer, 1994).

These core faculties generate many of the universal cognitions that allow

118

cross-cultural communication and make anthropology possible at all. For example, even neonates assume that a naturally occurring rigid body cannot occupy the same space as another (unlike shadows), or follow discontinuous trajectories when moving through space (unlike fires), or change direction under its own self-propelling initiative (unlike animals), or causally affect the behavior of another object without physical contact (unlike people) (Spelke *et al.*, 1995). When experimental conditions simulate violation of these universal assumptions, as in a magic trick, neonates show marked surprise (longer gaze, intense thumb sucking, etc.). Children initially expect shadows to behave like ordinary objects, and even adults remain uncertain as to how shadows move. This uncertainty often evokes the supernatural.

Religions invariably center on supernatural agent concepts, like gods, goblins, demons, witches, good fairies, bad fairies, and jinn. Here, I concentrate on the concept of *agency*, a central player in what cognitive and developmental psychologists refer to as "folk psychology" and the "theory of mind." Agency evolved hair-triggered in humans to respond "automatically" under conditions of uncertainty to potential threats (and opportunities) by intelligent predators (and protectors). From this perspective, agency is a sort of "Innate Releasing Mechanism" (Tinbergen, 1951) whose proper evolutionary domain encompasses animate objects but which inadvertently extends to moving dots on computer screens, voices in wind, faces in clouds, and virtually any complex design or uncertain circumstance of unknown origin (Guthrie, 1993; cf. Hume, 1756, 1957).

A number of experiments show that children and adults spontaneously interpret the contingent movements of dots and geometrical forms on a screen as interacting agents that have distinct goals and internal motivations for reaching those goals (Heider and Simmel, 1944; Premack and Premack, 1995; Bloom and Veres, 1999; Csibra *et al.*, 1999).[2] Such a biologically prepared or "modular" processing program would provide a rapid and economical reaction to a wide – but not unlimited – range of stimuli that would have been statistically associated with the presence of agents in ancestral environments. Mistakes, or "false positives," would usually carry little cost, whereas a true response could provide the margin of survival (Seligman, 1971; Geary and Huffman, 2002).

Our brains, it seems, are trip-wired to spot lurkers (and to seek protectors) where conditions of uncertainty prevail (when startled, at night, in unfamiliar environments, during sudden catastrophe, in the face of solitude, illness, or prospects of death, etc.). Plausibly, the most dangerous and deceptive predator for the genus *Homo* since the Late Pleistocene has been *Homo* itself, which may have engaged in a spiraling behavioral and cognitive arms race of individual and group conflicts (Alexander, 1989). Given the constant menace of enemies within and without, concealment, deception, and the ability to generate and recognize false beliefs in others would favor survival. In potentially dangerous or uncertain circumstances, it would be best to anticipate and fear the worst of all likely possibilities: presence of a deviously intelligent predator. How else could humans have managed to constitute and survive such deadly competitive groups as the Iatmul headhunters of New Guinea (Bateson, 1958) or the Nāga of Assam (northern India)?

All the Nāga tribes are, on occasion, head hunters, and shrink from no treachery in securing these ghastly trophies. Any head counts, be it that of a man, woman, or child, and entitles the man who takes it to wear certain ornaments according to the custom of the tribe or village. Most heads are taken not in a fair fight but by methods most treacherous. As common a method as any was for a man to lurk about the water Ghāt of a hostile village and kill the first woman or child who came to draw water. Every tribe, almost every village, is at war with its neighbor, and no Nāga of these parts dares leave the territory of his tribe without the probability that his life will be the penalty (Crooke, 1907, 41-43).

Throughout the world, societies cast their enemies as physically or mentally warped supernatural beings, or at least in league with the supernatural. Originally, *nāga* "applied to dreaded mountain tribes, and [was] subsequently used to designate monsters generally" (Werner, 1961, 284). The dragons of ancient India (*nāga*) and their Chinese derivatives (*lung*) are often depicted as half-human and half-animal creatures that emerge from the clouds to wreak havoc on humankind. Similarly, serpent-like devils and demons are culturally ubiquitous (Munkur, 1983), perhaps evoking and addressing a primal fear shared by our primate line (Mineka *et al.*, 1984).[3]

From an evolutionary perspective, it's better to be safe than sorry regarding the detection of agency under conditions of uncertainty. This cognitive proclivity would favor emergence of malevolent deities in all cultures, just as the countervailing Darwinian propensity to attach to protective caregivers would favor the apparition of benevolent deities. Thus, for the Carajá Indians of Central Brazil, intimidating or unsure regions of the local ecology are religiously avoided: "The Earth and underworld are inhabited by supernaturals... There are two kinds. Many are amiable and beautiful beings who have friendly relations with humans... The others are ugly and dangerous monsters who cannot be placated. Their woods are avoided and nobody fishes in their pools" (Lipkind, 1940, 249). Nearly identical descriptions of supernaturals can be found in ethnographic reports throughout the Americas, Africa, Eurasia, and Oceania (Atran, 2002a).

In addition, humans *conceptually create* information to mimic and manipulate conditions in ancestral environments that originally produced and triggered our evolved cognitive and emotional dispositions (Sperber, 1996). Humans habitually "fool" their own innate releasing programs, as when people become sexually aroused by make-up (which artificially highlights sexually appealing characteristics), fabricated perfumes, or undulating lines drawn on paper or dots arranged on a computer screen, that is, pornographic pictures. [4] Indeed, much of human culture – for better or worse – can be arguably attributed to focused stimulations and manipulations of our species' innate proclivities.

These manipulations can activate and play upon several different cognitive and emotional faculties at once. Thus, masks employ stimuli that trigger our innate, hyperactive facial-recognition schema. Masks also employ stimuli that activate, amplify, and confound emotions by highlighting, exaggerating or combining certain facial expressions. Moreover, like two-dimensional drawings of the Nekker cube for which there is no stable three-dimensional interpretation, masks can produce feelings of unresolved anxiety or "uncanniness." In many religious ceremonies, e.g., as a mask rotates away (e.g., clockwise) from an onlooker, who now gazes on the mask's hollow back, the onlooker perceives a three-dimensional face emerging in the other direction (counterclockwise) from inside the back of the mask (cf. Dawkins, 1998). Such manipulations can serve cultural ends far removed from the ancestral adaptive tasks that originally gave rise to those cognitive and emotional faculties triggered, although manipulations for religion often centrally involve the collective engagement of existential desires (e.g., wanting security) and anxieties (e.g., fearing death).

Recently, a number of devout American Catholics eyed the image of Mother Theresa in a cinnamon bun sold at a shop in Tennessee. Latinos in Houston prayed before a vision of the Virgin of Guadalupe, whereas Anglos saw only the dried remnants of melted ice cream on a pavement. Cuban exiles in Miami spotted the Virgin in windows, curtains, and television afterimages as long as there was hope of keeping young Elian Gonzalez from returning to godless Cuba. And on the day of the World Trade Center attacks, newspapers showed photos of smoke billowing from one of the towers that "seems to bring into focus the face of the Evil One, complete with beard and horns and malignant expression, symbolizing to many the hideous nature of the deed that wreaked horror and terror upon an unsuspecting city" ("Bedeviling: Did Satan Rear His Ugly Face?," *Philadelphia Daily News*, September 14th, 2001).

In all these cases, there is culturally conditioned emotional priming in anticipation of agency. This priming, in turn, amplifies the information value of otherwise doubtful, poor, and fragmentary agency-relevant stimuli. This enables the stimuli (e.g., cloud formations, pastry, ice cream conformations, sounds of dubious origin) to achieve the minimal threshold for triggering hyperactive schemata for facial-recognition, body-movement recognition, and sound-recognition that humans possess for identifying agents. I suspect that the "buzzing" associated with the Fátima Marian apparitions in Portugal in 1917, like Bernadette Soubirous's "visions" of the Virgin at Lourdes in France some decades earlier, were expressions of this pancultural disposition.

In sum, supernatural agents are readily conjured up because natural selection has trip-wired cognitive schema for agency detection in the face of uncertainty. Uncertainty is omnipresent; so, too, the "hair-triggering" of an agency-detection mechanism that readily promotes supernatural interpretation and is susceptible to various forms of cultural manipulation. Cultural manipulation and priming of this modular mechanism facilitate and direct the process. Because the phenomena created readily activate intuitively given modular processes, they are more likely to survive transmission from mind-to-mind under a wide range of different environments and learning conditions than entities and information that are harder to process (Atran 1998, 2001). As a result, they are more likely to become enduring aspects of human cultures, such as belief in the supernatural.

EXISTENTIAL ANXIETY: AN EXPERIMENT ON WHAT MOTIVATES BELIEF

If supernatural agents are cognitively salient and possess hidden knowledge and powers, then they can be invoked to ease existential anxieties such as death and deception that forever threaten human life everywhere. This section summarizes an experiment that I recently undertook with Ara Norenzayan and Ian Hansen linking adrenaline-activating death scenes to increased belief in God's existence and the efficacy of supernatural intervention in human affairs.

Our experiment builds on a study by Cahill and colleagues (1994) dealing with the effects of adrenaline (adrenergic activation) on memory. They showed college students a series of slides and a story line about a boy riding a bike. Some subjects were exposed to an uneventful story: the boy rides his bike home, and he and his mother drive to the hospital to pick up his father (who is a doctor). For the other participants, the story begins and ends in much the same way, but the middle is very different: the boy is hit by a car and rushed to the hospital's emergency room, where a brain scan shows severe bleeding from the boy's brain and specialized surgeons struggle to reattach the boy's severed feet. After exposure to the stories, and before being tested for recall, half the subjects were given either a placebo pill or a drug (propranolol) that blocks the effects of adrenaline. The placebo and drug groups recalled the uneventful story equally well. Only the placebo group, however, remembered the emotional story more accurately than the uneventful one.

Our hypothesis was that existential anxieties (particularly death) not only deeply affect how people remember events but also their propensity to interpret events in terms of supernatural agency. We primed each of three groups of college students with one of three different stories: Cahill *et al.*'s uneventful story (neutral prime), Cahill *et al.*'s stressful story (death prime), and another uneventful story whose event-structure matched the other two stories but which included a prayer scene (religious prime). Afterwards, each group of subjects read a *New York Times* article (October 2, 2001) whose lead ran: "Researchers at Columbia University, expressing surprise at their own findings, are reporting that women at an *in vitro* fertilization clinic in Korea had a higher pregnancy rate when, unknown to the patients, total strangers were asked to pray for their success." The article was given under the guise of a story about "media portrayals of scientific studies." Finally, students rated the strength of their belief in God and the power of supernatural intervention (prayer) on a 9-point scale.

Results show that strength of belief in God's existence and in the efficacy of supernatural intervention (Figure 1) are reliably stronger after exposure to the death prime than either to the neutral or religious prime, $F(2, 74) = 3.77$, $p = .03$ (no significant differences between either uneventful story). This effect held even after controlling for religious background and prior degree of religious identification.

Terror Management Theory (TMT) maintains that cultural worldview is a principal buffer against the terror of death. Accordingly, TMT experiments show that thoughts of death function to get people to reinforce their cultural (including religious) worldview and derogate foreign worldviews (Greenberg, *et al.*, 1990; Pyszczynski, *et al.*, 1999). According to TMT, then, awareness of death should enhance belief in a worldview-consistent deity, but diminish belief in a worldview-threatening deity. Our view suggests that the need for belief in supernatural agency overrides worldview defense needs for death-aware subjects.

To test this idea, in a follow-up to our study, 73 American undergraduates were told the prayer groups were Buddhists in Taiwan, Korea, and Japan. Supernatural belief was measured either shortly after the primes, or after a significant delay between the primes and the belief measures. When the primes

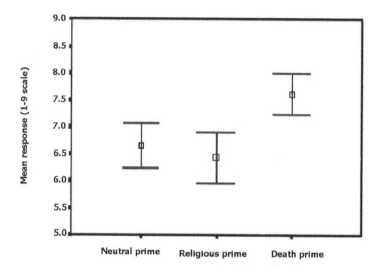

were recently activated, as expected there was a stronger belief in the power of Buddhist prayer in the death prime than in the control prime, $F(1, 33) = 6.65$, $p = .01$. Remarkably, death-primed subjects who previously self-identified as strong believers in Christianity were *more* likely to believe in the power of Buddhist prayer ($r(33) = .37, p = .03$). In the neutral (control) condition, there was no correlation between Christian identification and belief in Buddhist prayer. Given a choice between supernatural belief versus rejecting a foreign worldview (Buddhism), Christians chose the former. This finding is difficult to explain in terms of bolstering a cultural worldview.

In a cross-cultural extension, 75 Yukatek-speaking Maya villagers were tested, using stories matched for event structure but modified to fit Maya cultural circumstances. They were also asked to recall the priming events. We found no differences among primes for belief in the existence of God and spirits (near ceiling in this very religious society). Subjects' belief in efficacy of prayer for invoking the deities was, however, significantly greater with the death prime than with religious or neutral primes, $\chi^2(2, N = 75) = 10.68$, $p = .005$. Awareness of death more strongly motivates religiosity than mere exposure to emotionally nonstressful religious scenes, like praying. This supports the claim that emotionally eruptive existential anxieties motivate supernatural beliefs.

We found no evidence for differences in recall of priming events after subjects rated their strength of belief in God and the efficacy of supernatural intervention. With this in mind, note that uncontrollable arousal mediated by adrenergic activation (e.g., subjects chronically exposed to death scenes) can lead to Posttraumatic Stress Disorder (PTSD) if there is no lessening of terror and arousal within hours; however, adrenergic blockers (e.g., propranolol, guanfacine, possibly antidepressants) can interrupt neuronal imprinting for long-term symptoms, as can cognitive-behavioral therapy (work by Charles Marmar discussed in McReady, 2002, 9). Heightened expression of religiosity following exposure to death scenes that provoke existential anxieties may also serve this blocking function (Atran, 2002b). We plan to test the further claim that existential anxieties not only spur supernatural belief, but also that these beliefs are, in turn, effectively validated by assuaging the very emotions that motivate belief in the supernatural.

CONCLUSION

All of this is not to say that *the* function of religion and the supernatural is to promise resolution of all outstanding existential anxieties anymore than *the* function of religion and the supernatural is to neutralize moral relativity and establish social order, to give meaning to an otherwise arbitrary existence, to explain the unobservable origins of things, and so on. Religion has no evolutionary functions *per se*. It is rather that existential anxieties and moral sentiments constitute – by virtue of evolution – ineluctable elements of the human condition; and that the cognitive invention, cultural selection and historical survival of religious beliefs in the supernatural owes, in part, to success in accommodating these elements. There are other factors in this success, involving naturally selected elements of human cognition. These include the inherent susceptibility of religious beliefs to modularized (innate, universal, domain-specific) conceptual processing systems, such as folk psychology, that favor survival of the supernatural within and across minds.

Notes

[1] For each *natural domain*, there is a proper domain and (possibly empty) actual domain (Sperber, 1996). A *proper domain* is information that is the cognitive module's naturally-selected function to process. The *actual domain* of a module is any information in the organism's environment that satisfies the module's input conditions whether or not the information is functionally relevant to ancestral task demands – that is, whether or not it also belongs to its proper domain. For example, cloud formations and unexpected noises from inanimate sources (e.g., a sudden, howling gush of wind) readily trigger inferences to agency among people everywhere. Although clouds and wind occurred in ancestral environments, they had no functional role in

recurrent task problems with animate beings. Similarly, moving dots on a screen do not belong to agency's proper domain because they could not have been involved with ancestral task demands. Like clouds and wind, moving dots on computer screens belong to its actual domain. A parallel example is food-catching behavior in frogs. When a flying insect moves across the frog's field of vision, bug-detector cells are activated in the frog's brain. Once activated, these cells in turn massively fire others in a chain reaction resulting in the frog shooting out its tongue to catch the insect. The bug-detector is primed to respond to any small dark object that suddenly enters the visual field (Lettvin, *et al.*, 1961). If flying insects belong to the proper domain of the frog's Food-Catching module, then small wads of black paper dangling on a string belong to the actual domain.

[2] Psychoanalytic (Freud, 1990; Erikson, 1963) and attachment (Bowlby, 1969; Kirkpatrick, 1998) theories hold that primary deities are surrogate parents who assuage existential anxieties. But malevolent and predatory deities are as culturally widespread, historically ancient and as socially supreme as benevolent deities. Examples include cannibalistic spirits of small-scale Amazonian, sub-Saharan African, and Australian aboriginal societies as well as bloodthirsty deities of larger-scale civilizations that practiced human sacrifice, such as Moloch of the Ancient Middle East, the death goddess Kali of tribal Hindus, and the Maya thunder god Chaak.

[3] Another example from biology offers a parallel. Many bird species have nests parasitized by other species. Thus, the cuckoo deposits eggs in passerine nests, tricking the foster parents into incubating and feeding the cuckoo's young. Nestling European cuckoos often dwarf their host parents (Hamilton and Orians, 1965): "The young cuckoo, with its huge gape and loud begging call, has evidently evolved in exaggerated form the stimuli which elicit the feeding response of parent passerine birds.... This, like lipstick in the courtship of mankind, demonstrates successful exploitation by means of a 'super-stimulus'" (Lack, 1968). Late nestling cuckoos have evolved perceptible signals to *manipulate* the passerine nervous system by initiating and then arresting or interrupting normal processing. In this way, cuckoos are able to subvert and co-opt the passerine's modularized survival mechanisms.

[4] In every society, the auditory and visual hallucinations that our medical establishment associates with certain forms of temporal-lobe epilepsy and schizophrenia often take on a religious color. They become the "voices" and "visions" of personal revelation for the subjects themselves and, depending upon the society, they may become the charge of local religion as well. In other words, neuropsychological aberrations in the mental states of those who hear voices and see apparitions can also be a factor (Atran, 2002b).

References

ALEXANDER, R., "Evolution of the human psyche," in STRINGER, C. (ed.), *The*

Human Revolution, Edinburgh, The University of Edinburgh Press, 1989.

ATRAN, S., "Basic conceptual domains," *Mind and Language*, 4, 7-16, 1989.

ATRAN, S., "Folkbiology and the anthropology of science: Cognitive universals and cultural particulars," *Behavioral and Brain Sciences*, 21, 547-609, 1998.

ATRAN, S., "The trouble with memes," *Human Nature*, 12, 351-381, 2001.

ATRAN, S., *In Gods We Trust: The Evolutionary Landscape of Religion*, Oxford, Oxford University Press, 2002a.

ATRAN, S., "The neuropsychology of religion," in JOSEPH, R. (ed.), *NeuroTheology*, Berkeley, University of California Press, 2002b.

ATRAN, S. and SPERBER, D., "Learning without teaching," in TOLCHINSKY-LANDSMANN, L. (ed.), *Culture, Schooling and Psychological Development*, Norwood, NJ, Ablex, 1991.

BATESON, G., *Naven*, Stanford, Stanford University Press, 1958.

BLOOM, P. and VERES, C., "The perceived intentionality of groups," *Cognition*, 71, B1-B9, 1999.

BOWLBY, J., *Attachment and Loss*, vol. 1, *Attachment*, New York, Basic Books, 1969.

BOYER, P., *The Naturalness of Religious Ideas*, Berkeley, University of California Press, 1994.

CROOKE, W., *The Native Races of Northern India*, London, Archibald Constable & Co., Ltd., 1907.

CAHILL, L., PRINS, B., WEBER, M. and McGAUGH, J., "Beta-adrenergic activation and memory for emotional events," *Nature*, 371, 702-704, 1994.

CSIBRA, G., GERGELY, G., BÍRÓ, S., KOÓS, O. and BROCKBANK, M., "Goal attribution without agency cues," *Cognition*, 72, 237-267, 1999.

DAWKINS, R., *Unweaving the Rainbow*, Boston, Houghton Mifflin, 1998.

ERIKSON, E., *Childhood and Society*, New York, Norton, 1963.

FREUD, S., *Totem and Taboo*, New York, Norton, 1913, 1990.

GEARY, D. and HUFFMAN, K., "Brain and Cognitive Evolution," *Psychological Bulletin*, 128, 667-698, 2002.

GREENBERG, J., PYSZCZYNSKI, T., SOLOMON, S., ROSENBLATT, A., VEEDER, M., KIRKLAND, S. and LYON, D., "Evidence for terror management theory II," *Journal of Personality and Social Psychology*, 58, 308-318, 1990.

GUTHRIE, S., *Faces in the Clouds*, Oxford, Oxford University Press, 1993.

HAMILTON, W. and ORIANS, G., "Evolution of brood parasitism in altricial birds," *Condor*, 67, 361-382, 1965.

HEIDER, F. and SIMMEL, S., "An experimental study of apparent behavior," *American Journal of Psychology*, 57, 243-259, 1944.

HIRSCHFELD, L. and GELMAN, S. (eds.), *Mapping the Mind*, Cambridge, Cambridge University Press, 1994.

HUME, D., *The Natural History of Religion*, Stanford, Stanford University Press, 1757, 1956.

KIRKPATRICK, L., "God as a substitute attachment figure," *Personality and Social Psychology Bulletin*, 24, 961-973, 1998.

LACK, D., *Ecological Adaptations for Breeding in Birds*, London, Methuen, 1968.

LETTVIN, M., H., PITTS, W. and McCULLOCH, W., "Two remarks on the visual system of the frog," in ROSENBLITH, W. (ed.), *Sensory Communication*, Cambridge, MA, M.I.T. Press, 1961.

LIPKIND, W., "Carajá cosmography," *The Journal of American Folk-Lore*, 53, 248-251, 1940.

PINKER, S., *How the Mind Works*, New York, Norton, 1997.

THE ALIEN ABDUCTION PHENOMENON AND RELIGIOUS EXPERIENCES

— Ryan J. Cook —

A variety of commentators have expressed curiosity, perplexity, suspicion, and satisfaction about the affinities they see between religious experiences and reports of contact with aliens (see, e.g., Jung, 1957; Peters, 1977; Thompson, 1991; Whitmore, 1995; Denzler, 2001). Naturally, these affinities perturb those wishing to carry out a scientific study of unidentified flying objects, and please those seeking to place UFOs beyond the pale of science. The author proposes that rather than approach this topic via the heated scientific debate that surrounds it, the religious resonance of alien contact reports and UFO lore should be taken seriously.

INTRODUCTION

With this article I wish to present a brief overview of the religious affinities noted in U.S. alien abduction reports, specifically because of the distinction made between seemingly secular "abductees" and quasi-religious "contactees." Taking the religious aspects seriously highlights the interaction, in a fairly marginalized field, of people and theory from the science of society, the sociology of religion, and the stigmatized investigation of UFOs. It also invites us to critically examine how and why this religious framing is employed by those researchers. I will first lay out the context and contours for religious approaches to the abduction phenomenon in the United States, and then suggest a way to reframe those approaches so as to further multidisciplinary scholarship.

A CULTURAL-HISTORICAL CONTEXT FOR ALIEN ABDUCTION

Though it has a significant history in Western philosophy, theology, and literature (cf. Guthke, 1990; Dick 1982), the specific idea of contact with beings from other worlds has accumulated a great deal of credibility in broad sectors of Western societies only in the last century or so.[1] A number of factors have contributed to this growth in the U.S., among the most salient being:

> • *The proliferation of high technology*, especially technologies of communication and transportation that have increased flows of money, goods, information, and people in both scale and in scope (cf. Appadurai, 1996).

> • *The influence of scientific knowledge and experts*, not simply because of the efficacy of applied scientific findings, but also because of state and corporate sponsorship and the manner in which communications have connected scientists and facilitated non-expert access to (if not understanding of) scientific knowledge.

> • *The growth of new religious movements* open to influence from foreign traditions and scientific knowledge (cf. Beckford, 1989; Bruce, 1996), especially those incorporating aliens and UFOs (Lewis, 1995).

> • *The profusion of alien contact stories and reports* beginning in the mid-20th century, made plausible, first, by the popularity of science fiction (Guthke, 1989), second, by government-funded space exploration (both of these shaped by a Cold War atmosphere of imminent attack), and third, by the emergence of researchers trying to constitute the field of "Ufology" with themselves as experts (Denzler, 2001).

Quite early on, commentators remarked on religious overtones in the UFO field. Some noted the eschatological import of powerful extraterrestrials appearing in a time of nuclear danger, while others accused ufologists of a quasi-religious adherence to their so-called "extraterrestrial hypothesis." In fact, at around the same time that the "extraterrestrial hypothesis" consolidated among investigators and the American public in the early 1950s, figures labeled "contactees" emerged, claiming to have received important messages from the "space brothers" (Jacobs, 1975; Peebles, 1994). Those labeled "abductees" – to set apart their unpleasant and seemingly secular contacts with aliens – emerged only slightly later. After a series of landmark cases, abduction research has come to dominate American ufological research as well as popular conceptions of alien contact.

The largest group of American scholars interested in the religious aspects of alien contact came from the social sciences, psychology, and religious studies.

They were drawn to the "contactees" and the groups that formed around them (e.g., Festinger *et al.*, 1956; Balch and Taylor, 1977; Lewis, 1995). Other allied researchers have examined religious themes in the UFO field from the vantage points of psychoanalysis (Jung, 1957), folklore (Bullard, 1987; Rojcewicz, 1984) and cultural studies (Dean, 1998).

Another interested group came from the heterogeneous collective of ufology, claiming (almost) all UFO phenomena and dealing with their field's internal heterogeneity and external stigmatization (Blake, 1979; Denzler 2001). Avoiding contacteeism and UFO religious movements, American ufologists have come to focus preponderantly on abductees,[2] often linking their reported experiences to conspiracy theories about hidden alien influences on humanity (Jacobs, 1997). Yet despite leaving overt religious phenomena out, some researchers of a psychotherapeutic orientation (Mack, 1993; Mack, 1999) or New Age bent (Craft, 1996) have come to deal with the spiritual implications of abduction that I shall treat below.

GROUNDS FOR RELIGIOUS APPROACHES TO ABDUCTION

For researchers open to the religious aspects of abduction reports, the key lies in how the experience transforms abductees psychologically and spiritually, just as contact with spiritual beings does.[3] They note multiple points where abduction reports parallel reports of religious experiences – visionary, shamanic, and otherwise. These points break down into parallels of form, content, and effects:

Form – Reports of abductions and of contact with spirits feature a "trip" trope, inextricably linking the changes in state experiencers undergo to their (perceived) movement in space-time. In both genres, the trip begins in isolation from other humans, either by physical distance, altered state of consciousness, or some combination thereof (Jacobs, 1997; James, 1929). The space-time of the trip seems to be at right angles to that of ordinary experience, a place of "high strangeness" (Hynek, 1972), where the constants of everyday life do not apply. Aliens and spirits test the experiencers – in the case of abductees, with medical-type procedures (Pritchard *et al.*, 1994); in the case of shamans, with bodily dismemberment and reassembly (Eliade, 1974). The trip ends with the experiencer returned with profound, though often latent, changes (see below).

Content – The beings that take experiencers out of their everyday reality are superhuman, uncontrollable, overwhelming, and usually uninvited. Bright lights and odd sounds, or an equally odd absence of normal background noise, frequently accompanies them, as does other paranormal activity, e.g., the appearance of poltergeists or dead relatives. Both aliens and spirits say they need to engage humanity through specific people, manipulating this chosen few for some greater purpose. The beings frequently impart messages to experiencers, which the latter often interpret as a cue to spiritual and behavioral change (Mack, 1994; Porter, 1996).

Effects – Contact with these non-human "others" transforms the life world of the experiencers decisively. Their personalities are altered, not simply as a result of coping with the experience, but also due to the expanded worldview – and the new self-image – produced by contact.[4] These changes beget, and are in turn affected by, altered social relations. Once revealed as such, experiencers are frequently stigmatized by people around them and alienated from unaccepting family and friends. This same public disclosure, however, may also lead to membership in new communities, religious or therapeutic. Also resulting from these psychosocial changes are changes in how experiencers act in the world – on one end of the spectrum, withdrawing; on the other end, performing good works as part of a mission (James, 1929; Mandelker, 1995).

A REPORT-CENTERED APPROACH

Taking these professed parallels as our basis, I want to suggest a slightly different approach to the religious aspects of the abduction phenomenon. If there is one place where abduction and religious experiences can definitely be equated, it is in their careers as *reports*. As such, they are elaborated into narratives – that is, fitted into a larger context like a life history or a myth, circulated through various media and social fields, abstracted and then assimilated into folklore or entertainment. A report-centered approach allows us to seriously compare the two experience genres without reducing one to the other or taking apparent similarities and differences for granted. I will now lay out what I think should be the minimal components of this approach, all admittedly influenced by my training in the American tradition of cultural anthropology.

First of all, a report-centered approach must be thoroughly *comparative*, broadening the range of cultural phenomena at our disposal as comparisons. Certain ufological researchers portray abductees as shamans for the space age (cf. Mack, 1994). There is a plentiful anthropological literature upon which we can draw to test that contention.[5] A closer examination of the large literature on religious apparitions, like that of the Virgin Mary, is also in order, as some commentators (e.g., Vallée, 1968) have either linked apparitions to or subsumed them under the "UFO" rubric.[6] Other interesting comparisons lie in cults of possession and of affliction (e.g., Osterreich, 1966; Lewis, 1971; Stoller, 1989), wherein people try to manage the intervention of nonhuman "others." We should also examine the characteristics of therapeutic relationships (e.g., Torrey, 1974) for what they can tell us, not only about coping with contact, but about the conditions in which contact reports are fashioned. For instance, there is a certain "critical communication" (cf. Lehrer, 1982) between researcher-therapist and abductee-patient, through which both parties arrive at a common set of terms for understanding experiences and refashioning them into narratives. I would suggest a similar communicative process when religious experiencers attempt to convey their otherworldly experiencers to an interlocutor or belief community.

Second and related should be a close attention to *context*. We ought to take seriously differences between the historical and (sub)cultural contexts within which abduction and religious experience reports are produced. For instance, why do religious movements emerge from religious experiences and not from abductions (cf. Mandelker, 1995; Whitmore 1995)? One major factor may be that these reports come out of different interpersonal formations. Abduction reports are brought into – and elaborated within – a usually secular therapeutic setting, often solidified in group therapy.[7] Religious experience reports are shared within a belief community, and their elaboration, their "critical communication," often forms the basis for new belief communities. Likewise, we can trace out different channels for the diffusion of abduction reports and for religious experience reports. Abductees' reports reach others primarily through ufologists, with their media products and social networks, and secondarily, through popular entertainment and folklore. Religious experiences come to light through the social networks and media of religious communities or organizations.[8]

The next issue is that of methodological *rigor*, which is inextricably linked with close attention to context. We should insist on studying reports, because we do not have access to personal experiences of this or any kind except through those (semi)public statements made by experiencers and their investigators. Furthermore, we should guard against taking categories like "abduction experience" or "religious experience" – or the phenomena they subsume – as givens. Categories of thought (and the disciplines set up to study them) are constructed (Lincoln, 1999); they have builders and critics, beginnings and careers, all of which are necessary to understand how they currently exist.

One final aspect of a report-centered approach should be a respectful but thorough *critique* of all those involved, including ourselves. Accepting the criticisms of sociological explanations based heavily on interests (cf. Martin, 1993), we should nevertheless inquire about the goals of experiencers and the communities with which they affiliate. What do they hope to gain by reporting their experiences to or through the people they choose? For that matter, what is at stake in aligning abduction and religious experience reports? Another crucial point is that in Ufology (Blake, 1979; Denzler, 2001) or religious studies (McCutcheon, 1997) or any other discipline, we have investigators occupied with demarcating a field of research, making themselves experts in that field, and acquiring authority through that expertise. Experiencers become enrolled into the projects of these investigators as surely as their reports become assimilated into existing folkloric and entertainment narratives. And all of these actors, reports, and projects exist within an "ideological arena" (Hess, 1993) that involves other actors with their own ideas and goals, including those of us who study others in the field.

SUMMARY

Despite the brevity of this survey, I hope to have demonstrated first, that parallels in form, content, and effects between alien abduction reports and religious experience reports make an examination of the religious aspects of the abduction phenomenon legitimate, and second, that there exists an approach, based on reports made by professed experiencers, that respectfully addresses the subject by attending to matters of context and comparison with methodological rigor and a critical eye.

Notes

[1] This distribution, however, has not occurred uniformly across either this span of time or the range of societies involved. A thorough study of the alien contact idea would ask what factors have shaped the distribution and trajectory.

[2] That this is not the case for ufologists in other countries (cf. Vallée, 1993) suggests just how influential specific cultural contexts and historical trajectories can be on the forms both UFO reports and UFO research take.

[3] There are also some writers in fundamentalist or evangelical Christian circles

that have tackled abductions and UFOs in general from their particular theological perspective – that is, as evidence of satanic deception in the End Times (cf. Weldon and Levitt, 1975; Wimbish, 1990; Alnor, 1992). Since their interaction with both ufological and social-scientific research on abduction is limited, I will do no more than to mention them here.

[4] For a particularly vivid example of transformation in an abductee, see Fowler, 1980.

[5] I have suggested elsewhere (Cook, 1998) some factors working against the "shamanic explanation" for abduction, not the least being that abductees – unlike shamans – do not cultivate the ability to travel voluntarily to the aliens' realm on anyone's behalf.

[6] Vallée makes a pointed comparison between UFO sightings and the Fátima apparitions of the early 20th century.

[7] For a thought-provoking guide, see Clark and Loftus, 1996.

[8] It should also be noted that the two types of reports meet and mingle in at least one context, what has been termed the "cultic milieu" (Campbell, 1973).

References

ALLNUTT, F., *Infinite Encounters: The Real Force Behind the UFO Phenomenon*, Old Tappan, Fleming H. Revell, 1978.

ALNOR, W.M., *UFOs in the New Age: Extra-terrestrial Messages and the Truth of Scripture*, Grand Rapids, MI, Baker, 1992.

APPADURAI, A., *Modernity at Large: Cultural Dimensions of Globalization*, Minneapolis, MN, University of Minnesota Press, 1996.

BALCH, R.W. and TAYLOR, D., "Seekers and saucers: The role of the cultic milieu in joining a UFO cult," *American Behavioral Scientist*, 20, 839-860, 1977.

BECKFORD, J.A., *Religion and Advanced Industrial Society*, London, Unwin Hyman, 1989.

BLAKE, J.A., "Ufology: The intellectual development and social context of the study of unidentified flying objects," *The Sociological Review Monograph*, 27, 315-337, 1979.

BRUCE, S., *Religion in the Modern World: From Cathedrals to Cults*, Oxford, Oxford University Press, 1996.

BULLARD, T.E., *UFO Abductions: The Measure of a Mystery*, Washington, DC, The Fund for UFO Research, 1987.

CAMPBELL, C., *Cults, the Cultic Milieu, and Secularization: A Sociological Yearbook of Religion in Britain*, 1973.

CLARK, S.E., and LOFTUS, E.F., "The construction of space alien abduction memories," *Psychological Inquiry*, 7, 140-143, 1996.

COOK, R.J., Shaman and Abductee: American Ufology as Crypto-science and Counter-sociology, unpublished MA thesis, Chicago, University of Chicago, 1998.

CRAFT, M., *Alien Impact*, New York, St. Martin's Press, 1996.

DEAN, J., *Aliens in America: Conspiracy Cultures from Outerspace to Cyberspace*,

Ithaca, Cornell University Press, 1998.

DENZLER, B., *The Lure of the Edge: Scientific Passions, Religious Beliefs, and the Pursuit of UFOs*, Berkeley, University of California Press, 2001.

DICK, S.J., *Plurality of Worlds: The Origins of the Extra-terrestrial Life Debate from Democritus to Kant*, Cambridge, Cambridge University Press, 1982.

ELIADE, M., *Shamanism: Archaic Techniques of Ecstasy*, Princeton, Bollingen, 1974.

FESTINGER, L., RIECKEN, H., and SCHACHTER, D., *When Prophecy Fails*, Minneapolis, University of Minnesota Press, 1956.

FOWLER, R.W., *The Andreasson Affair*, New York, Bantam, 1980.

GUTHKE, K.S., *The Last Frontier: Imagining Other Worlds from the Copernican Revolution to Modern Science Fiction*, Ithaca, Cornell University Press, 1990.

HESS, D.J., *Science and the New Age: The Paranormal, Its Defenders and Debunkers, and American Culture*, Madison, University of Wisconsin Press, 1993.

HYNEK, J.A., *The UFO Experience*, Chicago, Henry Regnery, 1972.

JACOBS, D.M., *The UFO Controversy in America*, Bloomington, Indiana University Press, 1975.

JACOBS, D.M., *The Threat*, New York, Simon & Schuster, 1997.

JAMES, W., *The Varieties of Religious Experience: A Study in Human Nature*, New York, Modern Library, 1929.

JUNG, C.G., *Flying Saucers: A Modern Myth of Things Seen in the Skies*, Princeton, Bollingen, 1957.

LEHRER, A., "Critical communication: Wine and therapy," in OBLER, L.K. and MENNIN, L. (eds.), *Exceptional Language and Linguistics*, New York, Academic Press, 1982, pp. 67-79.

LEWIS, I.M., *Ecstatic Religion: An Anthropological Study of Spirit Possession and Shamanism*, Baltimore, Penguin, 1971.

LEWIS, J.R. (ed.), *The Gods Have Landed: New Religions from Outer Space*, Albany, State University of New York Press, 1995.

LINCOLN, B., "Theses on Method." In McCUTCHEON, R.T. (ed.), *The Insider/ Outsider Problem in the Study of Religion: A Reader*, London, Cassell, 1999, pp. 395-398.

MACK, J.E., *Abduction: Human Encounters with Aliens*, New York, Charles Scribner's Sons, 1994.

MACK, J.E., *Passport to the Cosmos*, New York, Crown Publishers, 1999.

MANDELKER, S., *From Elsewhere: Being E.T. in America*, New York, Birch Lane Press, 1995.

MARTIN, B., "The critique of science becomes academic," *Science, Technology, and Human Values*, 18(2), 247-259, 1993.

McCUTCHEON, R.T., *Manufacturing Religion: The Discourse on Sui Generis Religion and the Politics of Nostalgia*, Oxford, Oxford University Press, 1997.

OSTERREICH, T.K., *Possession: Demoniacal and Other*, Secaucus, NJ, Citadel Press, 1966.

PEEBLES, C., *Watch the Skies!: A Chronicle of the Flying Saucer Myth*, Washington,

DC, Smithsonian Institution Press, 1994.

PETERS, T., *UFOs – God's chariots?: Flying Saucers in Politics, Science, and Religion*, Atlanta, John Knox Press, 1977.

PORTER, J.E., "Spiritualists, aliens, and UFOs: Extraterrestrials as spirit guides," *Journal of Contemporary Religion*, 11(3), 1996, 337-354.

PRITCHARD, A., PRITCHARD, D.E., MACK, J.E., KASEY, P., and YAPP, C. (eds.), *Alien Discussions: Proceedings of the Abduction Study Conference, Cambridge, MA*, Cambridge, MA, North Cambridge Press, 1994.

ROJCEWICZ, P., The Boundaries of Orthodoxy: A Folkloric Look at the UFO Phenomenon, unpublished Ph.D. dissertation, Philadelphia, University of Pennsylvania, 1984.

SALIBA, J.A., "Religious dimensions of UFO phenomena," in LEWIS, J.R. (ed.), *The Gods Have Landed: New Religions from Other Worlds*, Albany, State University of New York Press, 1995, pp. 15-54.

STOLLER, P., *Fusion of the Worlds: An ethnography of possession among the Songhay of Niger*, Chicago, University of Chicago Press, 1989.

THOMPSON, K., *Angels and Aliens: UFOs and the Mythic Imagination*, New York, Ballantine, 1991.

TORREY, E.F., "Spiritualists and shamans as psychotherapists: An account of original anthropological sin," in ZARETSKY, I.I. and LEONE, M.P. (eds.), *Religious Movements in Contemporary America*, Princeton, Princeton University Press, 1974.

VALLÉE, J.F., *Passport to Magonia: On UFOs, Folklore, and Parallel Worlds*, Chicago, Henry Regnery, 1969.

VALLÉE, J., *Dimensions: A Casebook of Alien Contact*, New York, Ballantine, 1993.

WELDON, J., with LEVITT, Z., *UFOs: What on Earth is Happening?*, New York, Bantam, 1975.

WHITMORE, J., "Religious dimensions of the UFO abductee experience," in LEWIS, J.R. (ed.), *The Gods Have Landed: New Religions from Other Worlds*, Albany, State University of New York Press, 1995, pp. 65-82.

WIMBISH, D., *Something's Going on Out There*, Old Tappan, Fleming H. Revell, 1990.

RELIGIOUS APPARITIONS
AND ALIEN ENCOUNTERS
— COMMON THEMES

— Irene Blinston, Ph.D. —

Very little is known about the phenomenon of religious apparitions. The reason is the inability of researchers to duplicate the apparitional events in laboratory settings. Even less is known about the percipients of religious apparitions and how their lives are impacted. This is not the case with alien encounters. Numerous studies have been conducted on UFO and alien encounter phenomena. Articles and books have provided the results of studies looking at the psychological effects of alien encounters on contactees (see, e.g., Jacobs, 1992; Mack, 1994; Pritchard, Pritchard, Mack, Kasey, and Yapp, 1994; Sprinkle, 1988). Because of the lack of research specifically aimed at the experiencers of religious apparitions, there is very little data available with which to analyze and compare these two phenomena. In this paper, the author explores the linkages between religious apparitions and alien encounters suggested by her study of adults who experienced religious apparitions in childhood.

INTRODUCTION

In 2003, I began a study of adults who experienced religious apparitions as children. It was my desire to learn the impacts and lifelong aftereffects of such experiences. In my research, I used a three-part process to gather data: (a) a questionnaire that allowed for detailed answers and explanations (filled in by 24 participants), (b) verbal and nonverbal exercises involving the creation of an expressive arts piece and the submission of a three to 10 page written autobiography (13 of the 24 participants provided submissions), and (c) an interview process (involving one participant). An analysis of the submissions yielded 22 themes. One of the surprises of my findings was that the elements of those themes were also found in the stories provided by the seers of Fátima and in the accounts of the experiencers of alien encounters. All of the data I collected in my study were in the form of written, verbal, and non-verbal submissions provided by adults recollecting their childhood encounters.

Fernandes and d'Armada (2005) posited in *Heavenly Lights*, the first volume of their Fátima trilogy, that they had "no reason to value too highly Lúcia's capacity to remember as an adult" (p. 12). They were referring to her ability to accurately recount her childhood apparitional experiences. Findings from my research indicated that adults remember their encounter experiences in vivid detail. The only difference is that as adults experiencers have the ability to describe their accounts with an expanded vocabulary.

The three seers of Fátima, Lúcia, Jacinta, and Francisco, were young children under a great deal of duress from both (a) representatives of the Catholic Church and (b) public officials. They were repeatedly asked to tell their stories of the encounters. It is not known if the published reports were altered or enhanced by the adults who wrote them. One could speculate that they were; however, we are led to believe that they were not.

One of the argued deterrents of working with experiencers who are children is their limited vocabulary and their subsequent inability to explain their experiences in coherent detail. Considering the ineffability of apparitional encounters and similar profound experiences, articulate adult experiencers are challenged to provide adequate verbal descriptions of, or explanations for, these types of events (Rowan, 1983). In the case of Fátima in 1917, it is very possible that adults paraphrased what they were told when the children recounted the apparitions. Only Lúcia lived to adulthood. Jacinta and Francisco died as children. Consequently, the two young seers' versions of the story remain in the limited words of children and possibly were reworked by the adults who recorded the seers' telling of the events.

Because of the ineffability of apparitional and other profound experiences, the use of non-verbal means of recounting the details has proved effective. The expressive arts were used in studies of people reporting near-death-experiences (NDEs) by Rominger (2004) and people reporting Exceptional Human Experiences (EHEs) by Palmer (1999). In my own research, the expressive arts were used as a means of stimulating memories. The artwork, along with open-ended interview questions and written autobiographies, provided qualitative and artistic forms of inquiry into the accounts of the percipients. The studies conducted by Rominger, Palmer, and myself provided rich descriptions of the participant's unacknowledged human experiences. Common threads can be identified when comparing the data and findings of the above studies.

APPARITIONAL ENCOUNTERS

The results of my study of religious apparitional encounters provided interesting surprises. This section will detail three particular areas of interest. The areas include (a) the rate of occurrences of religious apparitional encounters, (b) beings seen in apparitions, and (c) descriptions of the encounters.

The Rate of Occurrences of Religious Apparitional Encounters

One of the surprises in my research was discovering that apparitional encounters occur much more frequently than we realize. For experiencers, apparitions can be a one-time occurrence or a repeating phenomenon. At least four of the recognized cases in Europe consisted of a series of encounters taking place on pre-determined dates: (a) Lourdes, France; (b) Fátima, Portugal; (c) Beauraing, Belgium; and (d) Medjugorje, Bosnia (Connell, 1997; Zimdars-Swartz, 1991). In my study, 52% of the respondents reported multiple encounters with the same religious figure or additional religious figures. Among my participants, 8% reported that their apparitions consisted of two or more religious figures.

From 1900 to 1999, at least 392 cases of apparitions of Mary were reported and subsequently investigated by authorities of the Catholic Church. Ninety-five of those cases involved children as percipients (Tierney, n.d.). Based on these figures, one may question how many cases were reported and not investigated. When I began my study of child experiencers of religious apparitions, I asked this very question. I also wondered how many cases were not reported to Church officials and subsequently kept secret by the percipient. Following that line of thinking, I pondered how many reported and unreported cases there were involving figures other than Mary, such as Jesus, saints, and other Biblical figures. As suggested by the above-reported statistics of apparitions of Mary, the numbers could be high.

Given the findings from the limited amount of research in the field, it is apparent that these experiences are not rare events after all. In the six months that I called for participants in my study of experiencers of childhood religious apparitions, 180 people from around the world attempted to qualify. Only two of those experiencers indicated they had reported their apparitional events to a Catholic authority. Of the two reported apparitional experiences, neither was investigated by a Church official. Due to the potentially large number of experiences that go unreported, researchers have no way of knowing how many events have actually occurred.

Beings Seen in Apparitions

Religious apparitional encounters can include Jesus, Mary, saints, angels, and other biblical figures (see, e.g., Blinston, 2005; Palmer, 1999; Sparrow, 1995; Wiebe, 1997). In my study, 30% of the reported encounters involved Mary, while apparitions of Jesus comprised 56%. The remaining 14% of the accounts consisted of Abraham, St. Theresa, and Moses. Throughout history, people from various cultures have reported having apparitional experiences. Those reported apparitions have included such figures as Buddha, Krishna, and Islamic notables. There are countless anecdotal cases involving apparitions of celestial-type beings, in addition to reported apparitions of God (Robb, 2006).

Apparitional encounters have affected not only the lives of the experiencers; their impacts have been felt on a global level. Two of the world's religions began with religious apparitions – Islam and Mormonism. Both Mohammad and Joseph Smith had visitations with an angel. Islam is now the second largest religion in the world, and its start was an encounter experience.

Comparing Apparitional and Alien Encounters

Throughout this section, excerpts from my participants' stories, those of Fátima, and those of alien encounter experiencers are used as examples. The examples demonstrate the common elements that are shared in their stories. When reading the story excerpts, please note that two of my participants have English as their second language and this is evident with their wording and sentence structure.

Descriptions of Apparitional Encounters

A substantial amount of knowledge can be gained about apparitional events by paying close attention to the descriptions provided by the experiencers. By comparing the descriptions of Fátima to those of other apparition experiencers, three common elements emerge: (a) light, (b) communication, and (c) some form of touch or physical contact. These three elements are also found consistently in descriptions of alien encounters. The following subsections provide examples for comparison of these three elements among the stories of Fátima, the participants in my study, and experiencers of alien encounters.

LIGHT IN APPARITIONS AND ALIEN ENCOUNTERS

Light was an important element in the apparitions at Fátima. Light was also an important element in the stories of the participants in my study. Additionally, the stories of alien encounters are abundant with reports of light (see, e.g., Jacobs, 1992; Mack, 1994; Sprinkle, 1988). Following are examples of light found in the stories of Fátima, my research, and alien encounters.

The Fátima Story

The children of Fátima told of an appearance of lightning when there were no clouds in the sky. In the following excerpt, Lúcia described the light she and the other two children saw at the first apparition of Mary:

> "[W]e beheld a Lady all dressed in white. She was more brilliant than the Sun, and radiated a light more clear and intense than a crystal glass with sparkling water when the rays of the burning Sun shine through it. We stopped astounded before the apparition. We were so close, just a few feet from her, that we were bathed in the light which surrounded her, or rather, which radiated from her." (dos Santos, 2005, p. 174)

This excerpt is taken from a book written by Lúcia dos Santos years after she saw the apparition. The excerpt provides a vivid and expressive description of the light she and the other two children witnessed. In October 1917, during the encounter, thousands of people had gathered in the area of the apparitions. A variety of reports were gathered from the people present, and many of their accounts included descriptions of light (de Marchi, 1952).

Stories from My Study

The following descriptions are verbatim excerpts of self-reports provided by the adult participants of my research. Following each excerpt are the name of the experiencer, his or her age at the time of the encounter, and the geographical location of the encounter. In order to maintain anonymity, the names of the experiencers are fictitious.

The experiencers provided the following examples of light:

> "[T]here's a light in our room near the window... and that light is getting stronger and stronger. I'm wondering that why there's a light in our room? We see a glittering white thing..." (Angelpauley, age 4, Philippines)

> "I saw a beautiful bluish white light fill the space next to my bed. I remember looking at it in awe... Everything was bathed in the bluish white light. The light was so lustrous and bright that it seemed like it should hurt my eyes." (Sarah, age 10, U.S.A.)

> "All of a sudden my whole room was filled with the most amazing light, brighter and clearer than any light I had seen before or since.

It was radiant. THE MOST AMAZING LIGHT, BRIGHT AND CLEARER THAN THE SUN ON THE WHITEST SAND, THE HARVEST MOON RISING, ALL THE SPOTLIGHTS ON A ROCK GROUP IN CONCERT [capitalized in original]." (Carol, age 10, U.S.A.)

"Suddenly, a bright light shone from under the bed. A beam of pure yellow, orange, and gold light shone through me. Colors of green, blue, orange, purple, red, and yellow swirled around me..." (Maxie, age 5, U.S.A.)

One of the most outstanding features of the light described by my participants was its brightness. The artwork created by 12 of my participants contained a light element. One of my participants, Carol, spent days searching different arts and crafts stores trying to find the perfect paint to depict the light she saw in her apparition.

Alien Encounter Stories

Contactees have provided detailed accounts of their experiences. Their stories can be found in autobiographical books and personal websites. Chronicled accounts are also available that were written by clinicians and researchers who put experiencers under hypnosis (Fowler, 1990; Hopkins, 1987; Jacobs, 1992; Mack, 1994; Ring, 1992). The following excerpts are taken from several sources. Each excerpt will be followed by a parenthetical citation of its source.

"The living room was very light... It's definitely got a bluish tint to it." (Mack, 1994, p. 146)

"All the air was lit up... It was the most incredible light. If there is such a thing as pure white. Totally pure, and it was everywhere." (Mack, 1994, p. 374)

"A brilliant ball of white light speckled with all the colors of the rainbow..." (Henriksen, 2002, p. 47)

Summary

The light associated with apparitions and alien encounters can be white or possess color and glittering qualities. Not all apparitional events have a light quality; however, 62% of the accounts in my research contained the element of light. If researchers look into other exceptional human experiences (EHEs), such as near-death-experiences (NDEs), and even kundalini awakenings and other forms of spiritual emergence, they will find similar qualities of light surface in the accounts (see, e.g., Greenwell, 1990; Krishna, 1970; Ring,

1992; Rominger, 2004). The similarity of the light depicted in the art of the participants in Rominger's (2004) research of NDE experiencers, and the light depicted in the art of my research participants was remarkable. It would be very interesting to compare the art of our participants with the art of experiencers of alien encounters. This additional information could add to the growing body of knowledge of EHEs, and allow for further comparison of the variety of experiences.

COMMUNICATION WITH APPARITIONS AND ALIEN ENCOUNTERS

Similar to the accounts of Fátima, communication has taken place in many apparitional encounters. The communication aspect of experiences is also found in a variety of EHEs, such as alien encounters and NDEs (Rominger, 2004; Ring, 1992; Sprinkle, 1988). The following three subsections use excerpts from the stories of Fátima, the experiencers of religious apparitions in my study, and experiencers of alien contact.

The Fátima Story

For those who are familiar with the Fátima story, the communication aspect of the many encounters was well publicized. There were a series of messages the apparition conveyed to the children. The apparition also conversed with the children, answering questions they asked regarding deceased friends and family members. Following is a short excerpt from Lúcia dos Santos (2005), describing the communication from the apparition during the first visitation at Fátima.

> "Then Our Lady spoke to us: 'Do not be afraid. I will do you no harm.'" (dos Santos, 2005, p. 174)

Lúcia asked the Being personal questions, inquiring if she and the other two seers were going to Heaven, and the Being replied:

> "'Yes you will... She [Jacinta] will go too... He [Francisco] will go there too, but he must say many rosaries.'" (dos Santos, 2005, p. 175)

In Fátima, the apparition shared certain messages with the children – secret messages. The children were to tell no one. Eventually, some of the messages were written down and provided to the Pope. Lúcia, however, took an unknown number of undisclosed messages to the grave when she died in February 2005.

Stories from My Study

Whether telepathic or verbal, communication was a prominent aspect of the experiences of my participants. In my study, 77% of the participants reported some form of communication with the figure in the apparition. The messages in the communications left lasting impressions on my participants, and they can recall the messages years after the encounters.

> "He spoke to me, but he did not speak through his mouth. He spoke to me through thoughts. He told me his name was Abraham. He told me many things." (Barbara, age 7, U.S.A.)

> "Jesus always walked with me, smiled to me and when I talked to him, he talked me back, mainly telepathically." (Tenshi, age 10, Japan)

> "She spoke to me in a lovely warm voice. She told me that I had a special purpose..." (Mamachen, age 6, U.S.A.)

> "He would sit on the other twin bed in my room, and tell me how I was never alone, and that no matter what, he'd always be there, all I had to do was call." (Angel, age 7, U.S.A.)

Sometimes, the child experiencer was told, or felt through that which was communicated, that he or she had a mission to fulfill in life. Other accounts detail how the experiencer was comforted by the communication from the apparition. Tenshi, my participant from Japan, indicated that she had normal, everyday conversations with Jesus.

Communication in Alien Encounters

Henriksen (2002) found four recurring themes in her study of alien communication. She analyzed 60 stories of alien encounters submitted by experiencers to a website on the Internet. The recurring themes she found in the messages were: (a) soothing or calming of the contactees while the aliens were passing on knowledge, (b) suggestions of malevolence, (c) indications that the experiencer was special in some way, and (d) making known the conditions affecting the future of the Earth and humanity (Henriksen, 2002, pp. 46-47). The experiencers in the sources I used were not identified by age at the time of the experience, so I am presuming that they were adults. All accounts quoted here will be considered adult events unless otherwise noted.

"I was making a declaration saying to myself, 'I am now ready to see a UFO, meet the beings in there that could assist and inform me in my inquiry.' A series of events started occurring over a 3-day period... On the third day, it was around 12:00 midnight... This voice came to me and said to me, 'if you really want to see a UFO, turn to your right.' I turned to my right and there was this very large ship. It was easily the size of a football field." (Chris, personal communication, October 11, 2006)

"He spoke to me, not with his mouth but in my head. He told me that everything would be okay and that he wanted to show me something. I then saw a picture in front of me like a TV screen or something..." (Henriksen, 2002, p. 44)

"I was told things and made to watch some sort of events that would be taking place here on Earth, in the future." (Henriksen, 2002, p. 46)

"I persisted in asking why they [continue to] take me. They heard me but ignored me until finally answering that I am 'one of the special ones' [quotation marks in original]." (Henriksen, 2002, p. 46)

The excerpts above resemble the communications found in religious apparitional encounters. This similarity is particularly true for those communications that were telepathic.

Summary

Verbal communication was reported in religious apparitional encounters and alien encounters. However, telepathic communications dominated the many stories I read. Further research of communication in apparitional and alien encounters may provide a larger sample from which to determine the verbal or telepathic prevalence. With the small sample sizes obtained through self-reports and anecdotal information found in the research for this chapter, I realized that further scholarly research is needed. The findings from additional studies may paint a better picture of the communication similarities found in apparitional and alien encounters.

TOUCH OR PHYSICAL CONTACT
IN APPARITIONS AND ALIEN ENCOUNTERS

Experiencers have indicated through their reports that they had been touched by the figure in their apparitions, or have had some form of physical contact including contact by energetic means. In my study, 62% of the participants reported being touched by the figure in their apparitions, either physically or energetically. Touch and physical contact is often mentioned in accounts of alien encounters.

The Fátima Story

The children of Fátima reported that they physically felt the light that emanated from the apparition. The feeling was reported as stronger when it was actually emanating from the hands of the apparition. The excerpt below describes how the children felt the light as it penetrated their bodies.

> "Our Lady opened her hands for the first time, communicating to us a light so intense that, as it streamed from her hands, its rays penetrated our hearts and the innermost depths of our souls. Then, moved by an interior impulse that was also communicated to us, we fell on our knees." (dos Santos, 2005, pp. 174-175)

Initially, an angel had appeared to the children prior to the apparition of the Being. Lúcia later elaborated in her book *Fátima in Lúcia's Own Words* about the physical feelings the seers felt while in the presence of both the angel and the apparition of the Being. Lúcia explained how the seer's physical and emotional feelings differed in intensity and character while in the presence of the apparition of the angel as opposed to the presence of the apparitions of the Being.

> "The force of the presence of God [in the presence of the angel] was so intense that it absorbed us and almost completely annihilated us. It seemed to deprive us even of the use of our bodily senses for a considerable length of time." (dos Santos, 2005, pp. 172-173)

> "I don't know why, but the apparitions of Our Lady produced in us very different effects. We felt the same intimate joy, the same peace and happiness, but instead of physical prostration, an expansive ease of movement; instead of this annihilation in the Divine Presence [of the angel], a joyful exultation; instead of the difficulty in speaking, we felt a certain communicative enthusiasm." (dos Santos, 2005, p. 173)

Lúcia's descriptions of the feelings felt in the presence of the two separate encounter figures are clear and vivid. The three child seers demonstrated identical behaviors and reactions as those experienced by adult mystics (Gaynor, 1973; Inge, 1899). The children's behavior and aptitude were contrary to those considered "normal" for children their ages, as dictated by the accepted developmental models that most psychologists and psychiatrists abide by today.

Stories from My Study

In my study, 61% of the participants who wrote autobiographies described a form of touch or physical contact. Their accounts included a variety of direct experiences with the figure in their apparitions. The following excerpts provide a sample of my participants' descriptions.

> "Then he reached out and touched my forehead with the tip of his index finger. Without a word, through touching me on my head, I felt as if I was filled with love." (Barbara, age 7, U.S.A.)

> "I could see the light but I could also feel it. I could feel and see a comforting hand run over my head and down my shoulder. It didn't feel like a hand but I could feel the soothing, healing energy calm my body and mind." (Sarah, age 10, U.S.A.)

> "He rose from the space under the bunk bed... As He rose, I rose with Him. Christ gently lowered me to the top bunk bed." (Maxie, age 5, U.S.A.)

Most of the touch and physical contact experienced by the participants in my study were felt energetically. Actual physical touch was reported by 21% of the original 24 participants. Although not all accounts of touch or physical contact were described in detail, the element of physical contact was a significant feature of the encounter experiences of the participants.

Physical Contact in Alien Encounters

Stories of physical contact in alien encounters convey experiences that are not always pleasant. Readers may be familiar with frightening stories of probes and other forms of invasion of the contactee's body. Henriksen (2002), however, found from her study that physical contact, in the form of experiments conducted on the contactees, was both positive and negative. Positive accounts included cures and healings while negative accounts were painful, left scars, and traumatized the contactee. In many cases, physical and psychical contact was used to calm the contactee, provide healing, and/or communicate.

> "I'm starting to feel pain in the back of my head through my neck. I'm feeling pain and pressure there, behind my ear. What is he doing

back there? I don't like it." (Smith, 1994, p. 57)

"It touched me right between my eyes. I then saw many different things." (Henriksen, 2002, p. 46)

"The next thing that happened was that the figure walked to the side of the bed and I felt something very cold and extremely sharp enter my back, pushing its way into my spine, however, there was no pain in all this." (Henriksen, 2002, p. 55)

"What they have taken from me repeatedly is my seed, my semen. I have gone from tremendously deep anger and resentment to an understanding... I have also come to believe that the beings wish us no physical or psychological harm... It is easier for us and for society to label it invasion, trauma, rape, than to think that we have somehow willingly participated in our own development." (Peter, 1994, p. 56)

There are reported cases in which the touch, painful or not, was looked upon as necessary. I have read numerous accounts of contactees who have come to a deeper understanding and acceptance of their experiences as part of their spiritual evolution. Truncale (1994) conducted a study of 53 child experiencers of alien encounters and found that 17% of the experiencers reported being touched by an alien being. Unlike Henriksen (2002), Truncale did not indicate if the children's experiences of touch induced in them negative or positive feelings.

Summary
The cases of touch in the reports from my research participants involved positive feelings, healing, and/or comfort. The same is true in the stories from Fátima. Alien contactees reported both positive and negative effects of physical contact.

CONCLUSION

It is no wonder that there is confusion concerning apparitional events and alien encounters; they are very similar in their descriptions and qualities. The elements described in this chapter outline only a few of those similarities. Further research may uncover more and better detailed parallels between the two phenomena. A great deal could be learned about the accounts if more stories from encounter experiencers are collected and compared. By dismissing experiencers' claims, a chance to broaden the understanding of encounter experiences and additional dimensions of the human potential are also dismissed. By listening to, honoring, and accepting experiencers' stories, researchers have an opportunity to make further contributions to the fields of consciousness studies, the study of exceptional human experiences, parapsychology, and human development. Including the stories of experiencers in a qualitative study may broaden the researchers' horizons across many fields. Data and findings from such studies may build a body of knowledge that would increase the understanding of the human aspect of encounter experiences and provide a better understanding of the variations of encounter phenomena.

References

BLINSTON, I., When Children Witness the Sacred: Spiritual and Psychological Impacts, Lifelong Aftereffects, and Disclosure Aspects of Religious Apparitional Encounters, *Dissertation Abstracts International*, 66(03), 1753B (UMI No. 3168454), 2005.

CONNELL, J., *The Visions of the Children: The Apparitions of the Blessed Mother at Medjugorje*, New York, St. Martin's Press, 1997.

FOWLER, R.W., *The Watchers: The Secret Design Behind UFO Abduction*, New York, Bantam Books, 1990.

FERNANDES, J. and d'ARMADA, F., *Heavenly Lights: The Apparitions of Fátima and the UFO Phenomenon*, Victoria, BC, EcceNova Editions, 2005.

GAYNOR, F. (Ed.), *Dictionary of Mysticism*, Secaucus, NJ, Citadel Press, 1973.

GREENWELL, B., *Energies of Transformation: A Guide to the Kundalini Process*, Saratoga, CA, Shakti River Press, 1990.

HOPKINS, B., *Intruders: The Incredible Visitations at Copley Woods*, New York, Random House, 1987.

INGE, W., *Christian Mysticism*, Whitefish, MT, Kessinger Publishing, 1995 (Originally published in 1899).

JACOBS, D.M., *Secret Life: Firsthand Accounts of UFO Abductions*, New York, Simon & Schuster, 1992.

KRISHNA, G., *Kundalini: The Evolutionary Energy in Man*, Berkeley, CA, Shambala Publications, 1970.

MACK, J.E., *Abduction: Human Encounters with Aliens*, New York, Charles Scribner's Sons, 1994.

MARCHI, J. de, *The Immaculate Heart: The True Story of Our Lady of Fátima*, New York, Farrar, Strauss & Young, 1952.

PALMER, G., Disclosure and Assimilation of Exceptional Human Experiences: Meaningful, Transformative, and Spiritual Aspects, *Dissertation Abstracts International*, 60(05), 2358B (UMI No. 9932122), 1999.

PETER, "Medical procedures," in PRITCHARD, A., PRITCHARD, D.E., MACK, J.E., KASEY, P., and YAPP, C. (eds.), *Alien Discussions: Proceedings of the Abduction Study Conference, Cambridge, MA*, Cambridge, MA, North Cambridge

Press, 1994, p. 56.

PRITCHARD, A., PRITCHARD, D.E., MACK, J.E., KASEY, P., and YAPP, C. (eds.), *Alien Discussions: Proceedings of the Abduction Study Conference, Cambridge, MA*, Cambridge, MA, North Cambridge Press, 1994.

RING, K., *The Omega Project: Near-Death Experiences, UFO Encounters, and Mind at Large*, New York, William Morrow & Co., 1992.

ROBB, P., *The Kindness of God*, Parker, CO, Outskirts Press, 2006.

ROBINSON, E., *The Original Vision: A Study of Religious Experience of Childhood*, New York, The Seabury Press, 1983.

ROMINGER, R., Exploring the Integration of Aftereffects of the Near-Death Experience: An Intuitive and Artistic Inquiry, *Dissertation Abstracts International*, 65(04), 2110B (UMI No. 3129588), 2004.

ROWAN, J., "The real self and mystical experiences," *Journal of Humanistic Psychology*, 23(2), 9-27, 1983.

SANTOS, L. dos, *Fátima in Lúcia's Own Words* (15th ed.), Fátima, Secretariado Dos Pastorinhos, 2005.

SMITH, Y., "Table experiences: Procedures involving the head," in PRITCHARD, A., PRITCHARD, D.E., MACK, J.E., KASEY, P., and YAPP, C. (eds.), *Alien Discussions: Proceedings of the Abduction Study Conference, Cambridge, MA*, Cambridge, MA, North Cambridge Press, 1994, pp. 57-58.

SPARROW, G., *I am with You Always: True Stories of Encounters with Jesus*, New York, Bantam, 1995.

SPRINKLE, R.L., "Psychotherapeutic services for persons who claim UFO experiences," *Psychotherapy in Private Practice*, 6(3), 151-157, 1988.

THAVIS, J., "Assessing Apparitions: Vatican considers guidelines to help bishops," *Archdiocese of Denver*, February 12, 2003, on the internet: *www.archden.org/dcr//news.php?e=11&s=1&a=177.*

TIERNEY, J., "Marian apparitions of the 20th century, The Mary page: All generations will call me blessed (last modified Friday, April 25th, 2003, at 13:57:04 EDT by Michael P. Duricy), Dayton, OH, The Marian Library/International Marian Research Institute, retrieved August 17th, 2003, on the internet: www.udayton.edu/mary/resources/aprtable.html.

TRUNCALE, D., "Alien/UFO Experiences of Children," in PRITCHARD, A., PRITCHARD, D.E., MACK, J.E., KASEY, P., and YAPP, C. (eds.), *Alien Discussions: Proceedings of the Abduction Study Conference, Cambridge, MA*, Cambridge, MA, North Cambridge Press, 1994, pp. 116-126.

WIEBE, P., *Visions of Jesus*, Oxford, Oxford University Press, 1997.

ZIMDARS-SWARTZ, S.L., *Encountering Mary: From La Salette to Medjugorje*, Princeton, NJ, Princeton University Press, 1991.

MARIAN APPARITIONS AND ALIEN ABDUCTION PHENOMENA — SOME COMPARISONS

— David M. Jacobs, Ph.D.[1] —

This paper compares two widely reported events, Marian apparitions and alien abductions, both of which consist primarily of anecdotal testimony and are considered extremely unlikely to occur. In addition, it discusses the subgroup of "contactees" that report that they receive messages from aliens. The purpose of the paper is to determine some key similarities and differences that might suggest similar or dissimilar causative factors either neurologically or experientially, although it is beyond the scope of this paper to attribute objective causative factors to apparitions or abductions.

The author describes some key characteristics of the Marian Apparition phenomenon. He then compares them with key characteristics of the alien abduction phenomenon. Finally, he discusses the contactees who share some of these characteristics.

Similar phenomena with long and complicated histories will vary widely both in the actual events and in the participants' perceptions of those events. No matter what the experience consists of, a great number of superficial similarities will arise – both events are perceived by humans, both events happen to males and females, both events happen in the daytime and evening, both events involve things seen and heard, and so forth. Furthermore, there are going to be a great number of consistent and perhaps important "touch points" about which the author must make the decision whether or not to include in the comparison. The author is aware that the elimination of touch points from analysis is a subjective decision and perhaps even an unconsciously political one, but they cannot all be included.

By necessity, the author incorporates some of the most well known Marian apparitions and some of the most agreed-upon events within them. Although there is less unanimity of agreement about abduction events, the author concentrates on those more commonly known.

Whereas most Marian apparition researchers assume that the events either did or did not happen as stated and they are or are not indicative of religious revelation, the author's assumptions about the appearance of the Virgin Mary are neutral. Similarly, most thinking about alien abductions is that they have happened as stated, or they are psychological in origin. The author has done the majority of his professional work in the UFO and abduction field wrestling with these models and uses much of his own research into abductions as the comparative base for this article.

MARIAN APPARITIONS

There is an extensive scholarly record of Virgin Mary visions throughout the centuries. Researchers have studied the visions' core events along with those that come after the initial visionary experience. Each vision represents a complex set of circumstances that can reverberate for many years and affect the seers, the community, the locale, and the Church, as well as people around the world.

Apparition Literature

Scholars have, over the years, analyzed these factors. For example, Paolo Apolito has studied the social construction of the 1985 Oliveto Citra vision and the mythology surrounding the events. He has looked at its meaning based on information transmission and on the narrative negotiation that takes place to give the vision a meaningful political and religious construct. Michael Carroll has analyzed the seers within a Freudian framework, assuming that their familial relationships gave shape to their visions. Sandra Zimdars-Swartz looked at the evolution of the apparition's geographical site as a sacred place and studied the effect both of the economics of the holy place, and also on the methods of worship of those affected.

Some authors have written about specific apparitions; others have concentrated on countries with a history of apparitions. Scholars have studied apparitions within specific centuries and others have looked at the consumer culture and popular culture surrounding visions and their locales.[2]

A few writers, including Roberto Pinotti, Corrado Malanga, and Joaquim Fernandes and Fina d'Armada, have taken more unconventional pathways by assuming that the visions of certain events existed in objective reality but were misinterpreted as religious phenomena when they might have been Unidentified Flying Object (UFO) sightings. And, Craig Lundahl compared the visions of Medjugorje with Near Death Experiences.[3]

Although theologians have been involved in disputes about whether the apparitions represent holy intervention in human affairs, some writers are convinced that they could be the work of the Devil to trick humans before the

Second Coming. Others have written reverential books about certain Marian apparitions assuming their religious significance and origin.[4]

Various researchers have catalogued thousands of apparition events dating from the 3rd century, but most agree that the vision at Guadalupe in 1531 was the first example of the modern Marian apparition phenomenon. Researchers have attempted to put these visions into specific categories. Sara Horsfall has identified 16 characteristics of what she calls "The Marian Apparition Life World." The characteristics include: "The Marian Apparition Life World is as Real as the Physical World"; it "Has a Force for Authority of Its Own"; and "The Logic and Order of the Marian Apparition Life World is Not the same as the Physical World." [5] Although one may or may not agree with her categories, the research on the subject takes much the same tack as research on alien abductions but without a potential supernatural explanation. In my own research of Marian apparitions, I have found that either a much longer or a much shorter typology could easily exist for these apparitions, depending on how finely one categorizes them. Similarly, typologies of abduction experiences have been fashioned since the late 1980s using a great variety of categories.[6]

Some Typical Apparition Characteristics

Typically, the Marian apparitions of the 19th and 20th centuries (e.g., Rue Du Bac [1830], Lourdes [1858], Fátima [1916-1917], La Salette [1846], Medjugorje [1981]) start with an outdoor sighting of what the perceivers believe to be an apparition. In several of the most famous cases, children were the initial percipients. The children may or may not recognize the apparition as that of the Virgin Mary, depending upon whether she identifies herself or whether she is clearly seen and identifiable as Mary. In virtually all cases there is communication between the apparition and the percipients. Indeed, at times only communication takes place and visualization is not reported.

Marian apparitions have some general similarities. Michael Carroll has found that the number of male and female percipients of the Virgin Mary is roughly the same around the world.[7] However, the number of children as original seers in some of the most well known cases is striking. Many of the seers come from the lower socio-economic levels in the society and they have been raised within a Christian tradition. The event, the messages, the controversy, and the investigation are all within the context of established Christian religious doctrine, and more specifically, most are within traditional Catholic teaching. Whatever the context, the visionaries are able to clearly remember what they saw and heard and then tell others about their experiences.

Many visions are not just single events – a series of other apparition sightings often follow. The Virgin Mary predicts some of the subsequent apparitions; others happen without prediction and are generally in the same locale as the original sightings. Although there are some exceptions, the apparition usually communicates with an original seer and, for the most part, others cannot hear the actual messages (at Fátima, others said they heard a buzzing noise). The most prominent seer usually transmits the Virgin Mary's communications to others. Sometimes, if the original event was a multiple visionary sighting, one or more of the others might at future dates have their own visions and communications.

Invisibility and Visibility

The Holy Family lives in an unseen universe. In order to be seen, the Virgin Mary must go from the invisible to the visible. She must transfer from one realm of existence to another. But that visible realm is not accessible to all. In many cases others cannot see her, so it is not necessarily a completely public event. However, when making an appearance, invisibility must of necessity be broken. Invisibility is central to Christianity and is an accepted space where souls of all people can eventually dwell. Thus, becoming invisible after an apparition is not considered an extraordinary occurrence.

Communication Categories and Forms

Marian communication takes characteristic forms, although it can vary in any given appearance. The Virgin Mary usually issues: (1) requests, (2) directives, (3) warnings, (4) prophecies, (5) secrets to be revealed later, and (6) personal communications for the visionaries. Communication takes place in the seers' languages. This means that visionaries "hear" the language in their heads and can understand it. They are able to tell others precisely what the Virgin Mary told them, although sometimes they embellish or add information later, as Apolito describes at Oliveto Citra.[8]

In the 19th and early 20th centuries, messages took a characteristic structure: The apparition would communicate that people are not paying enough respect to her Son, that they are not praying enough, that they are not saying the Rosary enough, and that they are not being religious enough. If this does not change, she warns that consequences will follow. She sometimes predicts famine, crop failure, or other disasters. Her secrets suggest knowledge of the world's activities. Her messages are sometimes in the form of prophecies.

At times, Mary will make a request that includes such tasks as simple as increased praying for both visionaries and for others. The message might be a special request to strike a medal on her behalf – as at the La Salette appearance.

Sometimes the request can be the far more complicated responsibilities of building shrines, chapels, or other religious structures on her behalf. When the townspeople comply, the building of the structure becomes not only a community event, but also an added attraction for the pilgrims' destination.

Finally, the Virgin Mary might say that she will return to the same location for a specified period of time. The returns attract many onlookers, who might or might not see evidence of Mary; however, the original seer almost always perceives the apparition. Sometimes, secondary visionaries see the apparition without the original seer being present, as in Lourdes. But other times so many people claim to see apparitions that the numbers threaten to weaken the original sighting's impact. In Oliveto, Church officials had to filter out the secondary seers – often pilgrims – to protect the original vision.[9]

From time to time, Mary will entrust secrets to the original visionary for later revelation. The secrets have had to do with political or military events that will occur in the future.

The prophetic messages and the one's requiring action from the apparition witnesses can be almost as important as the visitation. They allow for a validation of the Virgin Mary's appearance because their content is a form of proof of Mary's thought processes. They provide motivation and purpose for the Virgin Mary's visitation and they give meaning and narrative shape to the event. Indirectly, they also provide information about the Holy Family. Without a message, the Virgin Mary's appearance would be all but impossible to judge.

Miracles and Pilgrimages

A series of miracles often accompanies the Virgin Mary's appearance. The miracles often involve healings. For example, a spring comes forth at Lourdes that was never there before. The waters are said to have healing powers and visitors have reported cures of diseases, blindness, bone disorders, and other maladies at other holy sites.

Miracles increase the likelihood that the Virgin Mary actually appeared and enable where she appeared to become a special holy site whose ongoing curative powers give it an immediacy that continues long after the original vision. When word of miracles spreads, people journey to the holy locale to partake of its religious and healing significance. The pilgrimage can either disturb the economy of the local area or help it. Events that occurred at such places as Lourdes and La Salette become major tourist attractions and enter into international popular culture beyond that of a local holy place. Since 1858, millions of people have traveled to Lourdes, one of the most popular tourist destinations in France. In the 20th century, two apparition events were made into Hollywood movies: *The Song of Bernadette* (1943) and *The Miracle of Our Lady of Fátima* (1952).

Investigating the Apparitions

Initial sightings of the Virgin Mary provoke controversy among the local people and clerics, especially if children are the seers. Most visions do not survive the initial controversy and investigators attribute them to natural or psychological causes. But serial visitations and messages might serve to reinforce the original event's unusual quality and therefore its verisimilitude. Eventually, local priests allow for the possibility that the mysterious vision could be worthy of further investigation.

The investigation can go forth because Christian faith is based on the doctrine of death and resurrection. The Catholic Church's position about Virgin Mary apparitions is, therefore, that appearances are possible because Holy individuals reside in a spiritual realm of Heaven and can come back to be seen and heard by mortals for whatever reasons the religious figures desire. Therefore, the Catholic Church must meticulously investigate every case for evidence that a particular vision is actually of a holy figure. The critical point is contained within the Church's paradigm that the possibility of apparitions always exists because Christ's irrefutable precedent has been set. This means that in spite of the often extremely skeptical attitude that Church officials initially assume over cases, it is possible that any case might be evidence of Mary's or other religious figures' (e.g., angels, saints, etc.) reappearance. Thus, the Church is required to admit the possibility of reappearance at any time and in any place.

Because of the overactive imagination of some people and the possibility of demonic activity, the Catholic Church has established a methodology for investigating sightings of the Blessed Virgin Mary. If the vision passes through initial screenings, a commission – usually of Bishops – is often convened to look into the events. The commissions have been extremely conservative in their review of the evidence and they have officially recognized only a small number of apparitions as being evidence that the Virgin Mary has appeared.

Message investigation is just as important as that of the vision. Some people have heard "locutions" from the Virgin Mary without actually seeing the apparition. Others have had sudden insight into the mind of the Christian Church as communicated presumably through a Holy figure. If the investigators find that the messages contradict traditional Catholic teachings, the history of the Church, or Church salvation, they judge the locution as unworthy of belief. Whereas most visions and locutions are found to be unworthy of belief, the Church's thorough review using scientific principles will occasionally result in an event of this nature being deemed "worthy of" although not mandatory for belief.

Depending on what list one reads and which clerics undertook the investigation and issued the findings, from nine to over 30 "approved" Marian apparitions have occurred. Local Bishops from the visionary's geographic locale approve some of these events. Most events have not gained official approval but they have achieved fame nonetheless and even some local clerics treat them as examples of holy visitation.[10]

The Visionaries

The seer, or at least the one who has risen to be the most prominent, who witnesses the original vision and/or the after-visitations, becomes critically important in the ongoing events. The seer witnesses the appearances and proclaims Mary's messages to others, who are often in close proximity and awaiting the messages. Whether they want it or not, this puts the visionaries in the event's center. Whereas before they might have been passive witnesses, upon relating their accounts and sharing the messages, they become active intermediaries between Mary and the people, between Heaven and Earth, and between the sacred and the profane. By interpreting and passing on information, they unwittingly place themselves in close resemblance to mediums and those who "channel" information from spirits and deceased people. They sometimes achieve a special status as a quasi-sacred person and worshipers often look to the visionaries to heal them or to intercede on their behalf with Mary. As vision researcher Chris Eipper has pointed out, the private or semi-private event becomes a public event. [11] Thus, the visions and surrounding activities leave a life-changing impression on both the visionaries and on the believers in the event's physical reality and meaning.

For the most part, the visionaries appear to be convinced of the reality of their visions. It is clear that for most of the seers, life is not the same after reporting the vision. Some elect to lead pious lives in the clergy or continue to have visions and to interpret the Virgin Mary's messages and their meanings.

Depth of Information about Event

Within approved and even unapproved visions, seers relate little depth of knowledge about the internal circumstances within Marian apparitions. They are, of course, recipients of the visions and communications and they sometimes do ask questions and receive answers. But the communications have a limited amount of information about what is going on behind the appearance. There is little sense of an existence beyond that of the appearance, although logically there must be because the Being knows about current human life and thought. Similarly, there is no information about such matters as how the religious figure gets energy, where the apparition resides when not appearing, what its routine daily existence (assuming there is one) involves as a religious being, as well as insights into other lesser religious entities, the relationships between entities, and so forth. It is as if the appearance itself comprises a completeness of event without knowledge of where the Virgin Mary was just before showing herself.

The appearance, communication, and miracles serve as both religious instruction and validation. Information is not known about how Mary decided upon the form in which to appear, e.g., choosing in some instances to appear full figure and in others only partially visible. It is not known why she sometimes wears clothes appropriate to the era in which she is seen and sometimes not. Although the virtue of existing in a supernatural state presupposes miraculous abilities, it is still worthy of discussion. The reasons are puzzling why she appears primarily to people who are within the Christian community, and not also to those who are not Christian thereby gaining converts rather than chastising believers for not praying with sufficient fervor. In many cases the visionaries and the Church questioned why the particular seer was chosen, but in general they did not raise other questions about Mary's existence apart from her appearance and her messages.

THE ABDUCTION PHENOMENON

The alien abduction phenomenon first came to public attention in the early 1960s with the famous Barney and Betty Hill case in the United States. UFO researchers were also made aware at that time of a 1957 case from Brazil. Since then, thousands of cases have been reported which occurred before and after the Hill and Brazil cases and researchers have been able to trace the phenomenon back to the late 19th century.

At first UFO researchers were hostile to its existence, fearing charlatanism. They began to admit reluctantly that it might be happening only after reports increased to the point where they could not be ignored. By the late 20th century, abduction reports had begun to dominate UFO research as the evidence mounted for abduction activity's existence and suitable psychological models to fit that evidence could not be found.

Among the most well known of the abduction phenomenon's physical characteristics are that people are physically missing from their normal environment when they are abducted, they are returned sometimes with scars, bruises and puncture wounds on their bodies, they are abducted singly and in groups, and members of the group can confirm each other's abduction.

The abduction phenomenon exists in an environment of ridicule and extreme incredulity. The scientific community considers it unworthy of study and has paid almost no attention to it. The public considers its existence to be possible but it is thought to be most probably an odd mentally generated phenomenon promulgated by popular culture and media. Researchers, however, have uncovered what they consider remarkable complexities and depth in the details of various accounts that, they say, point to a possible extraterrestrial origin.

Abduction Literature Categories

The literature on UFO abductions is not nearly as extensive as that of Marian apparitions. Books and articles about the UFO abduction phenomenon are divided between first person accounts, primary investigation studies, and secondary author works, both pro and con.

Abductees have been writing a growing body of dramatic, sincere, and informative first-person books about their experiences. Many, however, either do not remember clearly what has happened to them or they unwittingly fill in the unknown areas with "channeled" (dissociative) information. Dissociative information is usually an example of the unconscious generation of voices or communications that the conscious mind treats as coming from elsewhere. Therefore, researchers must be cautious with their recollections.[12]

Primary researchers fall into two categories: Those who know how to do abduction hypnosis and those who do not. The ones who are lacking in skills to do this type of research tend to take channeled information at face value. Those who understand the problems of abduction hypnosis are far more skeptical about recovered memories and have adequate controls in place to minimize dissociative material and to overcome the block against remembering the event. Primary authors such as Budd Hopkins, Karla Turner, Raymond Fowler, and John Mack have all contributed to insights about the abduction phenomenon through primary investigation.[13]

Secondary authors like T. Edward Bullard, John G. Fuller, Philip Mantle, and Nick Pope have provided good overviews of abductions investigated by other researchers. Bullard's work has been particularly thoughtful about the abduction phenomenon's cultural position in relation to myth and folklore.[14] Secondary authors dedicated to debunking the phenomenon assume abductions are psychological in origin and mount arguments for that supposition.

The Problem of Knowing and Remembering

In most cases, the abductees forget the abduction as soon as it ends. They know that something has happened to them and might remember a few seconds of the event. They might have an odd image in their minds associated with the event. They know that they cannot account for two or three hours or more of missing time. They tend to categorize the experience according to what the society allows. They think they have traveled on the astral plane, or that they have seen a strange ghost or a deceased relative. They interpret their sighting as an angel, a devil, or a religious figure. The problems of memory are evident and the verisimilitude of abduction accounts is a serious problem for any abductee and researcher.

In general, however, with proper investigation, most abduction researchers would agree that the narratives remain consistent about the structure of the abductions. The experiences begin in infancy and continue into old age. They occur repeatedly with increasing or decreasing frequency. Thus, to the global abductee population, abductions are not rare events.

Abductees report that they are taken when at home, in a car, in small groups, asleep, and awake. They say that they are taken out of their normal environment and transported directly through walls, windows, and roofs to a waiting UFO. They are rendered passive during the event and have no ability to fight or flee.[15]

Invisibility and Visibility

Although people (particularly family members) see others being abducted with them, most people on the outside cannot see the abduction. This is similar to Marian apparitions. For abduction researchers, invisibility has proven to be a difficult aspect of the phenomenon to deal with. Without the religious precedent of dwelling in an unseen realm, invisibility becomes somewhat incomprehensible. For researchers, the general assumption is that invisibility maintains the abduction phenomenon's clandestine quality without which there would be no abductions. It is a result of advanced physics rather than a supernatural and miraculous appearance.

Descriptions of Abduction Procedures and Activities

On board, the UFO abductees see four types of aliens: gray beings, insect-like beings, reptilian-like beings, and human-like beings. The task-oriented beings perform procedures on the abductees within physical, mental, and reproductive categories. Each category has a long series of complex procedures and experiences that are recognizable within disparate narratives.

Unlike Marian visionaries, most abductees do not understand what is happening to them and they do not know that other abductees are saying the same thing. They do not have a wider perspective on the reasons why they are continually being abducted. They do not know why they have had a lifetime of abduction experiences. They do not know where the aliens are from; they do not know alien names; they do not know alien intentions; they do not know what specific procedures are for; they do not know when they will stop; they do not know what has motivated the aliens to strive toward whatever goal they wish to achieve. Above all, they are frightened by the experience. They want to protect their families. They want it to stop.

Before they learn about the abduction phenomenon, many spend a lifetime living in a world that is filled with what they think are alternative realities complete with strange missing time sequences and odd bits and pieces of memories. For others, the abduction phenomenon passes almost unnoticed in their lives, although they know that something odd occurs to them from time to time.

Healings and Miracles

With the abduction phenomenon, there are no miracles and no miraculous healings. However, there are some rare instances of healings as a function of the abduction event. They are not public healings and they are not considered miraculous by abductees. Some people report that they are cured of their upper respiratory illnesses during the abduction, although there is evidence presented that the cure is not purposefully accomplished.

On even rarer occasions people will report more dramatic healings, such as accounts of diphtheria cures when the abductees were children in the 1930s. Many abductees view healings as simply maintaining the specimen as opposed to a concern with helping humans. Abductees have died of cancer, AIDS, and many other maladies and do not consider the abduction experiences to be curative.

The Abductees

Unlike most Marian visions, abductions are global and accounts come from both Christian and non-Christian countries. Christianity, however, plays no role in abduction accounts; the phenomenon spans the major religions. Regardless of where abductees are from or what their beliefs are, they all have one commonality: Their mother or their father was an abductee. Thus, the phenomenon is intergenerational and this means that the children of an abductee will be abductees as well. Therefore, rather than a special event followed by after-events, the abduction phenomenon begins in childhood and continues into old age. People are abducted with greater and/or lesser frequency throughout the course of their lives. Thus, the general public might think that abduction claims are rare events but for abductees they are extremely common. A poll taken by the Roper Organization in 1991 seemed to add statistical weight to this notion. It suggested that upwards of two percent of the American public has had experiences that could be indicative of abduction events. When people were asked directly if they were ever abducted, a small percentage of Americans answered affirmatively. The percentage translates into about one million people. [16] Even without formal polling, anecdotal evidence points to a widespread phenomenon. Researchers have been contacted by many thousands of individuals from around the world who think they might be involved in the abduction phenomenon. The people who have been investigated tend to span religious, economic, political, intellectual, educational, social, ethnic, and racial lines. Thus, the scale of the abduction phenomenon is very much larger than that of Marian apparition events.

Abductees range from professionals like psychiatrists, psychologists, therapists, physicians, professors, teachers, attorneys, police officers, military personnel, business executives, and clerics, to people who are undereducated, inarticulate and who cannot hold a job. There is no particular overt aspect of a person's life that would enable one to be an abductee other than parentage.

Children

With the more publicized Marian apparitions, children played a critical role as seers and as messengers. Children play only a peripheral role in abduction reports. They often alert their parents that "bad doctors" or "egg people" are coming into their rooms and taking them places. The parents often pass off these complaints as dreams. UFO researchers do not investigate children's abductions for ethical reasons; children are particularly prone to filling in memories when they do not remember; they are extremely suggestible; and they often wish to fill adults expectations about what happened to them. Therefore, their memories are unreliable. However, when the children become adults researchers can investigate these early accounts.

The Problem of Recovering Memories

Abductees' memory problems are a crucial difference between the Marian visions and alien abductions. In the vision phenomenon, the percipients remember everything. They remember what Mary wore, how she moved, and many details of her appearance. They remember what she said, including her overt and secret messages.

Abductees usually remember nothing, and if they do, it is only a sliver of what happened to them. Therefore, from the very start of encountering the phenomenon, memory problems constitute a great amount of methodological difficulty, abductee anguish, skeptical criticism, and ridicule from the general public. Hypnosis emerged as the best instrument for allowing the person to remember what has happened to him/her even though most serious researchers in the area are especially aware of the problems of hypnosis. Thus, when individuals describe abduction events, it is in two ways: they remember them through their conscious memories or they remember them through hypnosis. Neither way is perfect.

When abductees remember in the course of a competent investigation they recall entire events in great detail. The events and their details dovetail precisely with other accounts told by people who were not aware of the previous testimony. Most accounts are richly described and paint a coherent picture from beginning to end.

Investigating Abductions

Investigations of abductions have been slow to develop and few researchers have ventured into these untrodden grounds. Unlike the impetus for the Catholic Church, there is no established reason for scientists to study abductions other than people relating strange anecdotal accounts. In the late 1960s, astronomer J. Allen Hynek, the Air Force's consultant to its UFO investigation group Project Blue Book, described the "mental set" in the Air Force about the UFO phenomenon as, "It can't be therefore it isn't." With abductions, most scientists will admit that their extraterrestrial origin is theoretically possible, but since in their opinion it is extremely unlikely and because they believe it has never happened before, no irrefutable precedent has been set and therefore evidence of it, especially anecdotal, is *ipso facto* false. Thus, the "mental set" is "It never has been and therefore it is not."

Because it is almost impossible to admit of the possibility, the scientific community has mounted no studies of abductions. Scientists think it is a waste of valuable time and resources. Perhaps more importantly, there is no institutional funding or backing of studies of the phenomenon that might leave open the possibility that abductions are occurring. The only studies that receive funding are based on the overall premise that abductions are psychologically generated from such factors as sleep paralysis, temporal lobe lability, or other internal mechanisms.

Depth of Information about Abductions

Abduction researchers have been able to accumulate information over the last 40 years that has led to a considerable amount of knowledge about the phenomenon's background. Unlike Marian researchers, abduction investigators have begun to build a story about the aliens' work life, their abduction tasks, their motivations, goals, problems, mistakes, and other aspects of their lives.

Abductees describe logically how the system works, how the aliens go about their duties, the types of machines and devices used, and the content and methods of all the procedures they undergo. Experienced researchers understand many of the well defined and commonly used procedures administered to abductees. In the beginning of the abduction phenomenon, investigators thought that if it represented extraterrestrial life, it might be impossible to fathom what was happening. But although they do not know the answers to some basic questions, they have found that they can understand most of what abductees have described and that it appears to be consistent, rational, and related to a specific, goal-directed program. [17]

Lack of Religious Interpretation

When abductees tell their clergymen about their experiences, they sometimes receive a religious interpretation: demonic possession. This diagnosis does not seem to fit what has been happening and although a few accept it, most reject this explanation. In general, when abductees understand what has been happening to them, they do not ascribe it to a religious causative factor, whether angelic or demonic. Religiously minded abductees, including clerics, have the same nonreligious experiences as all abductees. At rare occasions during an abduction event, a person will ask an abductor a religious question. The answer almost always indicates that the aliens have absolutely no concern with religion of any type. Some abductees try to come to terms with the phenomenon by giving it a religious context ("God made everything in the Universe; He must have made aliens and therefore they must be good"), but most are nonplussed by the experiences and accept them as alien with an agenda of which they are ignorant.

Some people assume that the half-remembered person they saw standing in their room one evening was a deceased relative. These memories are within the Christian paradigm that allows for heavenly souls to reappear on Earth. The memories of loved ones coming back to say good-bye or to reassure them that everything is all right can be a cherished part of an abductee's life. Upon investigation, abductees invariably recognize their "relative" as an alien and they understand that an abduction is ongoing. This can be profoundly sad for the abductee who might have been heavily invested in the memory of their relative.

Locale of Abductions

In great contrast to the Marian sites, the location of the abduction is almost meaningless for subsequent interest. People have claimed abductions from their homes, cars, hotels, parks, and even busy city streets. It does not matter where they were during the abduction, although they tend to report more abductions in non-work related situations when they are alone or with their families. Urban and rural areas have an equal amount of abductions. When the abduction phenomenon first began, researchers would carefully examine the environment as they had done in the past with UFO sightings.

Some skeptics have suggested that psychological states such as sleep paralysis might be a cause of abduction fantasies and therefore the location of where the abduction claimant sleeps might be of significance. Others have suggested that the changes in Earth's magnetic field might trigger electrical impulses that cause temporal lobe instability, which in turn can cause abduction hallucinations. Therefore, the location of the event might assume importance for its proximity to geological activity. [18] In general, however, abduction sites are of no interest to the general public and of little interest to researchers. Furthermore, abductees are unable to control aliens by asking for a special appearance at a prescribed time and place.

Language and Communication

The language spoken to the abductee is in his or her native tongue and communication is conducted through what the abductees describe as telepathic. Although most Marian visionaries describe hearing words, abductees say that they receive an impression in their minds that automatically converts it to words so that they know what the aliens are saying. Thus, perhaps similarly to Marian communication, allowing the abductee to acquire communication in their own tongues mitigates the problem of differing languages. The difference is subtle but significant. In one case the apparition talks, in the other the alien "thinks."

Messages

The content of the communication is profoundly different between Marian apparitions and alien abductions. Within a competently investigated abduction context, no messages are given. People's questions are most likely to go unanswered. When conversations with aliens take place, substantive information is rare. The exception is that abductees report that substantive conversations are much more likely with more human-like beings.

At times, abductees say that they are privy to odd discussions of the future. Abductees have said that they are shown screen-like devices in which human-like aliens are together with humans. They "hear" that in the future everyone will be together in a happy co-mingling with human-like aliens. This characteristic monologue scares and disturbs abductees.

When the event is over and amnesia sets in, the opportunity to spread a message, should one be given, is automatically lost with the memory of the experience. Once abductees understand what has been happening to them, rather then spreading the news of their experiences, the vast majority of abductees prefer anonymity. They learned in childhood to keep quiet about the strange memories for fear of ridicule. As adults, they often do not tell their husbands or wives, even though the events are continuing.

Those who have not had their memories competently investigated remember bits and pieces of abductions that might be distorted or even false. Their accounts are often a combination of reality, false memories, New Age popular culture, and channeling. Within this context, the abductee will sometimes relate information about how aliens are here because the Earth is being destroyed ecologically, or the threat of atomic war imperils the Earth, or the Earth is in danger, whether naturally or through human folly. As a result, the aliens have had to intercede on Earth's behalf.

CONTACTEES AND REVEALED KNOWLEDGE

A subset of the alien abduction phenomenon is one in which people say that they are in constant contact with aliens through communication (locutions) rather than through actual abductions. There are some striking parallels between the contactees and some Marian apparitions. These similarities are particularly in evidence through message delivery. In channeled communiqués, the aliens deliver elaborate monologues to contactees, in which they explain who they are, where they are from, why they are here, why the Earth is in danger, and why humans need help from them. They discuss the history of aliens on other planets, the reasons that aliens were required to come here, the aliens' struggles with evil aliens, the aliens' love of humanity, and their vision of the future.

In most message accounts, contactees relate a strong religious component, which frequently takes the form of a validation of Jesus's life and an affirmation that there is one God. Finally, a warning is usually attached to contactee messages: If humanity does not do the right things, the consequences could be disastrous. [19]

Information flows smoothly in these stories. When the aliens deliver their message, they tell everything in considerable detail. All contactee questions put to the aliens are answered; all knowledge requested is given. The information is complex, complete, and wide-ranging.

Messages are regularly given to contactees who spread them to all who will listen. They write books and articles. They form groups around their messages. Their roles as messengers assume primary importance. They have been chosen by all-powerful beings and they become the intermediaries between aliens who do not profess to be gods (contactees reaffirm that there is only one true God) but who possess the knowledge and wisdom of the Universe. The chosen contactees enjoy a special relationship with aliens as their emissaries and message purveyors. Some of these contactees have formed groups around them to spread the message. The groups have sometimes formed themselves into cults like the Canadian-based Raelians and the suicidal cult that emerged in the 1990s, Heaven's Gate.

Most UFO and abduction researchers deem these messages and information to be dissociative and illegitimate. They consider contactees to be generally destructive of legitimate abduction claims because scientists and the public cannot tell the difference between the two. This hurts attempts to legitimize the subject.

CONCLUSIONS

It is clear that Marian apparitions and abductions are very different. Touch points exist, however, between the two and even more so in the peripheral aspects of the alien contact phenomenon. Whereas the comparative fit between abductions and apparitions is difficult to make, one can see many more similarities with contactees and apparitions. The message is the most obvious and powerful parallel. Both messengers gain information through revealed knowledge. They both transmit the remembered information to those who wish to hear. They both place themselves in positions of importance as intermediaries between the supernatural and the mundane. Although apparition visionaries often do not want this attention, contactees often seek it through their writings and public speaking appearances.

RESEARCH DIRECTIONS

Thus, although on the surface it might appear that the two phenomena are related in substance and genesis, the differences far outweigh the similarities. But in one area, the similarities conform more closely: the centrality of communication and messages with the contactees, but not with abductees. The meaning of this comparison requires more study both within the neurological sciences, religious studies, and popular culture. This suggests that a great number of unapproved Marian apparitions might have the same dissociative causative factors. This is an area where more research should be done.

Of course, the abduction phenomenon with its global aspects and enormous number of claimants would benefit greatly from commissions of competent investigators to look into the accounts, as the Catholic Church does for Marian apparition claims. But there is an even more accessible arena of research that might span both worlds. Abductees frequently remember the beginning or the end of an abduction event before their memory ceases. When they do not know what is happening to them, they think that they have seen a figure standing near them. Within a context that makes sense for their lives, they report that they have seen angels, Mary, and other religious figures. For the unaware abductee, this can be absolute evidence of the physical reality of God and His representatives. If that is the case, those religious figures, like in Marian apparitions, have chosen this particular person through which to make themselves known. They then can see themselves as special individuals to whom Jesus or others have chosen to reveal themselves. For researchers, the question is not only, as some writers have suggested, are apparitions evidence of UFO sightings, but from the point-of-view of the abductee, how many of these events have impelled the percipient to enter into a life of religious devotion? Thus, research needs to be done among the clergy, nuns, monks, and others who have devoted their lives to God, to see if the incidence of private apparitions is higher among them than in the general population and if the private apparitions are indicative of abduction activity. If researchers find a correlation, then it is possible to build bridges between the two worlds.

Notes

[1] I am grateful to Irene Jacobs, David Harrington Watt, Shelley Nutaitis, and Jean Therese Joyen for their suggestions for this article.

[2] APOLITO, P., *Apparitions of the Madonna at Oliveto Citra: Local Visions and Cosmic Drama*, University Park, PA, The Pennsylvania State University Press, 1998; CARROLL, M. P., *The Cult of the Virgin Mary: Psychological Origins*, Princeton, Princeton University Press, 1996; "The Virgin Mary at La Salette and Lourdes: Whom did the children see?," *Journal for the Scientific Study of Religion*, 24(1), 56-74, 1985; GARVEY, M., *Searching for Mary: An Exploration of Marian Apparitions Across the U.S.*, New York, Plume, 1998; CHRISTIAN, W. A., *Visionaries: The Spanish Republic and the Reign of Christ*, Berkeley, University of California Press,

1996; KAUFMAN, S. K., *Consuming Visions: Mass Culture and the Lourdes Shrine*, Ithaca, Cornell University Press, 2005; ZIMDARS-SWARTZ, S.L., *Encountering Mary: From La Salette to Medjugorje*, Princeton, Princeton University Press, 1991.

[3] FERNANDES, J. and d'ARMADA, F., *Heavenly Lights: The Apparitions of Fátima and the UFO Phenomenon*, Victoria, BC, EcceNova Editions, 2005; MALANGA, C. and PINOTTI, R., *I Fenomeni B.V.M.: Le Manifestazioni Mariane in una Nuova Luce [The B.V.M. Phenomenon: Marian Apparitions in a New Light]*, Milan, Mondadori, 1990; LUNDAHL, C.R., "A comparison of other world perception by Near-Death Experiencers and by the Marian visionaries of Medjugorje," *Journal of Near Death Studies*, 19(1), Fall 2000.

[4] RIPP, B., *End Time Deceptions*, Mandeville, LA, Twin Light Ministries, 1996; ODELL, C. M., *Those Who Saw Her: Apparitions of Mary*, Huntington, IN, Our Sunday Visitor Publishing Division, 1995.

[5] HORSFALL, S., "The Experience of Marian Apparitions and the Mary Cult," *The Social Science Journal*, 37(3), 375-384.

[6] BULLARD, T. E., *UFO Abductions: The Measure of a Mystery*, Mount Rainier, MD, The Fund for UFO Research, 1987; JACOBS, D.M., *Secret Life*, New York, Simon & Schuster, 1992; TURNER, K., *Taken*, Roland, AR, Kelt Works, 1994.

[7] CARROLL, M.P., "Visions of the Virgin Mary: The effect of family structures on Marian apparitions," *Journal for the Scientific Study of Religion*, 22(3), 205-221, 1983.

[8] APOLITO, P., op. cit., pp. 41-43.

[9] APOLITO, P., op. cit., pp. 50-51.

[10] Lists of Church-approved apparitions can be found on a variety of websites. These include: www.udayton.edu/mary/resources/aprindex.html, www.catholic-forum.com/saints/indexapp.htm, www.catholic.net/rcc/Periodicals/Faith/may-june99/Apparitions.html, www.cin.org/archives/cinbvm/199712/0007.html, www.franciscansfo.org/ap/Appariti.htm, www.catholicity.com/links/categories.html?catid=124.

[11] EIPPER, C., "The Virgin, the visionary, and the atheistic ethnographer: Anthropological inquiry in the light of Irish apparitions," *Anthropological Forum*, 11(1), 2001.

[12] Some examples of this literature are CARLSON, K., *Beyond My Wildest Dreams*, Santa Fe, NM, Bear & Company, 1995; COLLINGS, B. and JAMERSON, A., *Connections: Solving Our Alien Abduction Mystery*, Newberg, OR, Wild Flower Press, 1996; HALEY, L., *Lost was the Key*, Tuscaloosa, AL, Greenleaf Publications, 1993; STRIEBER, W., *Communion*, New York, Morrow, 1987.

[13] HOPKINS, B., *Missing Time*, New York, Marek, 1981; HOPKINS, B., *Intruders: The Incredible Visitations at Copley Woods*, New York, Random House, 1987; HOPKINS, B., *Witnessed: The Brooklyn Bridge Abductions*, New York, Pocket Books, 1996; JACOBS, D.M., *Secret Life*, op. cit.; JACOBS, D.M., *The Threat*, New York: Simon & Schuster, 1998; MACK, J.E., *Abduction: Human Encounters with Aliens*, New York, Charles Scribner's Sons, 1994; TURNER, K., *Taken*, op. cit.; FOWLER, R.W., *The Allagash Abductions*, Tigard, OR, Wildflower Press, 1993.

[14] BULLARD, T.E., *UFO Abductions: The Measure of a Mystery*; BULLARD, T.E., "UFOs: Lost in the Myths," in JACOBS, D.M. (ed.), *UFOs and Abductions: Challenging the Borders of Knowledge*, Lawrence, KS, The University Press of Kansas, 2000; FULLER, J.G., *The Interrupted Journey*, New York, Dial Press, 1966; POPE, N., *The Uninvited: An Exposé of the Alien Abduction Phenomenon*, London, Simon & Schuster, 1997; NAGAITIS, C. and MANTLE, P., *Without Consent: A Comprehensive Survey of Missing Time and Abduction Phenomena in the UK*, London, Ringpull Press, 1994.

[15] The routine of abductions can be found in JACOBS, D.M., *Secret Life*, op. cit. and in JACOBS, D.M., *The Threat*, op. cit.

[16] HOPKINS, B., JACOBS, D.M., MACK, J.E., WESTRUM, R., and CARPENTER, J., *Unusual Personal Experiences: An Analysis of Data from Three National Surveys Conducted by the Roper Organization*, Las Vegas, NV, Bigelow Holding Corporation, 1992. The figure of one million self-reporting abductees comes from a private Roper Poll taken in 1991 and then duplicated by the National Institute of Discovery Sciences in 1997.

[17] JACOBS, D.M., *The Threat*, passim.

[18] CLANCY, S., *Abducted: How People Come to Believe They Were Abducted by Aliens*, Cambridge, Harvard University Press, 2005; PERSINGER, M.A., "The UFO Experience: A Normal Correlate of Human Brain Function," in JACOBS, D.M. (ed.), *UFOs and Abductions: Challenging the Borders of Knowledge*, op. cit., pp. 262-302.

[19] Some examples of this type of literature are SUMMERS, M.V., *The Allies of Humanity: The Message that Cannot Wait*, Boulder, CO, The Society for the Greater Community Way of Knowledge, 2000; SUMMERS, M.V., *The Allies of Humanity, Book Two*, Boulder, CO, The Society for the Greater Community Way of Knowledge, 2005; ROYAL, L. and PRIEST, K., *Visitors from Within*, Phoenix, AZ, Royal Priest Research Press, 1993; ROBINSON, J.M., *Alienated: A Quest to Understand Contact*, Murfreesboro, TN, Greenleaf Publications, 1997; KANNENBERG, I.M., *Project Earth: From the E.T. Perspective*, Newberg, OR, Wildflower Press, 1995.

ANGELS AND ALIENS — ENCOUNTERS WITH BOTH NEAR-DEATH AND UFOs

— Janet Elizabeth Colli, Ph.D. —

The intersection of information deduced from accounts of extraterrestrial encounters and near-death experiences could lead us to several important clues about the eventual common background of these human landscapes. It is the author's suggestion that by means of these symptomatic portraits, affirmed by deeply rooted quantitative data, behavioral alterations detectable in subjects involved in such experiences can be specified and predicted. Of relevance within social psychology, yet not limited to it, are the results revealed herein, which, when compared with other significant examples of experiences of this nature, accentuate several formal constants and contents of such phenomena.

"To experience light (love, higher consciousness, nirvana, God) on Earth,
I have had to see and touch a bit of Heaven." – Judith

As a transpersonal psychotherapist, my clinical practice encompasses both clinical psychology and the psychology of spiritual experience. During the past 10 years, I have counseled those who are awakening to the reality of their relationship with the subtle realm. I have researched the role of trauma in entering transpersonal realms, including UFO sightings and encounters with so-called alien beings. I am among the most skilled clinicians in America's Pacific Northwest helping people who experience non-ordinary events.

Given my clinical expertise, I embarked upon extending Kenneth Ring's landmark research study, "The Omega Project: Near-Death Experiences, UFO Encounters, and Mind at Large," undertaken over 10 years ago. Ring is a social psychologist and one of the foremost researchers of near-death experiences (NDEs). Social psychology research has thus given us comparative studies of those who have experienced *either* near-death or UFOs. "Angels and Aliens" investigates those who have experienced *both*.

As for the NDE itself, about one-third of those who come close-to-death report that "something happened." That "something" is the *transcendental* NDE, where persons believe they have left their physical bodies and transcended the boundaries of the ego, and the confines of time and space. A 1982 Gallup Poll estimated that at least 8 million people have experienced NDEs, though it is now believed to be closer to 13 million in the United States alone. NDEs have been reported for centuries throughout the world's manifold cultures and religious traditions. Although no two NDEs are identical, a discernable pattern does exist. For quantitative measures of the NDE, a 16-item, scaled-response questionnaire has been developed (Greyson, 1983). The NDE Scale differentiates those who unequivocally have had NDEs from those with qualified or questionable claims. The NDE Scale is clinically useful in differentiating NDEs from organic brain syndromes and non-specific stress responses. It measures criteria such as the following:

> • *A life-threatening event or an event that is perceived as such.* The subjective perception that a life-threat is occurring can be enough to initiate an NDE, irrespective of the objective nature of the event. For example, the NDE of one of my research subjects resulted from an imminent car accident, though she did not actually sustain an injury during the accident. The research subjects in "Angels and Aliens" reported NDEs from such events as near drowning, concussions, coma, domestic violence, fever, and food poisoning.

> • *Feeling that the 'self' has left the body and hovers overhead – referred to as an out-of-body experience (OBE).* During such a state, people are often able to witness and later describe medical procedures of which they had no prior knowledge.

> • *Moving through a dark space or "tunnel."*

> • *Encountering a golden or white "light," usually described as magnetic and loving.*

> • *Meeting others, such as deceased loved ones or relatives, sacred beings ("God"), or "beings of light."*

> • *Life review, where every single event is re-experienced, sometimes from the perspective of all the lives that intersected*

with one's own. This poses a challenge to current memory research in terms of the sheer amount of instantaneous and empathetic information recall. "A Quantum Bio-Mechanical Basis for Near-Death Life Reviews," co-authored with Thomas E. Beck, theorizes how the physical body allows such non-local communication via the quantum vacuum or electromagnetic zero-point field (ZPF).

• *Boundary or barrier is reached that may not be crossed if one is to return to life*. The decision to return may be voluntary or involuntary.

It has been estimated that approximately seven years are required to fully integrate the after-effects of an NDE into one's ordinary, daily life. In summary, NDEs permanently alter a person's perceptions of what constitutes reality. As "Joan," a study participant, said, "I am not afraid of dying anymore. When I was in my NDE, it was so calm, peaceful, and serene that I could have stayed in that state forever. No, pain, fears, nothing but serenity."

Ring's study helped to determine the after-effects of NDEs on one's personality, social functioning, and physiology. By using the same questionnaire as "The Omega Project," my additional group of subjects who have experienced *both* NDEs and UFOs can be compared to Ring's findings. Eighteen subjects thus far have agreed to participate in the study. It is admittedly a small sample; in hopes of enlarging it, "Angels and Aliens" is an on-going study. The findings to date, however, are quantitatively significant. Seven quantitative charts and a sample of different kinds of items on the questionnaire are included in this paper, as well as a few brief vignettes from the case studies. "Angels and Aliens" thus consists of quantitative (statistical) and qualitative research, based on my own clinical observations. It should be noted that experiences with "UFOs" includes UFO sightings, however brief, as well as what can be considered a full-fledged "close encounter" with so-called alien beings. According to "Joan," a study participant, "I do know now that 'they' are *real!*"

Yet one need not be a "true believer" in the objective reality of UFOs to appreciate the significance of my research findings. "Angels and Aliens" seeks to unpackage the subjective belief system of people who believe they have had both experiences, and the psychophysical changes that they undergo. What kind of person makes these claims? How do they differ from those who have had only an NDE? Psychological studies have already proven that near-death experiencers (NDErs) do not suffer from dissociative disorders.

Though a non-specific stress reaction may result from those who come close-to-death *without NDEs*, the syndrome is generally not severe enough to be diagnosed as post-traumatic stress disorder (PTSD) (Greyson, 2001). The positive emotions that distinguish NDEs from other dissociative experiences may mitigate subsequent PTSD symptoms.

Moreover, we know from psychological studies that those who claim to be "alien abductees" are not mentally ill. The studies of both Slater and Parnell found no psychiatric disorders in such subjects. Nine subjects were selected who reported having been abducted by aliens. The subjects were administered a battery of objective and projective tests by a clinical psychologist who was not informed of their abductee status. Slater found subjects to "share brighter than average intelligence and a certain richness of inner life that can operate favorably in terms of creativity or disadvantageously to the extent that it can be overwhelming." Upon being informed of the subjects' shared belief system, Slater wrote an addendum to her original report.

The first and most critical question is whether our subjects' reported experiences could be accounted for strictly on the basis of psychopathology, for instance, and mental disorder. *The answer is a firm no.* In broad terms, if the reported abductions were confabulated fantasy productions, based on what we know about psychological disorders, they could only have come from pathological liars, paranoid schizophrenics, and severely disturbed and extraordinarily rare hysteric characters subject to fugue states and/or multiple personality shifts. It is important to note, as cited by Laibow, that not one of the subjects, based on test data, falls into any of these categories.

Parnell also found no overt psychopathology in 225 UFO experiencers (UFOErs) when administered the MMPI and the Sixteen Personality Factor Questionnaire. Parnell found that subjects who claimed to have had encounters with aliens (as opposed to UFO sightings) had a significantly greater tendency to endorse unusual feelings, thoughts and attitudes; to be creative and imaginative; and to be suspicious and distrustful. Given the negative cultural response to such claims, it is not surprising that these qualities have been correlated with experiencers.

For further findings about the psychological makeup of such subjects, we turn to "Angels and Aliens." Ring initially developed an extensive questionnaire in order to compare those who have experienced either near-death or UFOs with two control groups, near-death control (NDC) and UFO control (UFOC), made up of subjects who expressed a mere *interest* in either NDEs or UFO experiences. The questionnaire's inventories are as follows:

1. Experience and Interest Inventory
2. Childhood Experience Inventory
3. Home Environmental Inventory
4. Psychological Inventory
5. Psychophysical Changes Inventory
6. Life Changes Inventory
7. Religious Beliefs Inventory
8. Opinion Inventory

Other areas of focus have arisen as the research progressed. What can Ufology learn from the field of Near-Death Studies, and vice versa? For example, according to foremost NDE researcher P.M.H. Atwater, "Yes, there were those who said they experienced UFO phenomena before their near-death episodes, but this is rare." Given my research findings, however, that is simply not so. Exactly half of my subjects experienced UFO phenomena *before* their NDE. I believe that a relatively simple explanation exists for the discrepancy. Though Atwater's research is based on several thousand subjects responding to a call for NDErs, because of my expertise in Ufology, I had access to subjects who had "alien abductee" experiences since childhood. Indeed, 10 out of 18 had UFO experiences during childhood, eight of which consist of ongoing contact.

Do both NDEs and UFOs ever come together in the same experience? Is there evidence that the two phenomena are linked? Atwater, after interviewing about 3,000 subjects, found only two subjects who described an alien-type being as part of their near-death scenario. Again, Atwater's research results radically differ from my own. In fact, the very first subject I interviewed gave a lucid account of an alien being as part of his NDE. Our interview, which was quite long, was nearly complete when "Duane" suddenly said, "Oh, by the way, when I left this body and I was in the tunnel, *I wasn't human.*" Duane had perceived on either side of him two alien beings popularly known as "Grays." At the time of Duane's UFO experience, there were no "Grays" depicted in American popular culture. Duane's perception of his "self" was not totally distinct because he was out-of-body. Duane reports that he was escorted through the tunnel by two aliens, however, and he was aware that he, himself, was that kind of creature.

These gray beings functioned as guides as Duane traveled through the tunnel. While these aliens were apparently not figures that came from his cultural background, his "personal" experience with them continued to unfold after his NDE, when a conscious "close encounter" introduced their ongoing role in his life. Morse found, in a study of 150 NDErs, that 12% have regular contact with the "guardian angels" that they met during their NDEs. Apparently, "angels" are not the only beings that experiencers continue to contact. "Connie" feels a deep love and respect for a being that somewhat resembles a praying mantis. "When I looked up at his head, I saw only bright, white light. Like it was too bright for me to see. This same being was next to me when I woke up in the ICU [Intensive Care Unit] after the accident."

In spite of Atwater's extensive subject pool, my expertise in Ufology enabled me to access this particular subject, whose report significantly impacts the field of near-death studies. I have thus far found three subjects whose experiences directly link near-death scenarios with UFOs. Researchers must be willing to compare and contrast transpersonal phenomena such as NDEs, OBEs, and UFO experiences. Cross-disciplinary studies of such phenomena will likely advance consciousness research and prove to be the future trend.

What do encounters with both near-death *and* UFOs reveal about human nature and the nature of reality? "Angels and Aliens" provides preliminary observations about a) psychophysical, life, and value changes that such subjects undergo, and b) their view of material, physical reality.

Psychophysical Changes Inventory (PCI):
1. Physical Sensitivities
2. Physiological and Neurological Functioning
3. Psychoenergetic Functioning
4. Emotional Functioning
5. Expanded Mental Awareness
6. Paranormal Functioning

The Psychophysical Changes Inventory reveals that almost two thirds of NDE/ UFOErs (compared to about one-half of Ring's experiencers and about 15 percent of his control groups) claim that their nervous system now functions differently than it did before. Over one-half (compared to about a third of Ring's experiencers and about 8 percent of his control groups) also assert that their brains are "structurally different" than before. NDE/ UFOErs also emphatically declare that they have undergone a kind of mind expansion.

Percent Endorsement of Items on Psychophysical Changes Inventory

	NDE / UFOE	UFOE	NDE	NDC	FOC
Neurological Changes Difference in:					
Nervous System	<u>61.0</u>	47.4	51.4	18.5	12.8
Brain Structure	<u>55.5</u>	25.1	36.5	7.7	7.4
Expanded Mental Awareness Increase in:					
Mind Expansion	<u>86.5</u>	48.5	58.1	27.8	30.8
Information Flooding	<u>77.7</u>	56.7	48.6	20.4	17.9

Let us take a closer look at physiological and neurological functioning. It is frequently reported that wristwatches and computers of NDEers and UFOErs malfunction. Needless to say, ordinary life demands certain adjustments. One (UFOE) subject, "Joy," routinely experienced electrical anomalies with household appliances. Compared to the control groups, NDE/UFOErs are *seven to 10 times* more likely to assert that they cause electrical malfunctions. But Joy would have to wait nearly 20 years before clinical research studies connected this phenomenon to close encounters. Meanwhile, in the 1970s, Joy had to stop wearing watches because "none of the watches would work. Even battery-run. Nothing would work on my body." She was plagued with the same difficulties when it came to household appliances. Joy swears that their malfunctioning resulted in burnt toast – or no toast – as appliances either worked erratically or not at all.

One medically based theory could account for such electrical sensitivity. NDEs appear to alter the subject's electromagnetic (EM) field. Melvin Morse, a pediatrician and prominent near-death researcher, found in his study of 150 NDErs that more than one-fourth (compared to 4% of "normal" adults who had never had an NDE or paranormal experience) said that they could not wear wristwatches. Morse postulates that the Light encounter – with its alteration of the body's EM field – is responsible for such transformative after-effects as higher intelligence, positive personality changes, and increased paranormal

178

experiences.

Physicist Janusz Slawinski has, in fact, demonstrated that dying organisms emit a burst of electromagnetic energy at death. Morse hypothesizes that the Light phenomenon involves an excitation of the body's EM field that serves to "rewire" the brain's circuitry, and open previously unused neural pathways in the right temporal lobe, the area he calls "the seat of the soul." Morse attributes the paranormal abilities that are residual from NDEs to the opening of this circuitry. "[T]he full resources of the human mind have yet to be tapped and the near-death experience activates that part of the brain that has our dormant psychic abilities." Remarkably, 80 percent of NDE/UFOErs (compared to just over half of Ring's experiencers and about one-quarter of the control groups) report that their psychic abilities increased after their encounters.

Percent Endorsement of Items of Electrical-Sensitivity Syndrome

	NDE / UFOE	UFOE	NDE	NDC	UFOC
More Psychic	80.5	51.5	60.8	31.5	17.9
Healing Gifts	69.4	52.6	41.9	11.1	23.1
Sensitivity to Light	58.6	49.5	48.6	20.4	25.6
Mood Fluctuations	42.1	34.0	28.4	13.0	10.3
Electronic or Electric Malfunction	72.2	37.1	24.3	7.4	10.3

What is physiologically happening with these people? One of my research subjects relates that when he and his brother were young, they used to stick pins and paper clips into electrical outlets, repeatedly – just to feel the energetic "rush." They were not physically harmed, he said, it just "vibrated or tickled." Needless to say, I do not recommend that as a way to achieve an energetic shift, but I do offer it as an example of how my research subjects relate differently to EM fields.

P. M. H. Atwater has developed a 47-item, in-depth questionnaire to explore the electrical sensitivity phenomenon. Atwater has also voiced the need for physiological testing of experiencers to validate their subjective self-reports. For example, Norman Don and Gilda Moura's landmark study of the electro-encephalograms (EEGs) of UFOErs revealed patterns previously only measured in an advanced yogi during "samadhi," a profound meditative state of Unity consciousness. Magnetic resonance imaging (MRI) has allowed the examination of the neuroanatomical correlates of both veridical and illusory memories (Gauthier *et al.*). Positron emission tomography (PET) scans, and event-related brain potentials (ERPs) recorded with scalp electrodes could be the next stage of testing of NDE/UFOErs.

Until such studies can be conducted, however, subjective reports of Kundalini phenomena provide some measure of evidence of physiological changes. Kundalini, a term derived from the ancient tradition of tantric yoga, literally means "coiled up" like a serpent. It is said to be a subtle form of bioenergy that usually lies dormant at the base of the spine, but can be activated by various spiritual disciplines. Though its arousal may be destabilizing, the awakening of Kundalini can lead to experiences of profound ecstasy and cosmic awareness. Sandro, a study participant, experienced "this intensity, like my whole body, every cell, was just vibrating. It was very powerful." Symptoms are variable, but include the following items on the Kundalini Scale:

In summary, the data suggest that experiencers have undergone a *psychophysical* transformation, that is, changes to their physiology and central nervous system have allowed a higher level of consciousness to manifest. The general implication of these changes is voiced by Ring in the following: "*Extraordinary encounters appear to be the gateway to a radical,*

Percent Endorsement of Items on the Kundalini Scale

	NDE / UFOE	UFOE	NDE	NDC	UFOC
Energy in Hands	<u>94.4</u>	37.1	47.3	14.8	15.4
Deep Ecstatic Sensation	<u>61.1</u>	32.0	35.1	14.8	15.4
Severe or Migraine Headaches	<u>23.5</u>	34.0	17.6	9.3	10.3
Energy Currents Flowing through Body	<u>83.3</u>	44.3	50.0	13.0	20.5
Sensations of Tingling, Tickling On/Under Skin	<u>83.3</u>	54.6	39.2	3.7	30.8
Aware of Internal Lights or Colors	<u>61.1</u>	32.0	43.2	9.3	17.9

biologically based transformation of the human personality." According to Stacie, "We as a species are being forced to recognize a larger reality in direct conjunction with the indigenous prophecies of the coming Earth changes. It is my opinion that we are being prepared for a major transition. I am not referring to the cosmic community's presentation of themselves, but rather a much larger shift dimensionally [that] affects the entire planet."

Even more so than Ring's experiencers, people who have had both NDEs and UFOErs appear to be accelerated human beings. NDE/UFOErs may be the evolutionary forerunners that will usher in higher consciousness on a *collective* level on this planet. I liken them to *cultural dopants*, from the term in materials engineering, referring to a substance that, when added in minute quantities, changes the resulting substance dramatically. "Angels and Aliens" considers just how a global change of consciousness is taking place, one person at a time. Judging by the consensus on the following items of the Opinion Inventory, subjects would agree.

Percent Agreement to Items of the Opinion Inventory

NDE / UFOE	UFOE	NDE	NDC	UFOC

The widespread occurrence of UFOE is part of a larger plan to promote the evolution of consciousness on a species-wide scale

NDE / UFOE	UFOE	NDE	NDC	UFOC
88.8	60.8	52.7	50.0	56.4

My UFOE was "arranged" or "designed" by a higher agency or by my higher self

NDE / UFOE	UFOE	NDE	NDC	UFOC
88.8	59.8	63.5	44.4	43.6

My UFOE occurred so as to awaken me to the existence of larger cosmic forces which are affecting our lives

NDE / UFOE	UFOE	NDE	NDC	UFOC
83.3	56.7	50.0	44.4	51.3

There are higher order intelligences that have a concern with the welfare of our planet

NDE / UFOE	UFOE	NDE	NDC	UFOC
88.8	76.3	48.6	44.4	71.8

The Life Changes Inventory found significantly greater changes for the following value clusters: appreciation for life, self-acceptance, concern for others, materialism (decrease), quest for meaning and spirituality ("I feel more at peace now with myself and my loved ones"). There was widespread agreement among NDE/UFOErs that such experiences are an integral part of an evolutionary growth spurt towards greater spiritual awareness and higher consciousness. As one NDE/UFOEr, Daphne, put it:

> My life has been forever altered in every area imaginable: spiritually, mentally, physically, and other areas which are yet to be revealed. It's as if I've been given a rare (but not so rare) opportunity to see beyond this little life on Earth, and that somehow I'm to aid in some special growth or understanding, or spiritual revisitation by others who are here. I've always been into holistic/homeopathic remedies, wildlife protection, animal rights, wilderness protection, habitat restoration, etc. Maybe this is just a facet of life for those of us who will help the world grow intellectually?

Net Value Shifts on the Life Changes Inventory (LCI)

	NDE / UFOE	UFOE	NDE	UFOC	NDC
Self-Acceptance	1.37	0.92	1.13	0.81	0.80
Concern for Others	1.32	0.92	1.21	0.65	0.92
Materialism	-0.74	-0.37	-0.58	-0.17	-0.39
Ecological Concern	1.47	1.29	0.99	0.87	0.79
Concern for Planetary Welfare	1.82	1.44	1.21	1.03	0.86
Spirituality	1.60	1.21	1.22	0.86	1.09

In summary, compared to the control groups, NDE/UFOErs are *three to 10 times* more likely to report that they now experience the following elements of the Electrical-Sensitivity Syndrome: psychic abilities, healing gifts ("The whole thing was about speeding up my healing process"), sensitivity to light, mood fluctuation, and electric and electronic malfunctions. The changes that such subjects report as a result of their experiences are significant *increases* in the following categories (compared to Ring's experiencers of solely near-death or UFOs): psychophysical changes, psychic or healing gifts, Kundalini scale, and value shifts (social responsibility, concern for planetary welfare). Duane expressed ecological concerns such as "understanding the need to limit our population and to raise our young in an entirely different way... [and] the need to limit our consumption of our planetary resources."

How does this view of reality differ from someone who has had *only* an NDE or UFO experience? Due to subtle realm intrusions into daily life, subjects seem to have an expanded view of physical, material reality; that is, they believe in a more fluid continuum rather than a dichotomy of *subtle realm versus material, physical reality*. They also more readily believe in a multitude of beings ("We are not alone") and more actively engage in interspecies communication. According to Connie:

> The veil between realities is much thinner, if that makes sense... In my daily experience, I feel like I am in many different realities all at once, just more focused here. So, it is not so bizarre or strange to me when voices, shadows, odors, etc., leak through the veil from another reality. It surely makes experiencing this reality much more interesting and entertaining.

Percent Agreement to Items of the Psychophysical Changes Inventory

	NDE / UFOE
3. I became more sensitive to "other realities, other dimensions."	100
4. I seemed to become aware of multiple, overlapping realities at the same time.	77.7
45. I felt I had flashes of cosmic consciousness.	72.2
48. I became more aware of other entities or non-physical beings.	94.1

Interestingly, the awareness of "other realities" began for many NDE/UFOErs in childhood. The most common paranormal event, according to Morse, is the OBE – as 16% of Americans claim to have left their bodies at least once in their lifetime. NDE/UFOErs are over four times as likely (68.7%) to claim they have left their bodies during childhood. Stacie said, "I experienced a lot of physical trauma as a small person, so apparently it was easy to take me out and bring me back."

Percent Agreement to Items of the Childhood Experience Inventory

	NDE / UFOE
3. I felt that I had a "guardian angel" or special spirit friend that watched over me.	61.1
5. I seemed to know things that were going to happen in the future – and they did.	82.3
8. I was able to see into "other realities" that others didn't seem to be aware of.	55.5
14. I was aware of non-physical beings while I was awake.	56.2
15. I had out-of-body experiences.	68.7

What special challenges might arise as a result of experiencing both near-death and UFOs? While having watches malfunction and lights blow out are only minor inconveniences, it can become increasingly obvious that something unknown is intruding into their lives. Due to such intrusions into daily life, these experiences call for a deeper level of integration, as evidenced by an increased need for healing activities that extend into their livelihood. For example, three out of 18 are healthcare workers (including two licensed or registered practical nurses), two are masters or doctoral-level psychotherapists, and three have functioned as medical intuitives or clairvoyants. Morse also found that his sample of 150 NDErs were often in helping professions like nursing; however, as in all other categories, NDErs/UFOErs show significant increases over those that have had only NDEs or UFOErs. As Judith, a study participant, wrote:

> My exceptional human experiences [EHEs] have repeatedly shown me that everything is in a process of changing, unfolding, and evolving and that there is an infinitely bigger picture than the one I (we) operate from in the realm of physical reality. My EHEs represent a body of knowledge, and when viewed in sequence, one can easily see why I have chosen to work as a personal growth consultant, utilizing clairvoyant, clairsentient, and clairaudient skills to give [people] hints about their multi-dimensional being, and connect them to a larger life story. Because I have the privilege of seeing our divinity, I have come to trust the Mystery.

References

ATWATER, P.M.H., *Beyond the Light: What isn't being said about the Near-Death Experience*, Secaucus, NJ, Carol Publishing Group, 1994.

BECK, T.E. and COLLI, J.E., "A quantum bio-mechanical basis for near-death life reviews," *The Journal of Near-Death Studies*, 21(3), 169-189, spring 2003.

DON, N.S. and MOURA, G., "Topographic brain mapping of UFO experiencers," *Journal of Scientific Exploration*, 11(4), 435-453, 1997.

GAUTHIER, I., HAYWARD, W. G., TARR, M. J., ANDERSON, A. W., SKUDLARSKI, P., and GORE, J. C., "BOLD activity during mental rotation and viewpoint-dependent object recognition," *Neuron*, 34, 161-171, 2002.

GREYSON, B., "The near-death experience scale: Construction, reliability, and validity," *Journal of Nervous and Mental Disease*, 171(6), 369-375, 1983.

GREYSON, B., "Posttraumatic stress symptoms following near-death experiences," *American Journal of Orthopsychiatry*, 71(3), 368-73, 2001.

LAIBOW, R.E., "Clinical discrepancies between expected and observed data in patients reporting UFO abductions: Implications for treatment," on the internet (1991): *www.geocities.com/Area51/ Rampart/2271/ fs-abduclaibow.html*.

MORSE, M., and PERRY, P., *Transformed by the Light: The Powerful Effect of Near-Death Experiences on People's Lives*, New York, Villard, 1992.

PARNELL, J., "Measured personality characteristics of persons who claim UFO experiences," *Psychotherapy in Private Practice*, 6(3), 159-165, 1988.

RING, K., *The Omega Project: Near-Death Experiences, UFO Encounters, and Mind at Large*, New York, William Morrow & Co., 1992.

SLATER, E., "Conclusions on nine psychologicals," in *Final Report on the Psychological Testing of UFO Abductees*, Mt. Rainier, MD, The Fund for UFO Research, 1985.

SLAWINSKI, J., "Electromagnetic radiation and the afterlife," *Journal of Near-Death Studies*, 6(2), 79-94, 1987.

INCOMMENSURABILITY, ORTHODOXY, AND THE PHYSICS OF HIGH STRANGENESS — A 6-LAYER MODEL FOR ANOMALOUS PHENOMENA

— Jacques F. Vallée, Ph.D. and Eric W. Davis, Ph.D. —

The main argument presented in this paper is that continuing study of unidentified aerial phenomena (UAP), including "apparitions" of a religious or spiritual nature, may offer a theorem that supports the existence of new models of physical reality. The current SETI paradigm and its "assumption of mediocrity" place restrictions on forms of non-human intelligence that can be researched in our environment. A similar prejudice exists in the ufologists' often-stated hypothesis that Unidentified Aerial Phenomena (UAP), if real, must represent space visitors. Observing that both models are biased by anthropomorphism, the authors attempt to clarify the issues surrounding "high strangeness" observations by distinguishing six layers of information that can be derived from anomalous events, namely, (1) physical manifestations, (2) anti-physical effects, (3) psychological factors, (4) physiological factors, (5) psychic effects, and (6) cultural effects. In a further step, they propose a framework for scientific analysis of unidentified phenomena that takes into account the incommensurability problem.

THE CHALLENGE OF HIGH STRANGENESS

The rational study of reported cases of Unidentified Aerial Phenomena (UAP), including religious apparitions such as the so-called "miracles of Fátima" and other Marian events, is currently at an impasse. This situation has as much to do with the incomplete state of our models of physical reality as it does with the complexity of the data. A primary objection to the reality of UAP events among scientists is that witnesses consistently report objects the seemingly absurd behavior of which "cannot possibly" be related to actual phenomena, even under extreme conditions. In that respect, the similarity is striking between contemporary events reported as UFO close encounters and the more traditional observations of entities described as "angels," elves, and fairies, or deities. Skeptics insist that superior beings, celestial ambassadors or intelligent extraterrestrial (ETI) visitors simply would not perpetrate such antics as are reported in the literature. This argument can be criticized as an anthropocentric, self-selected observation resulting from our own limited viewpoint as 21st century *Homo sapiens* trying to draw conclusions about the nature of the Universe. Nonetheless, the high strangeness of many reports and the absurdity attending religious miracles must be acknowledged.

Advocates of UAP reality, on the other hand, generally claim that the Extra-Terrestrial Hypothesis (ETH) centered on interstellar travelers from extra-solar systems visiting the Earth remains the most likely explanation for the objects and the beings associated with them. Accordingly, they would re-interpret Biblical stories and religious apparitions in the framework of visits from space aliens. This argument, too, can be challenged on the basis of the witnesses' own testimony: ufologists have consistently ignored or minimized reports of seemingly absurd behaviors that contradict the ETH, by selectively extracting data that best fits their agenda or version of the theory. Thus the ETH, just like the skeptical argument, is based on anthropocentric self-selection (Vallée, 1990). Here we are witnessing an interesting overlap between the SETI and UAP paradigms: each excludes consideration of the other when laying claim to the legitimate search for, and contact with, potential non-human intelligence.

In the view of the authors, current hypotheses are not strange enough to explain the facts of the phenomenon, and the debate suffers from a lack of scientific information. Indeed, from the viewpoint of modern physics, our Cosmic Neighborhood could encompass other (parallel) universes, extra-spatial dimensions, and other time-like dimensions beyond the common four-dimensional space-time we recognize, and such aspects could lead to rational explanations for apparently "incomprehensible" behaviors on the part of beings emerging into our perceived continuum. As it attempts to reconcile theory with the observed properties of elementary particles and with discoveries at the frontiers of cosmology, modern physics suggests that humankind has not yet discovered all of the Universe's facets, and we must propose new theories and experiments in order to explore these undiscovered facets. *This is why continuing study of reported anomalous events is important. It may provide us with an existence theorem for new models of physical reality.*

Much of the recent progress in cosmological concepts is directly applicable to the problem: Traversable wormholes (three-dimensional hyper-surface tunnels) have now been derived from Einstein's General Theory of Relativity (Morris and Thorne, 1988; Visser, 1995). In particular, it has been shown that Einstein's General Theory of Relativity does not in any way constrain space-time topology, which allows for wormholes to provide traversable connections between regions within two separate universes or between remote regions and/or times within the same universe. Mathematically, it can also be shown that higher-dimensional wormholes can provide hypersurface connections between multidimensional spaces (Rucker, 1984; Kaku, 1995). Recent quantum gravity programs have explored this property in super-string theory, along with proposals to theoretically and experimentally examine macroscopic-scale, extra-dimensional spaces (Schwarzschild, 2000). Thus, it is now widely acknowledged that the nature of our Universe is far more complex than observations based on anthropocentric self-selection portend. In this respect, ufologists and SETI researchers appear to be fighting a rear-guard battle. Both suffer from identical limitations in the worldview they bring to their own domains, and to their antagonism.

ANTHROPOCENTRIC BIAS IN THE SETI AND UAP PARADIGMS

The anthropocentric biases in the SETI program are evident in the present search paradigm. Historically, the founders of SETI defined the search paradigm from a series of complex arguments and assumptions that led to the creation of a "SETI orthodox view" of interstellar communication while applying the "assumption of mediocrity" to our known present technological capabilities (Oliver *et al.*, 1973).

This approach was predicated on the notion that it was economically cheaper and technologically easier to generate and receive radio-wave photons for interstellar signaling rather than engage manned interstellar travel or robotic probes. Indeed, the latter was considered economically and technologically improbable within the "SETI orthodox view." This has led to four decades of the SETI program following a dominantly radio/microwave (RMW) oriented search scheme.

Given the failure of this initial approach, in the last two decades alternative SETI programs have been proposed. They exploit coherent laser optical/IR (COSETI), holographic signals and worldwide web detection schemes, as well as ideas to search for ETI artifacts (SETA, or astroarchaeology) and visiting probes (SETV, V = visitation) in the solar system or on Earth (Tough, 2000).

There are new proposed search schemes based on the application of high-energy (particle) physics detection, such as modulated neutrino beams, X-rays, gamma rays, and cosmic rays, etc. Other search schemes propose looking for artificially generated excess radiation emissions from astronomical bodies in space or for high-energy radiation starship exhaust trails (Matloff, 1998).

These new programs have been at odds with members of the dominant RMW-SETI program, possibly because of concern over having to share scarce resources or compete with other non-RMW programs for the very limited private funding available for overall SETI research.

The community of UAP researchers is also driven by its own orthodoxy, which is only violated at great personal risk to the critic who proposes a deviant view, and by its own "principle of mediocrity" when attempting to categorize and hypothesize explanations for the phenomenon. For this reason, we prefer to use the term "UAP" rather than the more common "UFO," which is immediately associated with the idea of space visitors in the mind of the public and media. Yet a bridge could be formed between the disparate SETI and Ufology communities if both would only recognize a simple fact: *No experiment can distinguish between phenomena manifested by visiting interstellar (arbitrarily advanced) ETI and intelligent beings that may exist near Earth within a parallel universe or in different dimensions, or who are (terrestrial) time travelers.*

Each of these interesting possibilities can be manifested via the application of the physical principle of traversable wormholes since they theoretically connect between two different universes, two remote space locations, different times and dimensions (Davis, 2001). Traversable wormholes are but one example of new physical tools that are available for consideration of inter-universal, interstellar, inter-dimensional, or chronological travel.

This leads the present authors to speculate that a new synthesis can be found by examining the full context of anomalous phenomena – including the apparently "absurd" characteristics found in religious apparitions – in terms of a six-layer model. The model uses the framework of the incommensurability problem and concepts borrowed from semiotics.

UAP – THE NEED FOR A UNIFIED APPROACH

What we present here is a new framework for UAP analysis that takes into account the lessons from SETI. In any scientific question, it must be possible to ascertain to what extent a hypothesis, when tested and proven to be true, actually "explains" the observed facts. In the case of UAP, however, as in physics generally, a hypothesis may well be "proven true" while an apparently contradictory hypothesis is also proven true. Thus, the hypothesis that the phenomenon of light is caused by particles is true, but so is the opposite hypothesis that it is caused by waves. We must be prepared for the time when we will be in a position to formulate scientific hypotheses for UAP, and then we may face a similar situation.

The framework we present here is based on such an apparent contradiction, because we will argue that UAP can be thought of *both* as physical and as "psychic." We hope that it will prove stimulating as a unified approach to a puzzling phenomenon that presents both undeniable physical effects suggesting a technological device or craft *and* psychic effects reminiscent of the literature on poltergeists and psychokinetic phenomena. Here we use the word "psychic" in the sense of an interaction between physical reality and human consciousness. As one example among many, it will be recalled that the events at Fátima involved luminous phenomena, atmospheric and thermal effects, and descriptions of an apparently metallic disk in the sky, while many of the 70,000 witnesses also experienced spiritual and psychological effects. The main percipients reported psychic states conducive to a form of extrasensory communication with a non-human Being assumed to be the Virgin Mary.

The feeling of absurdity and contradiction in these two aspects is not worse than scientific puzzlement during the particle/wave or, more recently, quantum entanglement and multi-dimensional transport controversies. The contradiction has to do with the inadequacy of our language to grasp a phenomenon that defies our attempts at classification.

THE SIX LEVELS OF UAP ANALYSIS

Let us consider the characteristics of the sightings that are not explained by trivial natural causes; we can recognize six major "layers" in terms of our perceptions of these characteristics, as they can be extracted from earlier works about UAP phenomenology (Vallée, 1975a, 1975b) or from the current National Institute for Discovery Science database.

Layer I: First of all is the *physical layer*, evident in most witness accounts describing an object that:

- occupies a position in space, consistent with geometry;
- moves as time passes;
- interacts with the environment through thermal effects;

- exhibits light absorption and emission from which power output estimates can be derived;
- produces turbulence;
- when landed, leaves indentations and burns from which mass and energy figures can be derived;
- gives rise to photographic images;
- leaves material residue consistent with Earth chemistry;
- gives rise to electric, magnetic, and gravitational disturbances.

Thus, UAP, in a basic physical sense, are consistent with a technology centered on a craft that appears to be using a revolutionary propulsion system. It is the existence of this layer that has led mainstream ufologists to claim that UFOs and related phenomena are due to extraterrestrial machines.

Layer II: For lack of an adequate term, we will call the second layer *anti-physical*. The variables are the same as those in the previous category, but they form patterns that conflict with those predicted by modern physics. Objects are described as physical and material but they are also described as:

- sinking into the ground;
- shrinking in size, growing larger, or changing shape on the spot;
- becoming fuzzy and transparent on the spot;
- dividing into two or more objects, several of them merging into one object at slow speed;
- disappearing at one point and appearing elsewhere instantaneously;
- remaining observable visually while not detected by radar;
- producing missing time or time dilatation;
- producing topological inversion or space dilatation (object was estimated to be of small exterior size/volume, but witness(s) saw a huge interior many times the exterior size);
- appearing as balls of colored, intensely bright light under intelligent control.

It is the presence of such descriptions that leads most academic scientists to reject the phenomenon as the product of hallucinations or hoaxes.

Layer III: The third layer has to do with the *psychology* of the witnesses and the *social* conditions that surround them. Human observers tend to see UAP while in their normal environment and social groupings. They perceive the objects as non-conventional but they try to explain them away as common occurrences, until faced with the inescapable conclusion that the object is truly unknown.

Layer IV: *Physiological* reactions are another significant level of information. The phenomenon is reported to cause effects perceived by humans as:

- sounds (beeping, buzzing, humming, sharp/piercing whistling, swooshing/air rushing, loud/deafening roaring, sound of a storm, etc.);
- vibrations;
- burns;
- partial paralysis (inability to move muscles);
- extreme heat or cold sensation;
- odors (powerful, sweet or strange fragrance, rotten eggs, sulphurous, pungent, musky, etc.);
- metallic taste;
- pricklings;
- temporary blindness when directly exposed to the objects' light;
- nausea;
- bloody nose and/or ears, severe headache;
- difficulty in breathing;
- loss of volition;
- severe drowsiness in the days following a close encounter.

Layer V: The fifth category of effects can only be labeled *psychic* because it involves a class of phenomena commonly found in the literature of parapsychology, such as

- impressions of communication without a direct sensory channel;
- poltergeist phenomena; motions and sounds without a specific cause, outside the observed presence of a UAP;
- levitation of the witness or of objects and animals in the vicinity;
- maneuvers of a UAP appearing to anticipate the witness' thoughts;
- premonitory dreams or visions;
- personality changes promoting unusual abilities in the witness;
- healing.

Layer VI: The sixth and last category could be called *cultural*. It is concerned with society's reactions to the reports, the way in which secondary effects (hoaxes, fiction and science-fiction imagery, scientific theories, cover-up or exposure, media censorship or publicity, sensationalism, etc.) become generated, and the attitude of members of a given culture towards the concepts that UAP observations appear to challenge. In the United States, the greatest impact of the phenomenon has been on general acceptance of the idea of life in space and a more limited, but potentially very significant, change in the popular concept of non-human intelligence. In earlier cultures, such as medieval Europe or Portugal in the early years of the 20th century, the cultural context of anomalous observations was strongly colored by religious beliefs.

POSSIBLE NATURE OF UAP TECHNOLOGY

A framework for scientific hypothesis on the UAP observations can be built on the identification (admittedly very coarse) of the six major layers of UAP effects. If we must formulate a view of the problem in a single statement at this point, that statement will be:

Everything works as if UAPs were the products of a technology that integrates physical and psychic phenomena and primarily affects cultural variables in our society through manipulation of physiological and psychological parameters in the witnesses.

This single statement can be developed as follows:

a)   The phenomenon is the product of a technology. During the observation, the UAP is a real, physical, material object. It appears to use either very clever deception or very advanced physical principles, however, resulting in the effects we have called "anti-physical," which must eventually be reconciled with the laws of physics.

b)   The technology triggers psychic effects either purposely or as a side effect of its manifestations. These consciousness phenomena are now too common to be ignored or relegated to the category of exaggerated or ill-observed facts. All of us who have investigated close-range sightings have become familiar with these effects.

c)   The purpose of the technology may be cultural manipulation – possibly but not necessarily under control of a form of non-human intelligence – in which case the physiological and psychological effects are a means to that end. But the parapsychologist with a Jungian framework may argue that the human collective unconscious is also a potential source of such effects – without the need to invoke alien intervention.

THE INCOMMENSURABILITY PROBLEM

These considerations bring us back to consideration of the SETI paradigm. Many SETI workers now realize that we cannot be so presumptuous as to assume that ET cultures, possessing a cognitive mismatch with us, will behave as humans do in the 21st century. Specifically, there is no reason to restrict them to radio-based communications technology and to exclude travel through interstellar space, transmission of imagery or the sending of automated probes. Thus, the SETV/SETA program overlaps ETH-based Ufology. Both are dedicated to detecting non-human intelligence on or near the Earth, demonstrating a paradigm shift away from the "SETI orthodox view" and principle of mediocrity.

The view that ETs and humans may have such divergent ways of conceptualizing the world that there can be no mutual understanding is referred to as the "Incommensurability Problem" in the SETI literature (Vakoch, 1995, 1999). The cognitive mismatch or Incommensurability Problem between human and ET cultures will guarantee that the latter will develop communication techniques other than radio. ET cultures may be sending radio and optical signals to Earth now but they may also be sending signals in a variety of other forms such as holographic images, psychic or other consciousness-related signals, modulated neutrinos, gamma ray bursts, wormhole-modulated starlight caustics, signals generated by gravitational lensing techniques, modulated X-rays, quantum teleported signals, or some quantum field theoretic effect, etc. The Incommensurability Problem even applies to the problem of understanding UAP manifestations within the framework of the ETH.

At the core of the Incommensurability Problem is the view that no intelligent species can understand reality without making certain methodological choices, and that these choices may vary from civilization to civilization (Vakoch, 1995). If ETs and UAP entities have different biologies and live in considerably different environments from humans, they may well have different goals for their science, and radically different criteria for evaluating the success of their science. Their explanatory mechanisms, their predictive concerns, their modes of control over nature might all be very different, and their means of formulating models of reality should be expected to differ drastically from ours (Rescher, 1985).

In this regard, there is one additional feature that needs to be mentioned in support of alternative SETI paradigms. The SETI program's encryption/decryption emphasis on pictorial images or messages is predicated on the assumption that ETs have sight like humans vis-à-vis the "SETI orthodox view" (Oliver *et al.*, 1973). We observe that this emphasis is not so much a reflection of the primacy of vision in humans, but rather a reflection of the philosophical assumptions about the proper means of gaining knowledge. Hence, anthropocentric self-selection becomes manifest within the SETI and Ufology "orthodox view."

Michel Foucault asserts that human reliance on science is based on studying visible characteristics of objects (Foucault, 1966). The belief that true knowledge must be acquired from sight originated in the 17th century. This emphasis on sight led to eliminating the other senses as potentially valuable sources of scientific information.

Without even raising the question of whether ETs or UAP entities can "see," we may be wise not to overestimate the importance of pictorial representations for them. The same applies for ET/UAP transmissions to us. We can see and gain knowledge by sight, but ET/UAP signals potentially bombarding the Earth could be misunderstood, unrecognized or undetected because we are not employing paradigms involving our other modalities, such as psychic functioning. Many examples of this are found in interactions between humans from different cultures (Highwater, 1981) and in Marian apparitions where the prime witnesses are often uneducated, illiterate children (e.g., Fátima, Lourdes, Guadalupe).

This last observation places constraints on what we can expect an ET reaction might be to signals sent from Earth. Because we cannot be certain of the nature of ET/UAP recipients of our deliberate messages and they cannot be certain of our nature when sending us their messages *a priori*, it is difficult to construct pictures that will be unambiguous. To some extent, ET/UAP viewers of our pictograms may project characteristics from their own species-specific experiences onto our messages, and we certainly project our own species-specific experiences onto their messages. The former may be the cause for the lack of detected ET signals (save for those 100+ radio and optical signals that were not false positives but also not repeated by their source) while the latter can be the cause of the current impasse in the study of UAP phenomena.

SEMIOTICS

In his analysis of the communication problem SETI Institute psychologist,

Doug Vakoch, has advocated the application of semiotics, the general theory of signs (Vakoch, 1999), where a sign is something that represents something else, the signified. For example, the words "the coin" might represent a particular object you hold in your hand.

In interstellar messages, in terms of classical information theory, there is no innate relationship between the form of the message and the content borne by the message. Once the information of the message is decided upon, an efficient means of encoding it is sought. In this approach, there is a purely arbitrary connection between content and form of the message. Semiotic-based messages have a wider range of possibilities for relating form and content.

Semioticians categorize signs according to the ways that the sign and signified are related to one another. In the association between the sign "the coin" and its signified object, this relationship is purely arbitrary. The sign for this object could have well been "the poofhoffer." This is a purely conventional association. In semiotics, when the association between sign and signified is arbitrary, the sign is referred to as a symbol. With symbols, there is no intrinsic connection between the form of expression (the sign) and the content that is expressed (the signified).

There are alternatives to the arbitrary connection between sign and signified that are seen in symbols. One alternative is the icon, a sign that bears a physical resemblance to the signified. With icons, the form of the message reflects its contents. For example, the profile of the man on a modern American quarter is an icon for a specific man who was the first President of the United States. We can also represent the same man with the symbol "George Washington." In the former case, the image of Washington is an icon because it physically resembles the signified. Icons can also be used when the signified is less concrete. For example, the "Scales of Justice" icon represents the concept of justice because there is similarity between the sign (scales that balance two weights) and the signified (concept of justice, which involves a balance between transgression and punishment). At Fátima, the Being first described (in the 1915 sightings) as an "Angel of Peace" within a globe of light became a "Lady of Light" in the 1917 observations. In turn, she became identified with the symbol of Mary, and ultimately with the Virgin herself.

It is also helpful to realize that icons are not specific to the visual sensory modality. It is possible to have a sign that physically resembles the signified in a non-visual way. For example, the fly *Spilomyia hamifera* beats its wings at a frequency very close to the wing-beat frequency of the dangerous wasp *Dolichovespula arenaria*. As a result, when one of these flies is in the vicinity of a group of these wasps, the fly gains some immunity from attack by birds. The fly's mimicry of the wasps occurs within the auditory modality. It is not attacked by would-be predators because it sounds like the wasps. In short, the fly's defense strategy is based on producing an auditory icon, in which the fly's wing-beating (the sign) physically resembles the wing-beat of the wasps (the signified) (Vakoch, 1999).

Icons could function in any sensory modality. Given that we are not sure which sensory modality may be primary for ETs/UAP, a sign for communication that is not reliant on any particular sensory modality would be preferable. In SETI/CETI, electromagnetic radiation is used as an iconic representation, allowing a direct communication of concepts (Earth chemistry, solar system organization, human DNA, math, geometry, etc.) without encoding the message into a format specific to a particular sensory modality. In using icons, the message's recipients are pointed directly toward the phenomena of interest, and not toward our models of these phenomena.

From a more complete perspective, the sign and the signified are in a triadic with the interpreter of the relationship. Thus, the similarity that exists between an icon and its referent does not exist independently of the intelligence perceiving this similarity. Although in iconicity there is a natural connection between the sign and the signified, this connection cannot exist without intelligence to observe the connection.

Ultimately, the problem of iconicity is that similarity is in the eye of the beholder. And because we do not know what ETs/UAP are really like, we cannot be sure that what to us seems an obvious similarity will be seen as such by an intelligence with a different biology, culture, and history, possibly originating in a different universe. Thus, judgment of similarity is not purely objective, but is influenced by a variety of factors that impact conventions of interpretation.

THE UAP AND ABDUCTION PROBLEM

The aforementioned behavior of UAP is not fundamentally absurd. This apparent absurdity is merely a reflection of the cognitive mismatch or the Incommensurability Problem that exists between humans and the phenomenon.

In this particular case, UAP are sending the message and we are the recipients. The message(s) sent to us are icons – icons fashioned by the phenomenon and sent to us via various sensory modalities. The difference between our respective cultures, biologies, sensory modalities, histories, dimensional existence, physical evolution, models of nature and science, etc. may be directly responsible for our lack of understanding of the phenomenon and its message. We cannot see what UAP believe to be (iconical) similarities in the message that is intended for us. These stated differences directly impact our conventions of interpretation in such a way as to impair our recognition of the "similarity" between the sign and the signified contained within the icons of the UAP message, further impairing our ability to "see and understand" the potential message or pattern.

The difference between the sensory modalities of UAP entities and humans may be responsible for our inability to properly detect the UAP message (icons) and correspond with them. This difference may also prevent us from correctly interpreting what their icons are if we do in fact recognize them. In this regard, recall that we will project our own species-specific experiences onto their icons (messages), thus manifesting the appearance of "absurdity" during the human-UAP interaction.

UFO abduction cases may exemplify this, in the sense that the "absurd" activities (or scenes) concurrent with abduction events could merely be the iconical defense mechanism deployed by the UAP to protect itself from the subject much like the way *Spilomyia hamifera* protects itself from birds by mimicry.

Kuiper (1977) and Freitas (1980) suggest that ETs/UAP visiting Earth would find it necessary to hide themselves from our detection mechanisms until they have assessed our technological level or potential threat and hazards. They would employ an adaptive multi-level risk program to avoid danger. Low observable stealth such as simple camouflage through mimicry, which works well in nature, may be the technique of choice for visiting UAP/ETI experienced in surveillance (Stride, 1998). Examples of mimicry techniques are UAP/ETI entering the atmosphere with either the look or trajectory of a meteor or hidden within a meteor shower, behaving like dark meteors without the associated optical signature, hiding within an artificial or natural cloud or a satellite reentry, behaving as pseudo-stars sitting stationary over certain regions, or mimicking a man-made aircraft's aggregate features (Stride, 1998). Another possibility is mimicry techniques employed for the manipulation of human consciousness to induce the various manifestations of "absurd" interactions or scenery associated with the encounter. Yet another would be to appear as a being recognizable within the target culture as an angel, demon, or deity.

CONCLUSION

Modern engineering has made us familiar with display technologies that produce three-dimensional images with color, motion, and perspective through physical devices. We speculate that UAP are analogous to these display technologies but utilize a wider range of variables to operate on the percipients and, through them, on human culture. The long time scale and the global nature of the effects make it difficult to test hypotheses involving such cultural effects.

Science fiction has familiarized us with the concept of machines or beings projecting an image of them that systematically confuses observers. One could imagine that UAP represent physical craft equipped with the means to interact both with the surrounding atmosphere and with the senses of observers in such a way as to convey a false image of their real nature. One could argue that such an object could use microwave devices to create perceptual hallucinations in the witnesses (including messages that are heard or seen by a single individual in a group).

Even such a complex scheme, however, fails to explain all the reported effects and the subsequent behavior changes in close-range witnesses. We must assume something more, the triggering of deep-seated processes within their personality. The question then becomes: to what extent are these effects evidence of a purposeful action of the operators? To answer this question, and to test more fully the hypothesis that UAP phenomena are *both* physical and psychic in nature, we need much better investigations, a great upgrading of data quality, and a more informed analysis not only of the object being described, but of the impact of the observation on the witnesses and their social environment. In other words, we need to develop a multidisciplinary methodology that encompasses all six layers we have identified, and can be applied to SETI as well as to UFO phenomena and close encounters with the beings associated with them. Such a methodology would open the way to the rational testing of hypotheses in an important domain that has been sorely neglected by mainstream science for too long.

References

DAVIS, E.W., "Wormhole-Stargates: Tunneling Through the Cosmic Neighborhood," *MUFON 2001 International UFO Symposium Proceedings*, Irvine, CA, 32-50, 2001.

FOUCAULT, M., *The Order of Things*, New York, Random House, 1966.

FREITAS, R. A., "A Self-Reproducing Interstellar Probe," *JBIS*, 33, 251-264, 1980.

HIGHWATER, J., *The Primal Mind: Vision and Reality in Indian America*, New York, Meridian, 1981.

KAKU, M., *Hyperspace: A Scientific Odyssey through Parallel Universes, Time-Warps, and the 10th Dimension*, New York, Anchor Books Doubleday, 1995.

KUIPER, T.B.H. and MORRIS, M., "Searching for Extraterrestrial Civilizations," *Science*, 196, 616-621, 1977.

MATLOFF, G., personal communication, New York University, 1988.

MORRIS, M.S. and THORNE, K.S., "Wormholes in space-time and their use for interstellar travel: A tool for teaching general relativity," *American Journal of Physics*, 56(5), 395-412, 1988.

OLIVER, B.M., et al., *Project Cyclops: A Design Study of a System for Detecting Extraterrestrial Intelligent Life*, NASA-Ames Research Center, CR 114445, 1973, pp. 177-181.

RESCHER, N., "Extraterrestrial Science," in REGIS, E., Jr. (ed.), *Extraterrestrials: Science and Alien Intelligence*, Cambridge, Cambridge University Press, 1985.

RUCKER, R., *The Fourth Dimension: A Guided Tour of the Higher Universes*, Boston, Houghton-Mifflin Co., 1984.

SCHWARZSCHILD, B., "Theorists and Experimenters Seek to Learn Why Gravity is So Weak," *Physics Today*, 53(9), 22-24, 2000.

STRIDE, S. L., "SETV – The Search for Extraterrestrial Visitation: Introduction to a Heterotic Strategy in the Search for ETI," *JSE*, submitted, 1998.

TOUGH, A., on the internet: *members.aol.com/AllenTough/strategies.html*, University of Toronto, Canada, 2000.

VAKOCH, D.A., "Constructing messages to extraterrestrials: An exosemiotic approach," paper IAA-95-IAA.9.2.05, presented at the SETI: Interdisciplinary Aspects Review Meeting, 46th International Astronautical Congress, Oslo, Norway, 1995.

VAKOCH, D.A., SETI Institute, personal communication, 1999.

VALLÉE, J.F., *The Invisible College*, New York, E. P. Dutton, 1975.

VALLÉE, J.F., "The Psycho-Physical Nature of UFO Reality: A Speculative Framework," *AIAA Thesis-Antithesis Conference Proceedings*, Los Angeles, 19-21, 1975.

VALLÉE, J.F., *Confrontations: A Scientist's Search for Alien Contact*, New York, Ballantine, 1990.

VISSER, M., *Lorentzian Wormholes: From Einstein to Hawking*, New York, AIP Press, 1995.

OTHER TITLES AVAILABLE FROM ANOMALIST BOOKS:

The Yowie
In Alien Heat
Heavenly Lights
Strange Company
Columbus Was Last
The President's Vampire
Worlds Before Our Own
In Search of the Unknown
On the Trail of the Saucer Spies
The Unidentified and Creatures of the Outer Edge
The Field Guide to Bigfoot and Other Mystery Primates
A Psychic Study of the Mystery of Spheres
A Casebook of Otherworldly Music
On the Track of the Poltergeist
The Universe Wants to Play
Encounters at Indian Head
The Spirit of Dr. Bindelof
The Search for Yesterday
Our Pyschic Potentials
The Haunted Universe
Celestial Secrets
Strange Guests
Shadow World
Confrontations
Dimensions
Revelations
Miracles

AnomalistBooks.com

CPSIA information can be obtained at www.ICGtesting.com
Printed in the USA
LVOW05s2123301114

416285LV00031BA/1512/P